The Sociolinguistics of Development in Africa

MULTILINGUAL MATTERS SERIES
Series Editor: Professor John Edwards,
St Francis Xavier University, Antigonish, Nova Scotia, Canada

For more details of these or any other of our publications, please contact:
Multilingual Matters, Frankfurt Lodge, Clevedon Hall,
Victoria Road, Clevedon, BS21 7HH, England
http://www.multilingual-matters.com

MULTILINGUAL MATTERS 139
Series Editor: John Edwards

The Sociolinguistics of Development in Africa

Paulin G. Djité

MULTILINGUAL MATTERS LTD
Clevedon • Buffalo • Toronto

Library of Congress Cataloging in Publication Data
Djité, Paulin G.
The Sociolinguistics of Development in Africa / Paulin G. Djité.
Multilingual Matters: 139
Includes bibliographical references and index.
1. Sociolinguistics–Africa. 2. Multilingualism–Africa.
3. Language and education–Africa. 4. Africa–Economic conditions. I. Title.
P40.45.A35D56 2008
306.44096–dc22   2007040067

British Library Cataloguing in Publication Data
A catalogue entry for this book is available from the British Library.

ISBN-13: 978-1-84769-046-3 (hbk)
ISBN-13: 978-1-84769-045-6 (pbk)

Multilingual Matters Ltd
UK: Frankfurt Lodge, Clevedon Hall, Victoria Road, Clevedon BS21 7HH.
USA: UTP, 2250 Military Road, Tonawanda, NY 14150, USA.
Canada: UTP, 5201 Dufferin Street, North York, Ontario M3H 5T8, Canada.

The policy of Multilingual Matters/Channel View Publications is to use papers that are natural, renewable and recyclable products, made from wood grown in sustainable forests. In the manufacturing process of our books, and to further support our policy, preference is given to printers that have FSC and PEFC Chain of Custody certification. The FSC and/or PEFC logos will appear on those books where full certification has been granted to the printer concerned.

Typeset by Wordworks Ltd.
Printed and bound in Great Britain by MPg Books Ltd.

Contents

Acknowledgements

I would like to thank Terry Chesher, Joel Dehe, Robert Desiatnik, David Price and Langming Zhang for reading and commenting on earlier versions of this book. I hope their comments and advice are reflected in my writing.

My deepest gratitude goes to my children. Thank you for your interest and challenging discussions. Paul-Simon, you once expressed the desire to 'stay with grandma to learn the mother tongue, then join you guys later', because you were curious (and I guess unhappy) that we do not speak an African language at home. I hope this book helps you understand the historical and structural constraints within which our language identities have been constructed. Bruce, you often worried about my state of health, because of the long hours I spent in the study; maybe this book will allay some of your concerns. Sidney, you often queried me about the practical solutions to Africa's woes; I hope the suggestions in this book provide some answers to your questions. Above all, remember your father's middle name: GOU–PO–GNON or the malevolence of the *Other* shall not determine your destiny.

16 June 2007

Preface

What if half the world's languages are on the verge of extinction?
Let them die in peace.
Malik (2000)

Language is the beginning; it is part of who we are.
Rosen (2002)

Fairclough writes:

> Sociolinguistics is strong on 'what?' questions (what are the facts of variations?) but weak on 'why?' and 'how?' questions *(why are the facts as they are?* how – in terms of the development of social relationships of power – was the existing sociolinguistic order brought into being? *how is it sustained? and how might it be changed to the advantage of those who are dominated by it?*). (Fairclough, 2001: 6; my italics)

Fairclough goes on to discuss 'the general insensitivity of sociolinguistics towards its own relationship to the sociolinguistic orders it seeks to describe' and suggests that:

> When one focuses on the simple existence of facts, without attending to the social conditions which made them so and the social conditions for their potential change, the notion that the sociolinguist herself might somehow affect the facts hardly seems to arise. [...] the effect of sociolinguistic research might either be to legitimise these facts and so indirectly the power relations which underlie them, or to *show the contingency of these facts despite their apparent solidity, and so indirectly point to ways of changing them.* (Fairclough, 2001: 7; my italics)

In other words, sociolinguistic research needs to expand, to consider not only the language uses at issue, but also the social landscape in which they occur (see also Tollefson, 1995). Fairclough has a point here. Many of us have been trained in the tradition of sociolinguistic research, which seeks to establish the facts, and refrains from speculating as to 'why?' and 'how?' In the developing world, and especially in Africa, this has led to a trend, albeit a sad trend, whereby research is limited to frameworks dictated by constraints such as the sources of funding and/or target publication outlets, often overlooking the reality of day-to-day interactions. Makoni and Meinhof (2004) argue that seemingly progressive applied linguistic projects consolidate a Western view of the continent in postcolonial Africa and only mirror these myths. The brave few who managed to break the shackles of accepted theories and wisdom were often derided and ridiculed. For instance, as recently as 1989, countering the arguments of African scholars on the prospects of the French language in Africa, Chaudenson was writing:

> As distressing and painful as this choice may be for a number of African intellectuals, most of them know quite well that there is no better one and, *rather than dreaming of some impossible Edenic Africas*, it is imperative and urgent to plan and manage the present to the best of our ability, in order to make a future possible. (Chaudenson, 1989; my translation; my italics)

Dumont could only concur and added:

> There is nothing more annoying than reading or hearing, almost thirty years after independence, nice texts about language rights and the necessity to introduce African languages in the schools. These are rear-guard struggles and the battle is over, if not won. ... [for] ... *no one comes out of a century of French colonial administration unscathed.* (Dumont, 1990; my translation; my italics)

Dumont's last phrase echoes one of the French obsessions that, through the French language, 'all conquered peoples ... will become republicans' (Brunot, 1967: 186).

Hence, the imposition of the French language in Africa is seen and constructed by some as an unchangeable fact of life, even though less than 20% of the people in the so-called 'French-speaking Africa' are proficient in it. In the face of such bold pronouncements and mystifications about language passing for theoretical frameworks and operating prejudicially against the whole continent, Ngalasso (1989) could only lament that 'All the indications are that in this minor continent, there are no people, only tribes, no languages, but a plethora of dialects more or less unintelligible and lacking in written tradition.' Like Sartre (1948)[1], Robert (2004: 58) has an entirely different perspective on the issue. She believes that it is urgent Africans speak about their land, their people and their languages, in their own way, and that others should learn to listen for once. Africans must construct their own perception and aspirations for Africa; and the rediscovery of the continent must go beyond intellectual sophistry that glosses over the reality, only to force it into one's own prism of preconceived ideas and speculative pseudo-theories (Robert, 2004: 95). One has to be allowed to contribute to making and writing one's own history, not just be subjected to it, for 'as long as the lions will not have their own historians, the stories about hunting will always praise the courage of the hunter' (African proverb). It must be said, though, that the specificity of Africa lies in the fact that the continent never had a word in edgeways. Convinced of their authority and right to impose their vision of the world on others, some in the developed world have endeavoured and continue to crash and eliminate all those who dare to think and act differently. Only conceit stops one from learning from the *Other*. Nevertheless, Africa's future, just like its past and present, comprises a multiplicity of viewpoints, all of which deserve to be heard.

The fact remains that, 50 years on, Africa is the only continent where a school child can have access to knowledge and science only through a language other than the one spoken at home or in the wider community; the only continent where the majority of the people cannot have access to justice in their own language(s). This has led a number of African researchers seeking to break out of the mould of sociolinguistic and applied linguistic platitudes (e.g. contrastive analyses between French and African languages, new approaches to teaching/learning French, etc.) to look for research grants outside the three champions of monolingualism: France, England and the United States. Germany, the Netherlands, Sweden, Norway and others quickly answered the call for academic freedom.

Not long after it had been acknowledged that no language could be shown to be more accurate, logical or capable of expression than another, there were rumblings about how, in practice, some languages are more 'adapted', and therefore more valuable, than others, in that they – and they alone – can be employed in all functions and domains of modern civilisation. Only European languages were suited for literature, high culture and, more importantly, science and technology, and the possession of a written language correlates with development. African languages on the other hand did not even have a literary tradition, an ascription with implications for the cognitive potential and level of underdevelopment, illiteracy and poverty of the speech communities of these languages. Needless to say, these assertions would not include an analysis of the 'why' and 'how', or the historical and structural factors that contributed in a significant way to such a situation (Tollefson, 1991). But isn't it the case that some languages have simply not been *allowed* to develop as others have? Isn't it the case that evidence of literacy tradition in some languages has intentionally been destroyed (Battestini, 1997), forbidden (e.g. Ajami script) or ignored (e.g. the Timbuktu manuscripts)?[2] We must now be able to accept that these things did happen; after all, the objective of colonisation '[was] not to suppress inequalities between human beings, but to amplify them and make them into law', 'not equality, but domination' (Renan, 1882, cited in Césaire, 1956/89).

So, it is a cruel irony that African languages have thus far been a liability, and a cause of vulnerability, rather than a source of power. In an age of globalisation, many indeed find it difficult to understand the need for other languages, especially in Africa, and discussions about the link between language and development in Africa can be frustrating. In addition to the foregoing articles of faith, coming from those who are regarded as experts in African sociolinguistics, crucial evidence and obvious counter-examples are often blatantly overlooked. Hence, Pool (1972: 213) could still write that ' ... a country that is linguistically highly heterogeneous is always undeveloped, and a country that is developed always has considerable language uniformity', and have his argument bandied around for decades as scientific truth (Coulmas, 1992: 25; Fasold, 1984: 7; Gellner, 1983: 35).[3] Meanwhile, developed nations in the heart of Europe (e.g. Belgium and Switzerland), and in North America (Canada) were multilingual, and poor nations in Europe (e.g. Portugal and Spain)[4] were monolingual, at least until they changed their constitution (e.g. Spain) and joined the European Community, now the European Union. The argument also overlooks highly homogeneous polities in Africa (Burundi, Rwanda and Somalia) and elsewhere (Cambodia, Lao PDR and Vietnam) that are still underdeveloped. Significantly, some do acknowledge that this view is essentially 'based on *the high degree of coincidence* of virtual and, more importantly, *perceived* monolingualism and economic development observed in the industrialised world' (Coulmas, 1992: 25) not on science, even though they are prepared to put forth an even stronger version of the same argument. Hence, using data from the International Monetary Fund on reserve currencies, Coulmas (1992: 77–81) argues that 'the value of a language is determined in relation to that of other languages ... [and is] ... above all economic ... [in part] ... through its advances on the foreign language market', and concludes that '*there is an almost perfect match with the great foreign languages of the world*' [my italics]. This argument begs the following question: What language does the Euro speak? Furthermore, the argument ignores a trend in central banks around the world, the trend for diversifying their reserve currency base, as well as an even stronger trend that favours a rise of the euro as the preferred reserve currency. Secondly, the argument fails to acknowledge the fact that the true value of the languages of the European colonial powers – with the remarkable exception of Portuguese – is directly proportional to the role these powers played in the transatlantic slave trade and colonisation, as well as the size of their empires.

English and French, for instance, became 'economically valuable' at least in part because of these major historical, socio-political and economic events. Indeed, the current status of European languages is largely due to the fact that they have been imposed, under different guises, on the undeveloped countries of the world. What if there were a negative causal relationship between multilingualism and economic development? No real attempt is made to ask the questions that matter – 'why?' and 'how?' and, furthermore, as Fairclough would put it, how might this situation be changed to the advantage of those who are dominated by it, instead of recycling and elaborating on a number of linguistic fallacies and myths dating back from the days of colonisation? It is at times pointed out that, from a sociolinguistic perspective, African linguists should listen to speech communities that resist the use of their languages in education, in order to move beyond the 'impasse'. That some should call the neglect and complete relegation of African languages to non-languages an 'impasse' is disingenuous and places undue focus on the individual. Furthermore, it ignores more powerful historical and macrostructural factors that create and entrench social inequalities and injustices. The very observation about an 'impasse' often fails to fully acknowledge the insidious role the articles of faith and linguistic fallacies have played in the general perception of multilingualism in Africa. Therefore, the issue remains: what is the best way out of this 'impasse'?

In direct contradiction to the scientific evidence available, some, who are still wedded to myths about the 'superiority' and/or universality of a certain language – this used to be French; now it is English – even refuse to believe that there is an 'impasse'. In a critique of *Vanishing Voices* (Nettle & Romaine, 2000), Malik (2000) writes: ' ... most languages die out, not because they are suppressed, but because native speakers yearn for a better life. Speaking a language such as English, French or Spanish, and discarding traditional habits, can open up new worlds and is often a ticket to modernity.' In other words, the world community is better off embracing the (current) dominant language of globalisation (Van Parijs, 1999, 2000, 2002 and forthcoming). This is quite a categorical view: 'What if half of the world's languages are on the verge of extinction? Let them die in peace.' (Malik, 2000). The point is that, in the case of Africa, as is shown in this book, we are not exactly talking about languages on the verge of extinction. The presumption that multilingualism is a stumbling block to development is just that, a presumption – albeit engrossed with a certain vision of development as it ought to be pursued throughout the world, that is to say, through narrowly conceived economic theories and practices of development. Lieberson (1980: 12) points out that 'essentially no substantial causal linkage exists in either direction between changes in the nation's development and its level of linguistic homogeneity', whilst Nettle (2000: 344–346) argues that there is a 'lack of evidence for a direct causal interpretation ... *[and]* that attempts to enforce linguistic homogeneity cannot be justified on economic terms.' Nettle further writes that

> No data thus far produced give unequivocal evidence of a link between language and economy above and beyond that explained by their codetermination by geographical factors. A more realistic interpretation of the correlation would therefore stress that languages and economies coevolve under the constraints of physical and human geography. (Nettle, 2000: 344)

(Also see Grin, 1996, 1999 and 2003; Nettle & Romaine, 2000: 155; Skutnabb-Kangas, 2000: 242; Spolsky, 2003).

The stage is therefore set. We may now ask the fundamental questions, as patterns of language repertoire and use in developing nations, and now within the institutions of the European Union (Grin, 2004), amply demonstrate that the degree of communication effectiveness, and hence its critical importance to economic progress, is not necessarily a function of the number of languages spoken, but that of the availability of communication across the different language communities through multilingualism (Lo Bianco, 2002: 6). If the main argument seeking to tie multilingualism with difficulties in communication is essentially flawed, why should Africa continue to use European languages as the sole media of instruction and administration? How can African languages be used to improve outcomes in the areas of education, health, governance and the economy? What are the African languages that can bring about these outcomes? Is the aim of globalisation to transform the objective disempowerment of the African peoples into a subjective acceptance by these peoples of the view that they are incapable of empowerment? Does globalisation spell the demise of African languages?

The paradigm proposed in this book is to approach the definition and process of development in terms of the medium of transfer of non-prescriptive information and skills to the majority of the people, and the active participation of the latter in programmes that matter to their everyday life and wellbeing, so that the changes that are generated are sustainable. Despite the self-congratulatory claims of Francophonie and the Global English movement, African languages have survived, developed and spread (Organisation Internationale de la Francophonie, 2007). What does this say about the African people and their social and communicative practices of languages? What does it say about the prevailing definition of language?

Multilingualism in Africa

Fardon and Furniss (1994: 4) describe multilingualism as the African lingua franca, thereby stressing that multilingualism is the norm. Individuals use a variety of languages (indigenous languages, pidgins, creoles, popular varieties of national/official languages) in their daily interactions, with varying degrees of fluency, for different purposes, code-mixing and code-switching to adjust to new communicative situations.

After much hesitation, I have resolved to include in this foreword a brief autobiography, to underscore the point that the thrust of this book is not about a nostalgic dream for some imaginary revival of African languages, or a choice between the languages of the former colonisers and African languages. Born in Africa, the first languages I spoke were Wå and French, at home with my parents and siblings, and Yoruba, Baoule and Dyula, with other children of my age in the immediate neighbourhood and in other domains outside my home. All my primary and secondary schooling was in French, with English, then Spanish as subjects in secondary schools (English from the first year of secondary school and Spanish from the third year of secondary school). I soon added Attié, Gouro and Koulango as my father, a civil servant, took his family with him when he was sent to various regions across the country. As I moved away from home for my secondary and upper secondary schooling, I also picked up Dida and Bété.[5] My undergraduate studies were done mostly in French, with some English, and my graduate studies entirely in English – which meant that I spent three or four times the amount of time my American classmates took to go through the reading assignments. Later on, as an adult, for personal and professional reasons, I acquired 'passive knowledge' of other languages such as Ewe (a cross-border language spoken in Ghana and Togo)[6] and Laotian, and familiarised myself with Mandarin Chinese and Japanese, when my children studied these languages in primary and secondary school. Many educated Africans have followed a similar path, having to learn new languages altogether in order to attend tertiary institutions in Europe, the USA, the former USSR, China and Japan.

Over the years, and because of the way I use my language repertoire, French has taken over as my dominant language, and English as my second dominant language. I use the languages of my childhood only when needed, and although I am no longer proficient in some of them (some, like Spanish, have receded into passive memory) I cherish every word and phrase I can still recall. They are always a great source of satisfaction every time I get to use them to remind a childhood friend, or someone who speaks the language, that I am not a total stranger. And, all the while, I have never felt that I might lose fluency in Wå, as a consequence of having acquired all these other languages. My identity would be incomplete without the dispersed identities I have acquired through these languages. Better than Janus, I have several faces, each of which is an essential part of my personality, and with which I view and deal with the world around me. In my country of birth, and in other African countries, it is a matter of course that one should acquire all the communicative tools necessary to interact effectively with the people in whose environment one lives. It is a great irony that the English language I have embraced with a passion, in order to express my discontent with the hegemony of French in my country of birth, is itself displaying the same features and arrogance that I abhor so much.

This is not an exceptional linguistic experience in the context of my country of birth, or in the wider African context. Many African children are going through the same linguistic experience, and there is evidence to suggest that this dynamic of the patterns of language learning and use is spreading well beyond the lucky few of the late 60s and 70s.[7] But to what extent do such changes in language repertoires generate and are a reflection or a reconfiguration of 'elite closure' (Myers-Scotton, 1993: 149)?

It is sometimes suggested that I, and those Africans who have been through a similar linguistic experience, must be highly intelligent. But I am always reminded that this is very much akin to being a war veteran. Those who return home are not necessarily the bravest, and the heroes – the true heroes – die on the battlefield, just like all these brilliant minds I have come across in primary school, in secondary school and in my undergraduate years at university, who dropped out along the way for various reasons, including the failure to master the language of instruction.

Multilingualism in Africa is part and parcel of life and takes no account, a priori, of a hierarchy between the languages acquired. Most people select the language or variety of language most appropriate for a particular context of interaction and communities and identities are defined and change through particular practices and networks of communication. Batibo (2005: 1) gives the example of a Tshivenda speaker (South Africa) who may speak Tshivenda to his/her parents, but uses IsiZulu or Fanagalo when talking to workmates, and receives orders in Afrikaans from his/her employer, then uses English at a bank. Members of a speech community have a number of languages at their disposal and use them according to the subject matter and/or context, or to whom they are speaking. This complexity has led to assertions that defy common sense. There is therefore greater order in the apparent chaos of the African multilingual context than is generally realised, and the Somali, Rwanda and Burundi tragedies have finally turned on its head the argument that monolingualism or near-monolingualism is the bedrock of socio-political stability and economic prosperity for Africans. The reality is that local African languages help the masses survive, especially in the areas of health and the economy.

This reality is not exclusively African. Many children growing up in multilingual contexts the world over have similar childhood experiences with their languages. So conference interpreters, even in European countries, sometimes have to add a language to their repertoire, or improve it in a formal context, before sitting the entrance examination of the interpreting school. Sometimes this happens much later in their professional life, when they want to extend their language combination in order to enter a specific language market. Adding a language to one's repertoire is quite common and always enriching. Contrary to what some – mostly monolinguals – may think, speaking more than one language is not an act of religious faith; if one cannot be a committed Jewish practitioner and a devout Muslim, or a good Catholic and a strong Protestant at the same time, it is always rewarding to be able to speak to strangers in their own language and hence to build bridges instantly. The foregoing is evidence that the linguistic environment of the African child is a complex one. This multilingual complexity at the individual level is a reflection of the linguistic complexity of African societies at large. Is this sort of diversified linguistic repertoire an obstacle to efficient communication, and ultimately to development? What is development?

Introduction

... novelty shall not be suppressed for very long.
Kuhn (1962)

*As long as the lions will not have their own historians, the stories about
hunting will always praise the courage of the hunter.*
(African Proverb)

The aim of this book is to describe the place and role of African languages in
four areas traditionally considered as the pillars of development; namely,
education, health, the economy and governance. It argues that the role of
language in human societies contains its own imperative as the focus for
research in development, because language is the vehicle for the transfer of
knowledge, and because this transfer of knowledge is conditional upon the
efficiency of communication. Acknowledgement of this role would help
provide the masses with better literacy, numeracy and health care. This is
not just about African languages of wider communication, but also about
the gradual shifts in linguistic identities occurring in almost every African
society, based both on African languages of wider communication and on
European languages inherited from colonisation. The language practices of
individuals and communities exhibit an incredible capacity and resourcefulness in empowering themselves where and when it matters most. The
sociolinguistics of development suggests that an understanding of these
linguistic realities goes a long way towards helping to improve educational, health and economic policies and to resolve the crises of governance
in Africa.

Although the title of this book suggests an equal treatment of both
sociolinguistics and development, it is decidedly focused on development
in Africa. Development is often understood in terms of economic growth;
but the economy must rely on other key sectors such as education (an illiterate population cannot help itself out of the dungeons of poverty and
misery), health (an unhealthy population cannot provide a reliable
workforce) and good governance (the lack of basic human rights, good and
fair administration and political vision will seriously affect economic
growth). This book argues that language lies at the heart of all these sectors,
at least insofar as adequate and appropriate service provision is concerned,

and therefore at the heart of the economy and of development. Indeed, development is a process that requires a momentum of its own, if it is to endure. The help coming from well-meaning benefactors and aid donors will mean nothing, if it only goes to hands that receive, and not to brains that can conceive. This book also aims to question the present, in order to better understand the future.

Ki Zerbo (2003: 153) warned that 'The trees of growth must not hide the forest of development"; in other words, development must not be reduced to a question of 'economic possession' or 'power' to the detriment of a holistic and human vision. Development is first and foremost about 'being' and 'wellbeing', not just about a material dimension that leads to all sorts of absurdities. Although it is rich in mineral resources, the continent is better known in terms of poverty, inequality, exclusion, war and diseases; the sad reality is quite simply that development, in its current model, has stalled in Africa, and the current state of affairs can be summed up in one word: 'crippled'. The education systems, the health systems, governance and hence the economy are all crippled, and in no small measure, because of lack of genuine communication. Those at the top are *talking at*, not *to*, the population, using European languages that bring them power and prestige. For those at the bottom though, day-to-day life is a struggle that is made even harder, as they must face the challenge of learning and seeking medical help in a foreign language. Yet, there exists another Africa, an Africa of hard working people, and an Africa looking to the future with great anticipation. While this book may read at times like a litany of the continent's shortcomings, it is this thriving Africa that it aims to point to, through a discussion of the centrality of its languages in a sustainable development strategy, whilst arguing that development is much more than economic growth, and that development is viable only when it seeks to allow speech communities to realise their full potential, when it endorses and respects linguistic and cultural pluralism.

Each chapter of this book focuses on one of these sectors fundamental to economic growth and, ultimately to development, looking at the true place and role of African languages in these facets of the life of the African people. The subject of the first chapter, prolegomena to the sociolinguistics of development, is an attempt to summarise the main issues that have long stood in the way of African languages. Are the arguments justified and well founded? Is language neutral? This chapter argues that language is an inevitable site of ideology, which involves asymmetrical power relations between groups and individuals (Suleiman, 2004: 7); much more than just a means of communication, language binds a speech community with its history and a sense of identity through specific cultural practices that drive the imagination and creativity of the members of the community. Hence, language also serves as an instrument of power 'that shapes reality by influencing other people's perceptions of that reality, and of what counts as reality. Words are not empty talk; they are a form of action' (Suleiman, 2004: 218), and they express an ideological position. This is why no significant and lasting change can occur in Africa without her languages and without the full participation of the majority of her people. The solution to empowering the masses in Africa is not in making everyone fluent in English, French, Portuguese or Spanish, but in replicating their patterns of local language use in development policies and programs.

Empowering the people to take an active part in their own destiny begins with language literacy and education, both of which are critical indicators of development; so this topic naturally leads to a discussion of the role of language in the provision of literacy and education, the subject of Chapter 2. Most children of school age in Africa speak their mother tongues, and yet find themselves in schools where the language of instruction is not the language(s) they know, and so they will struggle to succeed academically. Many of them will drop out, or will be pushed out, for lack of success. This chapter revisits the issues raised by education in European languages and asks whether there is a case to be made for mother-tongue or bilingual education. Development is today perceived as the transformation of the world through the innovations of new information and communication technologies (World Summits on the Information Society in Geneva in 2003 and in Tunis in 2005). Hence, this chapter also discusses recent developments in Information and Communication Technologies (ICTs), which hold the promise of bridging the digital divide. ICTs now provide a pathway for accessing new knowledge through the languages that can articulate the creative and inventive instincts of the African child and offer the technical tools to address many of the constraints that held the African continent back, allowing a number of myths to develop and spread. Implementing a consistently democratic language policy through the enculturation of technology, such as software localisation, now appears as one of the critical components of the consolidation and expansion of democratic society in Africa, even, and especially, in a 'globalised' world.

Chapter 3 deals with language, health and development and discusses recent surveys (e.g. Sidaction, UNAIDS and WHO, 2005) and reports on local associations and community groups that are at the forefront of best practices in facilitating access to, administration and management of the antiretroviral drugs for the treatment of HIV/AIDS and other diseases in Africa. These programs are mostly implemented in the local languages and make up for gaps in a public health system that is completely overwhelmed in most African countries. The chapter also discusses the issues of medical infrastructure across Africa and the massive brain drain of African medical staff to Europe and the United States. However, the fundamental question here is about how the masses access health information in Africa, and how health is generally administered. What is the general pattern of doctor–patient communication, and to what extent is the language used critical to a successful outcome?

The topic of Chapter 4, language, the economy and development, has been an important one for quite some time now, and is increasingly being used to argue against the adoption of mother-tongue education in Africa. To what extent is economic analysis relevant to language? This book argues that the economic experiments of nearly half a century in Africa have failed, mainly because the actors of change have not been allowed to participate in the formulation and implementation of these development programmes. This is in part through the neglect of a sustainable strategy – the use of the languages most appropriate for the transfer of knowledge and technology in the African context. A look at language use in the informal sector of the economy suggests that at the micro-economic level African languages make good business sense. The informal sector involves an average of 2.7 million people or 76% of jobs in Cotonou (Benin), Ouagadougou (Burkina Faso), Abidjan (Côte d'Ivoire), Bamako (Mali), Niamey (Niger), Dakar (Senegal) and Lomé (Togo), and generates US$9 billion, or the equivalent of the combined GDPs of Senegal and Mali (see Afristat & DIAL, 2003). It occupies well over 90% of the active population, represents well over 70% of the GDP in several African countries, at least 43% of the African GDP according to the World Bank (2007) and is the lifeline for many communities in which African languages are the dominant vehicles of communication. This chapter examines whether policies mobilising and revitalising the languages that oil the machine of the informal economy can have positive implications for the formal economy and for economic development at large.

The chapter on language, governance and development, Chapter 5, looks at the need for the actors of development to understand and take an active part in the day-to-day running of their own affairs, through the language(s) they know, if good governance is indeed about people, all people, being able to talk to one another, and about participation, representation and benefaction. Current estimates of speakers of English, French, Portuguese and Spanish in Africa over the last 50 years vary between 20% to a low 5% (Bamgbose, 1971: 38-39; Heine, 1992: 27; Heugh, 1999: 75–76).[8] If this is true, then we are dealing with an elitist state of affairs, where the lucky few are talking to the majority of the people in languages that empower only those who do the talking. This chapter explores ways in which democracy and governance can be improved for the majority in Africa.

The final chapter suggests that language is a means by which the participation of the people in the process of development can either be facilitated or hindered. The question, when it comes to Africa, is no longer about what speech communities *need to do* with their languages, but what it is they *actually do* with them. This essential consideration has significant implications in terms of the place and role of European languages and their local varieties within the new, mostly young African speech communities; ignoring these in any future language plan will be as mistaken and costly as the language policy that is the target of this book. Language is an explicit contributing factor of development and needs to be taken into account in the formulation of innovative and visionary language policies in Africa for good education, health, economy and governance, all of which are conditional upon efficient communication.

What is the Sociolinguistics of Development?

In the preface to *English as Global Language*, David Crystal (1997: viii-ix) writes:

I firmly believe in two linguistic principles which some people see as contradictory, but which for me are two sides of one coin.

I believe in *the fundamental value of multilingualism, as an amazing world resource* which presents us with different perspectives and insights, and thus enables us to reach a more profound understanding of the nature of the human mind and spirit ...

I believe in *the fundamental value of a common language*, as an amazing world resource which presents us with unprecedented possibilities for mutual understanding, and thus enables us to find fresh opportunities for international communication ...

We need to take both principles on board if we are to make any progress towards the kind of peaceful and tolerant society which most people dream about ... . (Crystal, 1997: viii-ix; my italics)

There is indeed no contradiction in these two linguistic principles: safeguarding multilingualism, and having a common language at the same time. This is an age-old practice, which unfortunately has been tampered with across time and space by monolingual language policies.

Although the adoption of a national/official language or a medium of instruction is a complex process that requires the balancing of political and practical considerations, the available evidence does not suggest that since independence the African political classes have struck the right balance in this area. Language constitutes a key ingredient in creating a favourable context for sustainable and long-term endogenous development, and good education, health, economy and governance are all conditional upon efficient communication. So, it is one thing to argue that a common language is a necessary and sufficient requirement in nation building (Berdichevsky, 2004: 1) and another to suggest that development can occur in someone else's language. If multilingualism is valuable for nation building, instruction in African languages raises a number of issues and challenges that some advocates of this solution are not always fully aware of (Djité, 2006b). It would be wonderful if everyone could conduct all their affairs, including education, health, trade and governance, in their own language. The much more sobering reality is, however, is that the alternative of giving African languages a better status in education, health, the economy and governance requires considerable expenditure. Moreover, the correction of inequality, inequity and injustice is not always the motive for language-in-education planning. On the contrary, the available evidence suggests that language policy and planning have generally been carried out to establish or entrench a form of imposition or domination and, hence, to deepen the inequality, inequity and injustice. Therefore, the issue of instruction in African languages is one of power relations. Governments in Africa make language-related decisions in ways that can maintain and guarantee their control of power. The key question here is whether these decisions will lead to and foster development on the continent.

The sociolinguistics of development is an analysis of modernisation, informed by what constitutes the pillars of modernisation itself in the African context; namely, education, health, the economy, governance. The premise of the analysis is that each of these sectors is like a piece of a puzzle connected to the others. Education, for instance, provides the foundations for good governance. One cannot expect a country to attain any level of development when its people have no functional literacy skills, and no access to basic information about how to protect themselves against preventable diseases, when they cannot find employment, earn a decent wage and accrue assets, and are not able to participate in the public affairs of their own society. The language policy, language-in-education policy, the pattern of language maintenance and use, as well as language attitudes, form the basis of the analysis, and link all these sectors to the challenges of modernisation that face Africa.

The sociolinguistics of development calls for a paradigm shift in terms of the subject matter of the sociolinguistic study. It makes the point that the issue of language is vital and complex, because of its inextricable links with a society's education, health, economy and political life. It also acknowledges that language policy issues are highly political and politicised, and that language can be used as an instrument to provide or deny access to economic and political emancipation. Taking into account the language practices of the majority of the people concerned will make a critical difference in terms of effectiveness, relevance and sustainability. This is in no way an attempt to recover national and cultural pride (nationalism), but an attempt to facilitate the process leading to development, through a more appropriate language, for the majority of the population (nationism).

The sociolinguistics of development argues that a good language policy must be based on evidence from research and be defendable on the strength of this evidence. It must be realistic in terms of the resources available but, above all, it must be just and democratic and address the interest of the nation (Lo Bianco 1991). The premise of any scientific endeavour is to identify a problem and find a solution to it. Being able to identify a linguistic problem for what it really is, is a prerequisite to providing an accurate, organised picture of the overall linguistic situation and to making the prospect of language planning more realistic. Assumptions, no matter how close they may be to the truth, must be rejected, especially when they are not supported by evidence, and failing to acquaint oneself with the sociolinguistic reality or not taking it into account will not make it go away. Language is an implicit contributing factor to development, but the issues involved in the relevance of African languages in the modernisation of the continent are not simple and are most certainly beyond simplistic solutions.

Chapter 1

Prolegomena to the Sociolinguistics of Development

> *Western culture has made, through language, a provisional analysis*
> *of reality and, without corrective, holds resolutely to that analysis as*
> *final; the only correctives lie in all those other tongues which by*
> *aeons of independent evolution have arrived at different, but equally*
> *logical provisional analyses.*
> Whorf (1956: 244)

> *In broader terms, Africa that acknowledges its ethno-linguistic*
> *pluralism and accepts this as a normal way of life and as*
> *a rich resource for development and progress.*
> 'Vision for Africa' *–The Harare Declaration*
> (UNESCO, 2006)

Introduction

The interfaces between sub-Saharan Africa and the rest of the world have been, and still are, painful. In almost all cases (agriculture, trade, health, technologies, immigration), they present a negative balance. Indeed, everything pertaining to Africa is seen as a problem: its demography, its economy, its political systems, its languages. However, the most painful and absurd interface between Africa and the rest of the world is the language question, and the crucial nexus between language and development. In an age of globalisation, many find it difficult to understand the need for continuing to problematise and reflect on the issue of language in Africa. So much so that it is very hard to argue the case for the maintenance of African languages, let alone their development. It is even harder to generate interest in language policy issues about and on the African continent. Why is this so?

First, the African linguistic situation is genuinely a complex one: multilingualism is normal for the majority of the African population and language diversity is a feature of almost every country on the continent. Language policies, when they exist, vary considerably from one country to another, and the prevailing view around the world and in Africa is still that this continent is awash with a plethora of languages, the speech communities of which can hardly understand one another. Secondly, most African languages lack international currency and are put under severe strain by the languages of the former colonisers that arguably offer the African people economic and scientific advantages not available to them through their own languages. Thirdly, after independence, the hangover of colonial approaches to multilingualism has led many African countries to promote the use of European languages, to the detriment of the languages actually known and used by the majority of the people. Despite the occasional rhetoric about their importance, African languages have, until recently, been neglected and downgraded in almost all cases, as development intervention and pedagogical practices in education have been subordinated to the search for a way around the linguistic diversity of African countries (Robinson, 1996). Former British colonies by and large used local languages as languages of instruction in the first few years of education, whilst former French, Belgian and Portuguese colonies maintained French and Portuguese as the sole languages of instruction throughout the school system. These European languages, in essence the languages of power and high status functioning as boundary markers of socio-economic opportunity and mobility, largely excluded and still marginalise the vast majority of Africans from various aspects of everyday life that are considered the pillars of development. Indeed, knowledge of a European language is the sine qua non condition for higher education and socio-economic success, and African societies are currently split between those who speak the language of power and those who do not – a division that mirrors the dichotomy between literate versus illiterate, educated versus uneducated, urban versus rural, rich versus poor. And yet current language policies and practices show no real willingness to break away from the colonial systems, as many African governments seem hell-bent on pursuing the colonial practices and refuse to innovate in favour of mass education. Hence, 50 years on, the historical legacy still prevails (Bamgbose, 1991:70--71), and the current situation can be summed up as follows:

(1) timid or no use of local languages as media of instruction;
(2) dominant or exclusive use of the language of the former coloniser at all levels of education.

As a result, in most of Africa, one European language (English, French or Portuguese) always plays the most important role, at least in the official domain and mainly in the urban centres, placing those who are not proficient in European languages at a considerable disadvantage, and pushing majorities into separate and artificial existence. Comprehension and active use of French, English or Portuguese, the 'cultural [and economic] capital' seldom exceed 20% of the population and remain 'unattainable' for the rest (Alexander, 2000). This lack of proficiency in the official language is a powerful obstacle to individual and collective socio-economic improvement, as the majority of the people have no access to education, decent housing and health, and are denied full and active participation in the running of the affairs of state, simply because they cannot speak the official language.

Alexander (2005: 520) notes that Africa's linguistic dependence on Europe (Mazrui & Mazrui, 1998) was most apparent when the outgoing chairperson of the African Union (AU), Joaquim Chissano of Mozambique, caused a stir when he addressed the assembled Heads of States in KiSwahili, although it had already been resolved that KiSwahili would be one of the working languages of the AU. And there were even more rumblings in the audience when the incoming chairperson, Olusegun Obasanjo of Nigeria, proceeded to address the audience in Arabic, which has been an official language of the Organisation for African Union and the AU for a long time (*BBC News*, 2004). This supports the view of Mazrui and Mazrui when they write:

> [an] important source of intellectual dependence in Africa is the language in which African graduates and scholars are taught ... in non-Arabic-speaking Africa, a modern surgeon who does not speak a European language is virtually a sociolinguistic impossibility ... [A] conference of African scientists, devoted to scientific matters and conducted primarily in an African language, is not yet possible ... It is because of the above considerations that intellectual and scientific dependence in Africa may be inseparable from linguistic dependence. The linguistic quest for liberation must seek to promote African languages, especially in academia, as one of the strategies for promoting greater intellectual and scientific independence from the West. (Mazrui & Mazrui, 1998: 64–65)

The fundamental question has therefore always been, and still is, about the nexus between language and development. What, for example, is the most appropriate language(s) for disseminating information to the masses about health and hygiene and, most importantly, about preventive measures against diseases such as malaria, tuberculosis and HIV/AIDS? What is the most appropriate language(s) for passing on to farmers relevant information on the efficient and safe use of fertilisers and pesticides, or practical information on high-yield varieties of crops and cattle, techniques for stocking ponds, fish conservation and processing, rivers and artificial lakes, appropriate planting seasons, irrigation techniques and techniques for the preservation of land and soils? Quite simply, Africa cannot continue to ignore her own languages. Fifty years after colonisation began to come to an end, it is abundantly clear that the imposition of the languages of the former colonisers in the crucial areas of education, health, the economy and governance has failed to meet local needs.

The aim of this chapter is to separate facts from fiction, and to disentangle the language question in Africa from articles of faith passing for theoretical frameworks which, despite the appearance of intellectual complexity, are narrow and self-serving, because they fail to fully appreciate the complexities of language diversity. Nothing short of the full participation of the majority of its human capital will bring significant and lasting change to Africa; for, 50 years on, the solution to empowering the masses in Africa clearly does not lie in making everyone fluent in the languages of the former colonisers (i.e. English, French, Portuguese or Spanish). The issues raised in this chapter are:

(1) the assumptions underlying the rhetoric behind the marginalisation of African languages;
(2) the actual sociolinguistic picture of Africa, not just in terms of the number of languages, but in terms of the over-arching patterns of actual use, roles and statuses of these languages;
(3) whether language is neutral in the pursuit of development. In other words, can development be achieved in any language? Can civic information be efficiently disseminated? How much does the average citizen know about his/her country's political processes? Is the paucity of newspapers in local languages an impediment to political debate? What, in the final analysis, is development? Is the lack of development in Africa in fact an absence of solidarity?

What is Development?

Development, for the layperson, is quite simply finding solutions to everyday problems which human beings face, and improving their living conditions. In his Inaugural Address of January 20, 1949, after the devastation of World War II, US President Harry S. Truman described his thinking of Development Assistance as ' ... making the benefits of our scientific advances and industrial progress available for the improvement and growth of underdeveloped areas' (Truman, 1949). In other words, development was to be a process of transferring technical capability or expertise to stimulate local food production and industrial infrastructure. The developed world engaged in this process of transfer of know-how in Africa, seeking to replicate well-known and tried processes. This was inevitable, since economic theories of development and modernisation before the

Asian boom (Japan, Korea, Taiwan, Singapore, and now India and China) were mostly Euro-centric. Over time, it became abundantly clear to some that Africa's cultural and socio-historical circumstances are different, and that the paths to development on the continent may differ from those of the Western world. What are some of these cultural and socio-historical circumstances? Do they really matter?

All economic studies look at development in terms of the general level of education, the critical indicators of health, the growth of the economy and, most recently, good governance. The connection between language and development did not always feature in these studies, in part because development was first conceived as moral progress for 'primitive' or 'oral' societies. Yet economic history cannot be explained on the basis of economic factors alone; and language, being part and parcel of all spheres of life – thought processes, communication, education, health, the economy and good governance – cannot be excluded from economic history.

Development in Africa is often defined in technocratic terms that do not take language into account and hence marginalise the majority of the people, their concerns and legitimate aspirations, even though Africa is beset by a number of development issues that are language-related. Most approaches to development in Africa put the emphasis on economic growth, measured by traditional indicators such as the gross domestic product or the gross national product, and this is reflected in the definition of development one can draw from the practices of the Bretton Woods Institutions over the past six decades, namely, that development means export-led growth through structural adjustment, because for a long time development was determined by way of quantitative constructs such as gross national product, gross domestic product, growth and/or inflation rates and income per capita.[9] It was thought that technology (e.g. the green revolution), the economy (e.g. import substitution or comparative advantage theories), politics and the economy (e.g. the dependency theory, which sees a dependency link between politics and the economy), and/or demography were key factors of development policies.

Complicating matters further is the confusion created under the criteria of the World Trade Organisation (WTO),[10] where there is a certain degree of selection and interpretation of meaning of the terms 'developed' and 'developing' country, as countries choose to be either 'developed', 'developing' or 'least developed', because each of these statuses in the WTO brings certain rights and privileges. For instance, developing countries have the privilege of receiving technical assistance or the benefit from the Generalised System of Preferences (GSP) provided by developed countries (although it is the preference-giving country that decides which developing country will benefit from these preferences).

Development is therefore generally accepted as a moral evidence, universal aspiration and historical necessity. After nearly half a century of political independence, it has become painfully clear that development is certainly not the result of a quiet and easy stroll, inexorably promised to all. This is in part because, for far too long, development was an idea from developed countries 'projected', as it were, towards non-developed countries. Unfortunately, development in African countries was perceived by many as the hoarding of material wealth and consumerism, whilst the necessary changes of the productive social and organisational structures were overlooked. This kind of development has proven illusory for the majority. The current state of affairs in Africa clearly shows that there is something fundamentally wrong in this sort of approach and that one cannot set developmental goals that ignore the attributes and peculiarities of the target population.

This approach to development was first called into question in a report published in 1975 by the Dag Hammarskjöld Foundation,[11] as it became clear that communication is crucial in the process of technical or technology transfer. The report argued that, in order to be *sustainable*, development had to effect changes at three levels; namely: (1) at the level of the actors, (2) at the level of the methods used, and (3) at the level of the aims and objectives of the process. The report also stressed the need for a 'bottom-up' or participative approach to development, in which the target population and non-governmental organisations would become the main actors in development planning and projects. It was acknowledged that no one factor can define, account for or shape the development process, and that a shift had to be made from mono-causal and mechanistic theories of development to more holistic approaches, with the introduction of the 'human development indicator' encompassing several related development indicators. This type of development had to be firmly based on local knowledge and aimed at meeting local needs and aspirations. Languages are the cornerstones of communication and progress, and examining human development means examining how the communicative, and hence linguistic, dimension of development is understood. Participatory methods were therefore initiated, with a view to involving people in the identification and resolution of their own problems, and this gave rise to a number of methods of data collection, such as the Rapid Rural Appraisal (RRA), the Participatory Rural Appraisals (PRA) and the Participatory Learning and Action (PLA), all of which recognised the need to listen to the people and to share knowledge. The Participatory Rural Communication Appraisals (PRCA), a modified form of PRA, were also developed to focus on communications systems and improvement of communication sharing among all the stake-holders. The PRCA is a communication research method that uses field-based visualisation techniques, interviews and group discussions to generate information for the design of effective communication program-mes, materials, media and methods for development purposes. Needless to say, the PRCA requires the use of a shared language, and in rural and remote areas, an African language, to ensure, as the name of the method suggests, the full participation of the people in the process of needs anal-ysis, problems identification, possible solutions, understanding of the scientific, technical and developmental issues and, most importantly, the relevance to and sense of ownership by the people involved in such a process (Anyaegbunam *et al*, 2001: 18). Language in the PRCA serves as a vehicle for active participation of all the shareholders in the development process and influences decision-making.

The concept of *sustainable development* was again used in the 1987 Brundtland Report (WCED, 1987). In the 1990s, Mahbub Ul Haq developed the seminal concept of 'Development Index', a comparative standard means of measuring poverty, literacy, education, life expectancy, childbirth rates and other critical factors. As a result, in the UNDP 1992 *World Report on Human Development*, the UNDP changed the economic indicators (i.e. productivity, gross national product and infrastructure) through which the level of development of a society was assessed. Since then, the index has been used to measure: (1) life expectancy at birth, (2) adult literacy rate (with two-thirds weight) and the combined primary, secondary, and tertiary gross enrolment ratio (with one-third weight), and (3) gross domestic product per capita at purchasing power parity in US dollars. In other words, the Development Index is a measure of the extent to which the citizens of a country can lead a long and healthy life, be educated and enjoy a decent standard of living. It is therefore an indication of where a country is in terms of development.

This advance in the field of development theory acknowledges the link between language and socio-economic development. Human develop-ment has it roots in the social well-being approach and is understood as the process of opening up the people's opportunities and capabilities to enable them to lead rewarding, healthy and fulfilling lives. It is a process that includes empowering people to gain and maintain the skills necessary, not only to meet their basic needs (food security, safe drinking water, improved sanitation, health care, education), but also to show resourcefulness and inventiveness in taking up new challenges that directly or indirectly affect their lives. As a result, the UNDP is now of the view that:

Previous concepts of development have often given exclusive attention to economic growth – on the assumption that growth will ultimately benefit everyone. Human development offers a much broader and more inclusive perspective. It demonstrates that economic growth is vital. [...] But growth on its own is not sufficient – it has to be translated into improvements in people's lives. Economic growth is not the *end* of human development. It is one important *means*. [...] People contribute to growth, and growth contributes to human well-being. (UNDP 1992: 12; italics in the original)

The 1992 World Summit in Rio de Janeiro again insisted on the need, not only to include the people in development projects, but also to empower them to own and drive development initiatives from the start to the implementation stage. The Rio World Summit came up with a Plan of Action for the 21st century called *Agenda 21*, which defined the objectives and priorities of sustainable development and the action of the NGOs within that Plan of Action.

The concept of development itself was later extended to include issues such as empowerment, co-operation, sustainability and security (UNDP, 1996: 55–56). It has also been expanded to the role of culture in the development process, leading the UNDP to state that 'human development is concerned not just with people as individuals but also with how they interact and cooperate in communities' (UNDP, 1996: 55). In its 1996 Report, the UNDP (1996: 55) identified the imposition of a dominant language as a culturally repressive form of development, which destroys other cultures and languages in the pursuit of nation-building and stressed that the most successful states (e.g. Switzerland, Malaysia) tend to be those that acknowledge and respect cultural and linguistic diversity (UNDP, 1996: 4, 62). This view was reiterated in the 2004 UNDP report:

People want the freedom to practice their religion openly, to speak their language, to celebrate their ethnic or religious heritage without fear or ridicule or punishment or diminished opportunity. People want the freedom to participate in society without having to slip off their chosen cultural moorings. (UNDP, 2004: 1)

The 2004 report also warned that restrictive choices in language policies can lead to certain groups being excluded from society and therefore from development (UNDP, 2004: 60). Calling for a 'three language formula' for multilingual states, which would include an international language, a national lingua franca and a mother tongue in education and in government institutions (UNDP, 2004: 60–63), the report went so far as to say that 'development divorced from its human or cultural context is growth without a soul' (UNDP, 2004: 91). The UNDP is not alone is making such categorical assertions (see World Bank, 2005a, 2006a; ADB, 2006). This state of affairs comes as no surprise to the student of language, the education specialist, the health expert, the economist or the political scientist interested in Africa, who has witnessed teachers and their students, and doctors and their patients, struggling to communicate and politicians on television and radio talking *at* their people and aiming to impress the West, rather then talking *to* them and engaging them in a constructive manner.

What these major institutions were trying to suggest is that the mission of development is no longer the same and that the concept, just like the actions on the ground, has to change, along with the philosophy and practical approach. In the United Nations' 2005 *Human Development Report*, African countries occupied the last 23 places (from 154th to 177th) on the Human Development Index, with the best performers sitting at 51st (Seychelles) and 58th places (Libya) respectively.

Recent definitions suggest that development is a reduction in participants' vulnerability to things they do not control. Moreover, it is now generally agreed that people are to be placed at the centre of development, as development is increasingly seen as a general improvement of human life, including the general improvement of material well-being for the majority of the people in terms of food security, safe drinking water, improved sanitation, health care, education and better life expectancy. Human development can be understood as the process of opening up the opportunities and capabilities of people to enable them to lead rewarding, healthy and fulfilling lives. This process includes empowering people not only to gain and maintain the skills necessary to meet their basic needs, but to show resourcefulness and inventiveness to meet the challenges affecting their lives. Development is therefore not just economic, but also social and institutional, and incorporates elements of social practices, beliefs, values and customs, including languages. Only such a holistic approach can lead to the establishment of socio-political and economic systems and institutions that promote and guarantee human freedom (i.e. individual freedom, as well as freedom of choice), dignity, respect and social justice. Therefore, the concept of development cannot be dissociated from the need for active community participation in the process, as it comes down to the judicious utilisation of the available resources and human capital of the community. And, no matter how one defines development, it cannot be achieved without reference to language as an important factor, and real development is not possible in Africa without the integration of local languages and the full participation of all of her human capital. The people of Africa are the ones who will make it, or fail to make it, a developed continent.

Many organisations of the United Nations bodies now emphasise the fact that the recipients of development programs are not just passive receptors of knowledge and ready-made development solutions, but are active contributors to the designing of strategies to tackle specific problems. The fight to unlock the human potential of Africa is underscored in the 2004 UNDP Human Development report, _Cultural Liberty in Today's Diverse World_. The report highlights the potential of building a prosperous world, by bringing issues of language and/or culture to the mainstream of development thinking and practice; that is to say, 'Human development is first and foremost about allowing people to lead the kind of life they choose – and providing them with the tools and opportunities to make those choices' (UNDP, 2004: v). In the Foreword, Mark Malloch Brown, the UNDP Administrator, writes:

> If the world is to reach the Millennium Development Goals and ultimately eradicate poverty, it must first successfully confront the challenge of how to build inclusive, culturally diverse societies. _Not just because doing so successfully is a precondition for countries to focus properly on other priorities of economic growth, health and education for all citizens. But because allowing people full cultural expression is an important development end in itself._ (UNDP, 2004: Foreword: my italics)

The Report goes on to debunk some age-old myths according to which cultural and/or linguistic differences lead to social, economic and political conflicts, pointing out instead that managing such differences is a fundamental principle of human development. It notes that ' ... failing to address the grievances of marginalised groups does not just create injustice. It builds real problems for the future: unemployment, disaffected youth, angry with the status quo and demanding change, often violently.' (UNDP, 2004: vi). More often than not, social, economic and political conflicts erupt because of 'unequal access to economic assets, income or employment opportunities, social services or political opportunities' (UNDP, 2004: 41). Whilst being cautious and acknowledging that 'no state can afford to provide services and official documents in every language spoken on its territory', the report emphasises the need for multicultural policies in multilingual contexts by stressing another fundamental truth: 'Freedom of expression and the use of a language are inseparable' (UNDP, 2004: 60). Significantly, the Report argues that bilingual/multilingual education is a long-term investment whose costs are not as prohibitive as some would suggest, and gives the examples of the production of materials in Senegal, Guatemala and India to illustrate this point (UNDP, 2004: 62). It also deals with an important misconception (UNDP, 2004: 63), which, far too often, automatically compares language diversity to chaos, when in fact there is order in the apparent chaos of most multilingual polities. Djité (1988) and Prah (2000) have discussed the predominance of lingua francs and/or regional languages in multilingual contexts. These languages often transcend national boundaries (e.g. Bambara and Fulfulde in West Africa, Swahili in East Africa and Hausa in Nigeria, Niger, Chad and northern Cameroon) and are spoken by millions of people across territories much wider than those of many developed countries (e.g. Lingala in the Democratic Republic of Congo, Yoruba in Nigeria, Sango in the Central African Republic, Wolof in Senegal, and Xhosa and Zulu in South Africa). Another misconception is one that waves the spectre of banning European languages of wider communication, as was the case in Algeria in the early 1990s (Djité, 1992). In spite of all the optimistic 'guesstimates', the sociolinguistic reality remains that Africa speaks English and French today to about the same extent that medieval Europe spoke Latin (Coulmas, 1992: 52). More importantly, the goal of promoting multilingualism would be defeated if it meant banning European languages of wider communication. Instead, the goal is to give African languages the status they deserve in order to provide the majority of Africans with life-long functional literacy, numeracy and management skills, and to channel their entrepreneurial impulse for development into sustainable and long-term solutions. In as much as social wellbeing depends on the level of economic development, good economic performance is conditioned by an inversely proportional investment in human resources. Along the lines of the UNDP Human Development report, the UK *Commission on Africa* (2005) also calls for substantial new 'investments in [the] people' of Africa.

Much more than simply improving the standard of living, therefore, development is, in the final analysis, the sustained and continued improvement of the pillars of education, health, the economy and good governance (i.e. accountability) and a 'developing country' is a country *trying to achieve* some form of improvement of the human condition in the crucial areas of education, health, food, jobs, incomes and housing for the majority of its citizens, through its economic, political and social systems. The key terms here are the three words: *trying to achieve*, as not everyone is agreed that Africa has tried or is *trying to achieve* anything at all.

Can Africa Develop?

The continued decline of all the development indicators and the harrowing misery of the African people over the last five decades are good reasons to ask whether Africa really wants to develop. For a continent with a wealth of raw materials, oil, solar and wind energy, it is quite simply beyond the comprehension of many that Africa should still be wallowing in such misery. The African elite has and will blame the continent's predicament on an ongoing international conspiracy, which, from the transatlantic slave trade to colonisation and neo-colonisation, tries to control Africa's wealth and destiny. One wonders where one can find a drug that can make people so delusional, and many in Africa and abroad are beginning to tire of this line of argument, which essentially seeks to exonerate widespread mediocrity, incompetence, selfishness and greed in the society, and says that the problem lies squarely in the maladministration and systemic corruption of those elite (Kabou, 1991).

In her incisive _Et si l'Afrique refusait le développement_, Kabou (1991), among others (Ki Zerbo, 1990; Kodjo,1986; Memmi, 1989), asks whether Africa really wants to be developed and suggests that the evidence overwhelmingly points to the contrary. For her, Africa is under-developed and not developing, because of the lack of organisation, method and rigour characteristic of its economic, social and political structures. Kabou raises important issues having to do with a number of attitudes, excesses, paradoxes and contradictions underlining aspects of the prevalent mal-administration in many African countries, and pleads: 'Africa in the 21st century will have to become rational or there will be no Africa to speak of' (Kabou, 1991: 205). Ayittey (2005) shares this view and writes that there is much more than neo-colonialism and debt behind Africa's woes and, whilst arguing that a move away from the legacy of foreign colonial powers and contemporary Western-trained elites is vital, he accuses Africa's politicians of being largely responsible for the continent's problems. Smith (2003) goes so far as to state that if Africa is dying, this is a suicide that Africans alone are responsible for. Africans only have what they deserve, since as at the time of independence, 'Africa has been working for re-colonisation'. Unfortunately, everything in their material civilisation, their social organisation and their political culture acts as a braek to development. Manguelle (1989) adds that Africans have to acknowledge their own 'conscious' or 'unconscious' rejection of science and rationalism and undergo a radical 'cultural adjustment' before any development project on the continent can succeed.

But is it fair to say that Africans do not want development? Robert (2004) sees Africa as a victim of powerful external forces and conspiracies. According to her, one of the most serious problems in Africa is the presence on the continent of 'different (Western) ethnic groups that do not speak the same language, such as the World Bank, the IMF, the USAID and the French Ministry of Cooperation' (Robert, 2004: 27). In other words, far too many doctors who are not agreed on the right medicine to cure the patient. But clearly, Africa's underdevelopment is not due to disagreement between the donors or to lack of funding from the international community – otherwise, no one would be calling for debt forgiveness 50 years on. It is due to a lack of imagination, creativity and vision, and an inability to see the reality and accept oneself for what one is, and work towards sustainable and lasting solutions to one's ills. The political elite has distinguished itself by its zeal to out-Herod Herod, engaging in the building of prestigious white elephants with an almost kamikaze tendency to destroy everything preceding its term of office, and then to self destruct. It is an open secret that some leaders in these political elite are far richer than some of the wealthiest people in the developed world, and yet fail to help the most vulnerable citizens of their own countries, choosing instead, and with pride, to finance the political campaigns of their friends in Europe.[12] In almost all of Africa, key positions at all levels of government and administration, as well as university scholarships, are awarded not on merit, but by nepotism and favouritism. Government officials do not hesitate to write to Vice Chancellors and University Presidents overseas to request that their children be admitted in competitive courses without sitting the normal entrance examinations.[13] Some have argued that this ignorant and suicidal approach to governance was typical of an old generation of political leaders, who had sold their souls to the former colonisers. The jury is still out on the current political leadership, although the emerging trends are not encouraging. Wa Thiong'o (1986) suggests a decolonisation of the minds, whilst Djité (1994) argues that not only the political elite, but also the people need to be detoxified, because 'fish does not rot from the head alone, but also from the guts'. Indeed, corruption and greed are manifest not just in the embezzlement of public funds by government ministers, but also in the acts of the customs Officer, the traffic gendarme or policeman, and the office clerk, all of whom expect to be bribed before doing what they get paid for. It is manifest in the behaviour and philosophy of life of the masses who, in some countries, have come up with colourful expressions such as *'Qui est fou ?'* ('Who is mad?'), or *'Ce n'est pas le champ de mon père!'* ('It is not my father's farm!') – articulating their complete disregard for the proper functioning of public institutions.

These attitudes are reflected in the discourse of the political elite when it comes to language policy, and especially to language-in-education policy. Convinced of the superiority of European languages, they adopt the arguments of the colonial powers and use them in part to maintain and consolidate their own privileges, and to continue to divide and rule. And by dint of repeating and recycling such arguments, generations of 'English-seeking', not 'English-speaking', parents and children, have begun parroting their leaders, those they are endeavouring to emulate. Hence, many parents, especially in the rural areas, express the view that they send their children to school to learn the official language (English, French or Portuguese), and that a policy forcing them to learn an African language amounts to a dumbing down of their children to keep them at the bottom of the socio-economic scale. Therefore, arguing for the maintenance and development of African languages is a real challenge. It may not be enough to ask the right questions; one also has to engage in the much harder task of decolonising the minds of Africans. On all the available evidence, the latter task may indeed prove to be the hardest. And so the same questions remain. Must development be imported from the West, lock, stock and barrel? Must development be an intriguing, and sometimes contemptuous and arrogant, process that wants to dictate its own terms and conditions over and above those of the majority of the people? Must it ignore African culture and languages, African knowledge and know-how? This is one of the most important prolegomena that needs to be resolved for a sociolinguistics of development to be possible. And this endeavour requires an objective discussion of some of the myths (old and new) about why African languages are generally believed not to be conducive to development.

The Pathologising of Multilingualism: Old Myths about Language and Development in Africa

We define myths here as those commonly-held misconceptions that can be traced back to the era of colonisation and that are based either on the intrinsic value of language (i.e. linguistic factors) or the economic value of language (i.e. extra-linguistic factors, such as 'European languages are better suited for trade and globalisation'). These misconceptions, which are often based not on scholarship and research but on articles of faith, take on the characteristics of an ideology of contempt, trying all manner of ways to convince us that:

(1) African languages are barbarous, unintelligible forms of speech spoken by savage and low people, not worthy of God's creation and certainly not worthy of civilisation and industrialisation,[14] in part because they cannot express the complexities of modern scientific concepts, and also because there are so many of them that choosing any one of these languages as a national and/or official language will almost certainly lead to ethnic strife and division;

(2) Only European languages are rational, moral, civilised, and capable of expressing abstract thought, and therefore of articulating ideas pertaining to science, technology and development.

What is more, European languages are not only universal – as was at least claimed for the French language – they are also the only neutral languages able to inspire a feeling of nationhood in Africa.

These falsehoods and prejudices, all aimed at arguing the superiority of European languages, were planted in the minds of the African elite and ordinary people, and the colonial and neo-colonial literature is replete with negative descriptors ascribed to African languages and positive descriptors ascribed to the languages of the former colonisers.

The ad hoc nature of these generalisations was rarely questioned. Instead, as Hechter (1975) writes, they led to 'internal colonialism', whereby the African elite have reinforced the myths and negative images of African languages propagated by the colonial system. The protest of Aké Loba, a writer from Côte d'Ivoire, who declared: 'Let's speak French, English, Arabic, Chinese or Russian; but please, let's speak without wasting time' (cited in Person, 1982), is reminiscent of the famous cry of the Nama Chief in Namibia, who, in response to attempts to open schools using Nama as the medium of education, is reported to have said: 'Only Dutch, Dutch only! I despise myself and I want to hide in the bush, when I speak my Hottentot language' (Vedder, 1981: 275; cited in Ohly, 1992: 65). Internal colonialism is therefore as guilty as the colonial discourse on African languages in maintaining and spreading these myths that are now deeply rooted in the African psyche, as European languages continue to be associated with socio-economic advancement, whilst many Africans still do not believe that their own languages are capable of intellectualisation. Most African governments have retained the language(s) of the former coloniser(s) as their official language(s).[15] As a result, many, especially in the middle-class, are now bringing up their children exclusively in European languages, and many from the masses also seek to become, or have their children become, proficient in the same languages, having all come to the conclusion that the uplifting of their socio-economic status lies in these European languages.

The colonial legacy of linguistic ideology, the 'One Nation = One Language' equation, was so well articulated that some African languages have also been made more privileged than others (Blommaert, 1999a; Mazrui, 2003) on the African continent. Indeed, Blommaert (1999a) argues that Julius Nyerere's Ujamaa in Tanzania promoted the view according to which nation building required the reduction of language diversity 'to a workable degree', since ethnicity and its linguistic correlates were seen as remnants of the pre-independence situation. Although the wide use of KiSwahili, including as a medium of higher education (e.g. Open University of Dar es Salaam), disproved, in practice, the idea that African languages are not appropriate media for scientific discourse, the Swahilisation of Tanzanian society meant that the basic premises of colonial integrationist assumptions for efficiency and development were adopted. In other words, defining KiSwahili as a binding force for national unity also promoted the underlying belief that the fewer languages are spoken in a society, the more efficient that society is, and that a single national language should therefore be promoted, in order to stimulate the socio-political cohesion of the new nation. Language policy in Ujamaa society promoted Swahili exclusively, to the detriment of the other ethnic languages of the land, which were seen as symbols of tribal consciousness and obstacles to the hegemonic aim of the socialist ideology.

The curse of the Bible: Africa, the Tower of Babel

The Tower of Babel is a huge biblical architectural enterprise that Nebuchadnezzar II was never able to complete, because of communication difficulties within the workforce, who are said to have spoken the same language until divine intervention introduced other languages to confound the whole project. One of the most enduring myths about Africa is that, like the Tower of Babel, the continent has such a multitude of languages that it is impossible for any African country to choose a local language as its national or official language, or even as a medium of instruction. The problems of communication that made it impossible to complete the Tower of Babel are projected onto the African continent.

Without trying to deny the multilingual nature of Africa, it must be said that the identification of languages on the continent tends to be a loose free-for-all enterprise in which a new breed of explorers 'discovers' new speeches and labels them as they wish, hence creating new languages, in the name of their God-given right to do so, or as a necessary condition of despotism under which diversity of languages is consonant with a policy of divide and rule. As a result, dialects or phonological variations of the same language have been labelled separate languages (Djité, 1987), and the multilingual picture of the continent is blown out of proportion to suggest a linguistic Capernaum. Westley (1992) and Maho (2004), for instance, claim that at least 1400 languages are spoken in Africa, whilst Grimes (1992) believes that there are 1995 healthy languages on the continent. Batibo (2005: 2) acknowledges that:

(1)   many languages are known by several names, ... some [...] spelt with a variety of prefixes, and ... some [...] erroneously listed in categories to which they do not belong;

(2)   it is often difficult to distinguish between language, dialect and dialect clusters;
(3)   missionaries in the 19th century [...] established different orthographies' for each language variety 'thus separating them from each other;
(4)   the names of some languages are known only through documentation.

Batibo (2005: vii, ix) also asserts that about one third of the world's languages are found in Africa, where more than 2000 languages are spoken (see also Crystal, 1997; Grimes, 2000; Heine & Nurse 2000), giving each individual country 'an average of between 35 and 40 languages' (Batibo, 2005: 14). Batibo (2005: 3) further acknowledges that it is difficult to verify most of this information, especially in the absence of census data. Most of these figures are therefore the result of guesswork at best,[16] rather than principled linguistic analysis. The contradictions in the theoretical framework of Batibo's work are symptomatic of a number of locally-based African linguists, who claim not to be comfortable with some of the assertions or existing pseudo-evidence, but still use that pseudo-evidence in their work and, by so doing, help spread and entrench the very erroneous concepts and ideas they purport to disagree with. Although he comes to the conclusion that 'we just have to look inward', happily confusing the concepts of 'ethnic groups' and 'language groups', Simire (2003: 238), citing Onwuejeogwu (1987: 2–3), goes so far as to claim that 'The only place in the world that has over 300 ethnic groups is Nigeria.' Bobda following Tadadjeu (1990) compares Cameroon to a 'Tower of Babel' and writes:

> The linguistic landscape of Cameroon is uniquely complex, hardly paralleled by that of any other country in the world. [...] Indeed, the linguistic situation of Cameroon is not paralleled even by that of neighbouring Nigeria, a country of 130 million inhabitants, which has, in addition to English and Pidgin, over 400 languages. (Bobda, 2006: 357–358)

There is no doubt that counting languages is difficult, especially when it is a major challenge to find out how closely languages are related to each other (particularly in the case of unwritten languages). Whether two varieties should be considered independent languages or dialects of one language is a question to which it is almost impossible to find a uniform answer from native speakers, linguists, or politicians (Coulmas, 1992: 300). In an introductory note to his incisive *Language and Colonial Power*, Fabian (1986) begins with the following words: 'Writing on African history requires choices regarding nomenclature and orthography. Selecting and imposing names and ways of writing them, in fact, belonged to the exercise of colonial power over language.' He goes on to say that 'Any enumeration of distinct languages will be an artefact of linguistic classification rather than an accurate indication of communicative praxis' (Fabian, 1986: 82). The naming and development of languages in Africa were part of a conscious and premeditated plan to present the language situation on the African continent through European ideologies of racial and national essences' (Irvine & Gal, 2000: 47), and as separate and enumerable categories (Makoni & Pennycook, 2007: 2; also see Harris, 1980, 1981). Harries (1987) and Chimhundu (1992) have documented the inventions of Tsonga, Shona, Afrikaans, Runyakitara and ChiNyanja, whilst Irvine and Gal (2000: 47) have shed light on the description of Senegalese languages by 19th century European linguists. Makoni *et al.* (2006: 377, 385) also discuss the complex origins of terms such as Shona, and argue that Europeans appropriated African languages as a prelude to imposing these European variants of African languages on Africans.[17] Roy-Campbell (1998) describes how faulty transcriptions, some arising from missionary zeal and inaccuracies, occurred across the continent, resulting in a multitude of dialects of the same language being labelled as new languages. Makoni (2000) also criticises the role of missionaries in labelling certain speech forms fully-fledged languages, when they were known not to be fully-fledged languages. Brock-Utne (2005: 176) notes that Oshindonga and Oshikwanyama, north of Namibia, are listed as two separate languages and have two different written forms (when they are in fact the same language) simply as a result of the rivalry between the Finnish and German missionaries who visited and worked in the area. She adds that the maintenance of this artificial separation 'suited the divide and rule policy' of the apartheid government of the day. Prah (2003) is of the view that many of these inaccuracies are also due to a genuine lack of proper understanding of the languages transcribed and a failure to look at African societies outside the framework of the colonial boundaries. Examples of such arbitrary and artificial labelling can be found throughout Africa, from Malawi (e.g. ciNyanja and ciChewa), to Ghana (e.g. Akuapin, Asante, Fanti, Akim and Brong), to Côte d'Ivoire (e.g. Wobé, Guéré; Nyaboua and Nyédéboua or Bété and Dida) (Blommaert, 1999c; Bock-Utne, 2002; Djité, 1988: 1–13; Djité, 1987; Prah, 2002). According to the Centre for Advanced Studies of African Society (CASAS),[18] 85% of Africans speak no more than 12 to 15 core languages as their first, second and third language (Prah, 2000, 2002). Fenton (2004: 7, also cited in Makoni & Pennycook, 2007: 7) suggests that these language descriptions were, in many instances, no more than *interlinguistic descriptions* based on *European interlanguages*. Hence, missionaries and colonial administrators, who wrote grammars and textbooks, were able to learn their own versions of indigenous languages, which were sometimes given special names (e.g. *chibaba*, the variety of Shona spoken by the priests in Zimbabwe). Jeater (2001) shows that few whites (largely traders and farmers) had a poor command of the local languages in the early years of colonisation in Southern Rhodesia (1890–1935); yet, these were the very people used to translate and interpret in the public service. Hence, contrary to the old myth, Christianity did not work in favour of retaining and promoting local languages. Spolsky (2003: 86) notes for instance that it failed to save Amerindian languages, like Navajo, and almost wiped out the Mâori language in New Zealand. Hastings (2001) notes that there was comparatively very little published in African languages, except for church purposes and, in their enthusiasm to translate the Bible into African languages, different and/or competing missionary groups used their own idiosyncratic orthographies and spellings. In countless instances, this has led to the same speech form being represented in these different orthographies and spellings and often being labelled as 'full-blown' languages in their own right (Brock-Utne, 2000: 142). In a review of the effects of European colonisation on the language situation in Africa and elsewhere, and a critical analysis of the work of Christian missionaries in language contact situations, Errington (2001) discusses how, through standardisation different dialects of Shona were created by various Protestant and Catholic missionaries and then produced different languages in present-day Zimbabwe. This problem was exacerbated to a certain extent by the arbitrary geographical, ethnic and linguistic carve up of the continent by the colonial powers at the Berlin Conference in 1884, resulting in many countries (e.g. Benin, Cameroon, Chad, Côte d'Ivoire, Ghana, Liberia, Niger, Nigeria, Sierra Leone and Sudan) having peoples from adjoining states within their borders. It is all this evidence that leads Zeleza (2006: 14) to go so far as to say that 'African languages are inventions, mutually constitutive, existential and epistemic constructions'. Zeleza further contends that Christianity, hand in hand with anthropologists and the colonial administration, invented African languages, 'producing, regulating and constituting new languages and languages regimes [...] naming, codifying and standardising many of Africa's current languages' as part of their civilising mission (see Zeleza, 2006: 22). Since naming entailed counting, a 'census ideology' set in (Pennycook & Makoni, 2005; Makoni *et al.*, 2007), and languages and dialects were unified (e.g. Shona and Yoruba) or separated (e.g. Zulu and Xhosa, or Guéré, Wobé, Nyabua and Nyédébua) (see also Djité, 1988: 6–8), according to the imperatives of the colonial masters (Zeleza, 2006: 22). Christian missionaries therefore played a crucial part in assisting colonialism and neo-colonialism not only in destroying other ways of being, but also in terms of the language effects of their activities (Pennycook and Makoni (2005). Their choices of media of instruction were neither random nor gratuitous; they promoted European languages first and foremost and played a prominent role in the construction and invention of African languages to fit a certain European perception of a *Babelian* Africa. Fabian summarises the whole process and motivation thus:

> Missionaries did not describe (or even learn) African languages simply because 'they were there'; their linguistic, scholarly work was embedded in a communicative praxis which had its own internal dynamics. In very broad terms, it was characterised by a gradual shift from descriptive appropriation to prescriptive imposition and control. (Fabian, 1986: 76)

Romaine (1994, cited in Pennycook, 2002) alludes to speakers as cultural and political constructs when looking at Papua New Guinea where she found that speakers claimed to speak a different language when, linguistically, this language appeared identical to another language. She concludes:

> The very concept of discrete languages is probably a European cultural artefact fostered by processes such as literacy and standardisation. Any attempt to count distinct languages will be an artefact of classificatory procedures rather than a reflection of communicative practices. (Romaine, 1994, cited in Pennycook, 2002: 12)

Pennycook (2002: 14) concurs with Romaine, and suggests that the very notion that languages exist is highly questionable and most probably a reflection of European beliefs. Makoni and Pennycook (2007: 1) make a most interesting contribution to this debate, pointing out that beyond the fact that 'linguistic criteria are not sufficient to establish the existence of a language', *languages, conceptions of languageness* and the *metalanguages* used to describe them are 'inventions', that 'languages were ... invented ... as part of the Christian/colonial and nationalistic projects in different parts of the globe'. They add that these 'inventions' have had very real and material effects on how languages are understood and identified with, on how language and language-in-education policies are constructed and on social life. They suggest that these 'inventions' have to be 'deconstructed' and 'reconstructed' in order to find alternative ways to move forward (Makoni & Pennycook, 2007: 2, 3), for language is not 'a thing that leads a life of its own outside and above human beings' (Yngve, 1996: 28) and can be reduced to the simple arithmetic of enumeration. Makoni and Pennycook (2007: 6/7) also denounce the 'discovery attitude' (see Blommaert 1999b: 104), whereby whatever was there on the continent was there only as a result of European 'discovery'. Hence, languages were decreed into existence by those who, in Said's words, had 'been there' (Said, 1985: 156–157), an attitude that found its way into the French language (and psyche) when talking about Africa in terms of '*faire l'Afrique*' (literally, '*to make* Africa', meaning to 'have been there'), proving yet again that the German Anthropologist Leo Frobenius was right when he said that the idea of the barbarian black man was a European invention. If the aim of theory is to make things simple, why was it necessary to proclaim such complexity in the language situation of the continent? It would appear that language diversity led to the next logical step, albeit another myth, that multilingualism is a serious threat to national cohesion. It is to this other article of faith that we now turn.

Language diversity and the threat of inter-ethnic conflicts

A very common argument for the exclusion of African languages and maintenance of European languages in education and administration is that any attempt to impose the choice of a local language in these domains will exacerbate tensions among ethnic groups and lead to major conflicts. European languages are therefore often advocated as the best vehicles to draw the different language groups together into national consciousness and national integration. It is true that Africa currently leads the world in armed conflicts, but although many are quick to blame these events on ethnic and/or religious strife, it is yet to be demonstrated that any of these conflicts are based on language issues. Indeed, the worst and longest armed conflicts seem to have taken place in countries in which language diversity is not an issue to fight over (e.g. Burundi, Rwanda and Somalia). Furthermore, the acknowledgement and recognition of different legal statutes and the coexistence of multiple linguistic groups within the same territory is neither an African invention nor a curse. Multilingualism is a reality and part of the regular functioning of many countries (e.g. Albania, Belgium, Bosnia-Herzegovina, Bulgaria, Canada, China, Finland, Guatemala, India, Ireland, Israel, Pakistan, Paraguay, Switzerland and Sri Lanka, to name a few), including many in the heart of the developed world, demonstrating that the recognition and use of more than one language need not constitute an obstacle to national unity.

When in October 1830 for instance, a provisional government declared Belgium an independent state, splitting from the Netherlands, and bringing together Dutch-speaking Catholic Flanders and French-speaking Catholic Wallonia, the elite of the French-speaking minority dominated the affairs of the state, and all higher education was in French, until 1898, when formal equity was granted to the two languages, Dutch and French. Nevertheless, the Dutch-speaking population considered itself a junior partner in a state where French culture and language dominated every aspect of life (professional and socio-economic advancement). Even though the country was administratively separated into Dutch and French regions in March, 1917, the first university using Dutch as the language of instruction was not established until 1930, and Dutch did not become an official language of the army until 1938. Furthermore, a number of constitutional amendments and political reforms partitioned the country into four areas, all defined by language, after the Second World War (Dutch-speaking Flanders, French-speaking Wallonia, bilingual Brussels and a small German community district with local autonomy), and establishing three official languages: French (local variant Walloon, spoken by 33% of the population) Dutch (local variant Flemish, spoken by 60% of the population) and German (spoken by 1% of the population). In 1977, the country was divided into three administrative regions – Flanders, Wallonia and Brussels – but this new federation was not recognised in the constitution until 1980! And yet, today, there is no suggestion of a threat to Belgium's stability and prosperity, simply because of its linguistic organisation.

Switzerland is another good example of a multilingual, developed nation. Founded in 1291, Switzerland is a confederation comprising 26 relatively autonomous cantons and half-cantons. It is broadly divided into four linguistic zones. Its three official languages (Article 70 of the Constitution) are: French (spoken by 19.5% of the population), German (spoken by 63.9% of the population) and Italian (spoken by 6.6% of the population), while Romansh or Rhaeto-Roman, spoken by 0.5% of the population, is deemed to be an official language for communicating with Romansh speakers.[19] Three of the cantons are officially bilingual, while one is officially trilingual. Each canton has control over its own educational system. Cantonal school regulations require that every child learns a second national language, starting in primary school, although in practice English is increasingly taking over the 'other Swiss language' second-language requirement. The four languages within the territorial frontiers of Switzerland and the autonomous administrative system based on nationhood and clearly aimed at safeguarding religious, linguistic and cultural differences, have not hindered a strong sense of cohesion, solidarity and national unity; nor has the autonomy in the areas of education, mass communications and religious services. And although conflicts of interest plagued the early history of the country, these were never based primarily on the linguistic cleavage between French, German and Italian speakers, and Switzerland today enjoys the reputation of a most stable state with one of the world's highest standards of living. Another significant example is that of Spain which, after Franco, joined Belgium and Switzerland as an official multilingual country when she accorded official status to five languages – Catalan, Galician, Euskera (the Basque language), Valencian and Majorcan – in addition to Castilian (Spanish) in 1988. There is no evidence to suggest that this decision has weakened the country's institutions or dented the people's sense of cohesion and nationhood.

Finally, history teaches us that languages are not at the root of conflicts, because even people who speak the same language in the same territory did not always avoid major conflicts and wars. This was the case of England (1642–1645), the United States (1861–1865), Finland (1917–1918), Russia (1918–1920), Spain (1936–1939), Greece (1946–1949), Korea (1950–1953), Vietnam (1954–1975), Lebanon (1957–1958 and 1975–1990), Yemen (1962–1969 and 1986) and Somalia (since at least 1991). Somalia is a country widely considered to be the only truly homogenous nation in Africa, ethnically, culturally and linguistically. Indeed, these wars are testimony that the root cause(s) of conflicts often lie outside the language question.

Language(s) of international communication, science and technology

Early in the last century Jespersen (1926: 228) warned that: 'It would be unreasonable to suppose, as is sometimes done, that the cause of the enormous propagation of the English language is to be sought in its intrinsic merits'. This argument has become even more important with the growing need to keep abreast of developments in information technology, where European languages, especially English, are clearly dominant. Generally, European languages are the only ones to provide Africans with an interface for the exchange of information at international level. Given the marginalisation of their own languages, European languages are the prerequisites for Africans to attend universities at home and in other countries, to find work in international business or with humanitarian and non-governmental organisations, and to have access to a great number of other intellectual activities and endeavours. This growing reality has led to another article of faith, akin to a myth, according to which European languages are the only ones through which Africans can expand their world knowledge and the ability to communicate in a vastly wider context than they would ever be able to with African languages. One is almost tempted to suggest that, if taken to its logical end, such an argument can literally be extended to all other languages but English. Clearly, although history has placed some European languages at an advantage, no language has ever been shown to be more accurate, logical or capable of expression than another. Any language can be developed and used for higher functions, as is shown by the Finnish and Hebrew languages, which only recently developed into modern national languages. Likewise, some of the lingua francas in Africa – Bambara, Ewe, Hausa, Kinyarwanda, Kirundi, Kiswahili, Yoruba, Somali and Malagasy – are being considerably developed. Vocabulary expansion is an ongoing process in all languages, and even international languages (French is a case in point) are constantly undergoing elaboration in a changing world of science and technology.

Notwithstanding this, a number of African scholars have spent their lives trying to disprove the assertion that African languages are not appropriate vehicles for science and technology. Cheik Anta Diop and Ngugi Wa Thiongo are amongst the most prominent of these scholars. In an effort to show that African languages can be used for intellectualisation, Cheik Anta Diop translated Einstein's Theory of Relativity into Wolof (Senegal). Ngùgí Wa Thiong'o spent a number of years writing in his native Gikuyu. Others have pointed out that many texts, excluding the much older systems of Nubia, Egypt and Ethiopia, were written in Wolof as far back as 1732, and that Ewe, which is used in the government-owned newspaper _Azoli Yeye_ (or _La Nouvelle Marche_) in Togo, has a long tradition of literacy, with the first texts in the language dating from 1658. _Amegbetoa_, a novel written in Ewe in 1949 by the Ghanaian Sam Obianim, a best-seller reprinted eight times to date in that language, is currently being translated into French. Over the years, African countries have progressively allowed some local languages to play a significant role, especially in the broadcasting media.

Owing to their wide reach and their power to influence opinion, the media are an integral part of daily life, and an important tool for development. The languages associated with the media acquire an important status in society. Kenya has one daily newspaper in KiSwahili, whilst Tanzania has several. In Uganda, Luganda and other local languages have a strong presence in the media. In Mali, _Kibaru_, a rural newspaper, is written in Bambara, Peulh, Songhay and Tamasheq. Examples of the use of local languages, in community radio and on national radio and television for commercials or to disseminate practical information on health and hygiene or techniques of cultivation of land, abound across Africa. Even international broadcasters have joined in on the act. For example, the BBC (British Broadcasting Corporation) uses four African languages on its radio stations: Hausa, KiSwahili, Kinyarwanda and Kirundi. In the process, the BBC is making an active contribution to development of these languages, coining new words such as _'nyambizi'_ (meaning dive) for 'submarine', _'Kanjamau'_ ('a disease that emaciates those afflicted') for AIDS in KiSwahili, and phrases such as _'na'ura mai kwakwalwa'_ ('a machine that has a sharp brain') for 'computer', _'jirgi mai saukar angulu'_ ('a plane that lands like a vulture') for 'helicopter' in Hausa. The national languages of Tanzania

(KiSwahili), Botswana (Setswana), Ethiopia (Amharic), Somalia (Somali), and Afrikaans in South Africa also provide us with a good example of corpus planning and have demonstrated their capacity to render some of these new terms and expressions.

In 2005, the government of the Democratic Republic of Congo (DRC) and the Electoral Institute for Southern Africa produced a translation of the draft constitution in four local languages (Lingala, Ciluba, Kikongo and KiSwahili) in order to involve the masses in the democratic process. In June 2006, Microsoft Africa announced the launch of Microsoft Office 12 and Microsoft Vista in Wolof[20] as part of the Local Language Program of Microsoft International, which began in 2004. This is a major initiative seeking to create innovative partnerships with governments, universities and local authorities not only in Africa, but all around the world, as Microsoft International plans to have its Microsoft *Windows XP* and Microsoft *Office 2003* available in some 40 languages. In the final analysis, it is initiatives such as this that, by bringing African languages into the 21st century, are certain to close the debate on which languages are better suited for communication, science and technology.

Another aspect of the myth about the inherent inadequacy of African languages for communication, science and technology is that most of them have not been reproduced in written form, and may not have coined terms for scientific and technological advancement. Furthermore, engaging in corpus planning activities in these languages, and worse yet in several languages (that is to say, devising a writing system and lexifying and standardising the languages), developing educational materials, training teachers to use those materials, etc. will be prohibitively expensive for underdeveloped countries.

Firstly, history again teaches us that written communication was developed in some parts of the African continent (also see below). Although some will argue that written communication was introduced in Africa through religion and education (Christian and Islam in the 7th century), there is evidence that the Vai, a Mande-speaking people of north-western Liberia (a population of about 75,000) independently invented a phonetic writing system generally referred to as a script (Dalby, 1967; Gelb, 1952; Koelle, 1854). This script, a syllabary of 200 characters, with a common core of 20 to 40 characters, has been in active use, widely available to all members of the society and transmitted outside any institutional setting, for well over a century and a half, in the context of traditional rural life.[21] Another well known writing system, although now overshadowed by Romanised Hausa (Boko), is Ajami, an Arabic script that came into use in the 17th century and is still used today. Ajami is used to transcribe Hausa, a

Chadic language spoken by some 39 million people spread across northern
Nigeria and Niger, Benin, Burkina Faso, Cameroon, the Central African
Republic, Chad, Congo, Eritrea, Ghana, Sudan and Togo. Timbuktu,
Agadez and Sokoto have also been known as centres of intense writing
practices in Africa. Since the 15th century, they have resorted to the Arabic
script to transcribe business contracts, court decrees and judgements, as
well as correspondence in a number of local languages, and the library of
the Sokoto History Bureau holds a folder (No. 291) entitled '*al-murâsilât
billugat al-haoussâwiyya*' (correspondence in the Hausa language), which
contains some 20 manuscripts in the Hausa language, written in Arabic
script. Other well-known syllabaries in Africa are: Kpelle, Loma, Mende,
Ndjuká, Ojibwe and Yi.[22] Battestini (1997) notes that many African writing
systems were forbidden during the colonial era (e.g. Mum in Cameroon)
and some still are today (e.g. Kamara in Mali). Nevertheless, there was
then, as there is today, a certain degree of linguistic organisation. The
Timbuktu Manuscripts, for instance, provide a written testimony to the
continent's history and cultural heritage, as well as to the skills of African
scholars and scientists, in subjects such as astronomy, chemistry, clima-
tology, geography, history, Islamic studies, judicial law, mathematics,
medicine, optics, philosophy, physics and science. Written before European
colonisation, the Timbuktu Manuscripts constitute a rich legacy and a
unique cultural and intellectual heritage for the continent and provide
evidence for the idea that, contrary to the popular myths of a 'dark' continent of oral tradition alone, Africa had a thriving tradition of writing. Scattered in various locations in Timbuktu and its surroundings for the last 600
years – only 18,000 of an estimated 700,000 manuscripts are in the Ahmed
Baba Research Centre – virtually exposed to the elements of the desert,
these manuscripts have been in brittle condition for a long time and always
been in urgent need of restoration, preservation, translation and publication. However, it was not until 2001 that the President of South Africa,
Thabo Mbeki, on the occasion of a state visit to Mali, offered to help the
Malian government to preserve some 200,000 of these manuscripts.[23]

　　The story of the Timbuktu Manuscripts is an interesting one. First, it was
proposed and widely chronicled that Africans have essentially an oral
history. One could assume an innocent mistake had been made; but then
the colonialists stumbled upon the Timbuktu Manuscripts and had clear
evidence of the existence, not only of writing, but of scholarship of a higher
order. Yet, a deafening silence prevailed over this significant 'discovery' for
well over 600 years ... 600 years is a long time in anyone's conception of
time. Raising such an issue goes back to the heart of the claim of objectivity
and 'scientificity' of everything that had been said and written about the

Dark Continent and its people.[24] Only the brave will go on arguing that such significant oversights have not affected, directly or indirectly, the image the rest of the world now has of Africa, or the image most Africans have of themselves; for 'History [...] does not refer merely, or even principally, to the past. On the contrary [...] history is literally present in all we do. [...] it is to history that we owe our frames of reference, our identities, and our aspirations' (Baldwin, 1966: 173). To be so negligent and 'false to the past, false to the present, is to solemnly bind oneself to be false to the future' (Douglass, 1852). But fortunately, history does not disappear merely because we fail to acknowledge it.

Even when languages had a long tradition of writing and scholarship, colonialism would still denigrate them and ban them from schools and universities. This is indeed what the former USSR did in the Baltic States of Lithuania, Latvia and Estonia in the 1940s as well as in Georgia (19th century) and Ukraine (18th century), when it annexed these countries.[25] Despite the fact that the first written book in Lithuania dates back to the mid-16th century, the oldest known examples of written Latvian appeared in 1530, the Estonian language was standardised in the 19th century, Georgian writing was first seen in the 5th century and the recorded history of Ukrainian goes back to 988, the Russian Empire still imposed its own language, Russian.

Secondly, corpus planning activities are a necessity not just for African languages, but for all other languages, in underdeveloped as well as in developed countries. A case in point is the French language which, despite its long history of development, still manifests a constant need to invent new words, in order to cope with developments in the economic, scientific and technological fields. Hence, France has passed laws throughout the last two centuries and created a number of (Ministerial) Terminology Commissions, not only to make major changes to the French language (orthography and lexification), but also to make it an offence to use words/languages other than French.[26] Language development is therefore a continuous process in every language, including European languages, aiming to improve its efficiency in meeting the communication challenges of a changing world.

Historical Evidence from Africa

Myth-mongers about language and development in Africa ignore, or choose to ignore, not only the current and historical evidence in developed countries, but also what is well known about Africa. If it is true that the future of people depends in part on their history, it is also true that Africa's history did not start with colonisation and colonisation's myths about the continent and its languages. African languages may have increasingly been forced into a marginal position since colonisation, but there is no doubt that in pre-colonial Africa they were used as media of education, administration and trade. And African history is quite revealing of the fundamental role played by its own languages in the running of successful entities, some of which were larger than current states in both the developing and developed worlds. Ancient kingdoms and empires (e.g. Ghana, Mali, Songhay, Dahomey, Kanem-Bornu, Ashanti, Oyo, Tukulor, Zimbabwe and Axum), powerful, *developed* and highly organised centres of advanced civilisations (e.g. Mapungubwe and Great Zimbabwe), flourished as economic, political, cultural and religious centres, connected by trade to various parts of Africa, Europe and Asia for over a millennium. Needless to say, none of these ancient kingdoms and empires could have been run successfully for so long, if the assumption of linguistic chaos were true, and if the local languages could not assume any high function.

The Kingdom of Aksum (Axum), for example, began in the 3rd century and, by the 6th century, was exporting ivory, glass crystal, brass and copper items from Adulis, the port city on the Red Sea. Its agriculture and cattle breeding flourished, and Axum extended its rule to the northern Ethiopian Highlands and along the coast to Cape Guardafui. Some other small empires in Africa that have shown a degree of economic and political dynamism include the Dahomey kingdom (17th century), which became famous for its corps of women soldiers, and the Kanem-Bornu Empire (9th to 19th century). The first great West African empire was the Empire of Ghana or Wagadu (from 750AD to 1200AD), whose boundaries would have included most of modern Mali and parts of modern Northern Senegal and Southern Mauritania. This Empire became known as the 'Land of Gold', for its role as an economic intermediary within the gold trade from south to north, and the slave trade from north to south. The fame of Wagadu grew during the 10th and 11th centuries AD, when it was described by the Muslim writer, al-Bakre, as a great military power that could put 200,000 warriors in the field. In 990, Wagadu conquered Awdaghost, a Berber dominated city with ample water supply, where millet, wheat, grapes, dates and figs were grown, putting it at the peak of its power. Muslim tradesmen came to Awdaghost in caravans from Sijilmasa, Tunis and Tripoli in the north, through Taghaza, the Hausaland and the Lake Chad region, bringing salt, cloth, copper, steel, cowry shells, glass beads, dates and figs to the south. Kumbi, Wagadu's capital city, a Soninke town, became a commercial and intellectual centre in West Africa, and historical archives show that people in the north of Africa spoke of the king of Wagadu as the richest monarch in the world.

Another great West African pre-colonial empire, and perhaps the greatest, was the Empire of Mali, centred on Timbuktu, a point of trade for desert caravans, which rose out of the ashes of Wagadu in 1076AD. The Empire of Mali gained control of the trans-Saharan trade routes around 1200AD and at the peak of its power, comprised most of present-day Mali and Senegal, and parts of Mauritania and Guinea. It had control over the salt trade from Taghaza and the copper trade of the Sahara, as well as the trade in food stuffs such as sorghum, millet and rice. As the Empire of Mali dissolved in the 15th century AD, the Songhay Empire emerged under the able leadership of Sonni Ali, with about 70,000 residents and a 1000-boat navy. The Songhay Empire was based on the kingdom of Gao, a city founded around the 7th century as Kawkaw, which reasserted itself as the centre of a new empire (1350AD and 1600AD). Literally the largest Empire in the history of Africa, the Songhay Empire incorporated the former Ghana and Mali Empires and stretched all the way to Cameroon. It boasted an army of well over 35,000 soldiers, a large and elaborate bureaucracy, stand-ardised weights, measures and currencies, as well as new methods of farming. The Songhay Empire was also known as an example of political reform, order, stability and prosperity. It is during the Songhay Empire that the city of Timbuktu, which had become the centre of thriving trade in the 13th century, became a dynamic centre of Islamic learning, attracting scholars from around the world. The best known university of the Songhay Empire, the Sankore University, developed a reputation for scholarship in rhetoric, logic, Islamic law, grammar, astronomy, history and geography.

Despite all this evidence, African languages are today still subject to the same misconceptions and prejudices of the colonial days. How is it that Africans were able to run these great kingdoms and empires, large admin-istrations, armies and navies in African languages in pre-colonial times, only to be told after colonisation that they are no longer able to do so? What is it about the state of affairs of African languages that makes all these myths so hard to overcome?

The Present State of Affairs of African Languages

Just as Africa's history does not start with colonisation, so it does not end with it. And whilst many African languages have died out and some are on the brink of complete disappearance, the present state of affairs of many African languages, especially dominant regional and cross-border lang-uages, is anything but discouraging. Many mother tongues also continue to be quite healthy and play an important role in many spheres of family and community life. Yoruba, for instance, is spoken by millions of people, predominantly in south-western Nigeria and various communities across West Africa. Wolof is spoken by well over 80% of the population of Senegal as a first or second language (McLaughlin, 2001: 159), and is predominant as a language of commerce and urban life in Senegal, the Gambia and Mauritania. Amharic, the official language of Ethiopia, is spoken by 27 million native speakers.

Hymes writes that 'One must ask, not about genetic relationships among languages and objective linguistic demarcation of dialects, but about communication relationships among persons and groups' (Hymes, 1984: 8). And in Africa the masses have managed and developed networks of communication within national boundaries and across national borders, showing not only a willingness to identify themselves as members of a larger group, but also to co-operate with others who may be culturally and linguistically different. Because of these communicative and socio-economic realities, many of these dominant regional and cross border languages are perceived as neutral languages and are increasingly being learned as second languages. They are, in the true sense, the de facto media of wider communication, meeting the criteria of efficiency, adequacy and acceptability (Haugen, 1966: 61–63), to an arguably greater extent than European languages.

First, it can reasonably be argued that a number of African countries are (virtually) monolingual. This is the case at least for Somalia (Somali), Burundi (Kirundi), Rwanda (Kinyarwanda), Lesotho (seSotho) and Swaziland (siSwati).

Then, there are a number of lingua francas that which have arisen out of contact situations and enabled the majority of the people to communicate across ethnic barriers, and where there are imperatives of urbanisation, trade and travel. UNESCO defines a lingua franca as 'a language which is used habitually by people whose mother tongues are different, in order to facilitate communication.' Calvet (1987: 107–121) shows that they take precedence over minority languages, and over French, in the market place in some countries. In the Congo for instance, it is Lingala that is widely spoken on the northside of Brazzaville and Lari and/or Munukutuba on the south-side. In Niger, Hausa-Zarma, and its dialectal variant Songhay, are the languages of the market place in Niamey. Even within the family, Calvet (1987: 96–101) demonstrates that it is the external linguistic reality that influences the child, not the language(s) spoken by her parents. Here again, it is the lingua francas (Wolof in Senegal, Bambara in Mali and Hausa and/or Zarma in Niger, Dyula in Côte d'Ivoire, Ewe in Togo, Fon in Benin, etc.) that are clearly dominant, not the international and/or official languages. Some of these lingua francas are dominant at the national level.

This is the case for Kabuverdianu in Cape Verde (also a national language), seSotho in Lesotho, seSelwa in the Seychelles, Saotomense in Sao Tome and Principe (also a national language), Krio in Sierra Leone, Somali in Somalia, siSwati in Swaziland, Malagasy in Madagascar, Morisyen or Mauritian Creole in Mauritius, setSwana in Botswana, shiSona in Zimbabwe, Wolof in Senegal, Monokutuba in Congo, Amharic in Ethiopia, ciNyanja/ciChewa in Malawi and Sango in the Central African Republic (also a national language).

Finally, there are quite a few cross-border languages, such as Hausa in West Africa, that are demographically important languages shared across vast areas and often across national boundaries and are spoken by millions of people. Hausa has had a written system for more than 200 years, now in both a standardised Romanised (introduced in the 1900s by the British) and Arabic orthography (Ajami). With a total number of speakers estimated at 25 to 40 million in as many countries as Benin, Burkina Faso, Chad, Cameroon, Congo, Côte d'Ivoire, Ghana, Libya, Niger, Nigeria, Senegal, Sudan and Togo, Hausa is an official language in Nigeria, a main trade language in northern Nigeria and Niger, a subject in Nigerian secondary schools and universities, and a language of instruction in primary schools in Hausa-speaking areas in Nigeria. Several newspapers are published in Hausa, and it is present in over half of the radio and television broadcasting not only in northern Nigeria, but also in Cameroon. All international broadcasters, including the BBC, Voice of America, Deutsche Welle, Radio Moscow and Radio Peking use Hausa in their transmissions in West Africa. KiSwahili, in Eastern and Central Africa (the DRC, Kenya, Tanzania, Uganda, Southern Somalia, Northern Mozambique, the Comoro Islands, Burundi and Rwanda) is another major cross border language in Africa spoken or understood by 80 to 100 million people.[27] Lingala, with over 10 million speakers, is shared across Angola, the Central African Republic, the DRC and Congo). The cluster of Berber languages, spoken by 11 million people in northern and western Africa, includes Atlas Berber (Morocco and northern Algeria), Nefusi (western Libya), Siwi (Egypt), Tuareg (southern Algeria, Mali and Niger), Zenaga (south-western tip of Mauritania) and Zenati Berber (north-eastern Algeria, Tunisia, and north-western Libya), with dialects including Tamasheq (Algeria, Mali and Niger and Senegal), Shawia and Kabyle (Algeria), Amazigh (Tarifit, Tashlhiyt and Tamazightt) in Morocco, Shluh (Morocco and Mauritania) and Zenaga (Mauritania and Senegal) (also see Wolff, 1981). Standardised Berber has a writing system called Tifinagh. Table 1 summarises these and other important cross-border languages spoken by millions of people across territories much wider than those of developed countries, in some cases several times wider.

What these cross-border languages show is that languages have fuzzy boundaries, and that language classification, at least in this context, is speculative at best. Hence Fabian's 'Everything one learns about languages … militates against linguistic determinism (or fatalism), be it of the structural-semiotic or of the older 'Whorfian' variety,' since Shaba Swahili, the language he was studying, 'always shares its territory with several other languages', and 'is itself characterised by so much internal variation and lexical permeability (in the form of 'borrowing' or 'relexicalisation') that it simply makes no sense to regard it as a constant in language-and-culture studies' (Fabian, 1986: 5). All we can therefore say with any degree of

Table 1 Examples of cross-border languages in Africa

Language	Spoken in
Malinké/Dyula	Burkina Faso, Côte d'Ivoire, Gambia, Guinea, Guinea Bissau, Liberia, Mali, Senegal and Sierra Leone
ciNyanja/ciChewa	Malawi, Zambia and Zimbabwe
Crioulo	Cape Verde, Equatorial Guinea, Guinea Bissau and Sao Tome e Principe
Ewe	Ghana and Togo
Fang	Cameroon, Congo, Equatorial Guinea and Gabon
Hausa	Benin, Burkina Faso, Cameroon, Chad, Ghana, Mali, Niger, Nigeria, Sudan and Togo
Kanuri	Cameroon, Chad, Niger and Nigeria
KiRundi	Burundi, Rwanda and Uganda
KiSwahili	Burundi, The Comoro Islands, the DRC, Kenya, Malawi, Northern Mozambique, Rwanda, Southern Somalia, Sudan, Tanzania and Uganda
Kikongo	Angola, Congo and the DRC
Lingala	Angola, the Central African Republic, Congo and the DRC.
Luo	Kenya, Tanzania and Uganda
Moore	Burkina Faso, Côte d'Ivoire, Ghana and Togo
Pulaar/Fulfude	Benin, Burkina Faso, Cameroon, Chad, Gambia, Ghana, Guinea, Guinea-Bissau, Mali, Mauritania, Niger, Nigeria, Senegal, Sierra Leone and Togo
Sango	Cameroon, the Central African Republic, Chad and the DRC
Shona	Mozambique and Zimbabwe
Songhay	Benin, Mali, Niger and Nigeria
Somali	Ethiopia, Kenya and Somalia
Wolof	Gambia, Mauritania and Senegal
Yoruba	Benin, Nigeria and Togo

certainty about language classification in Africa is that it tells us more about the classifiers than the classified, about their power to impose, promote, control and restrict. The aim of colonisation was to establish and maintain power, to direct and regulate whatever was ultimately not eradicated and replaced (see Fabian, 1986: 83). However, 'the shape of [their] power must not be taken for the shape of reality (as is frequently done by those who wield power)' (Fabian, 1986: 8). Fabian also observes that 'The delusions of politicians and of grammarians are comparable, and often the two are allies – as, I believe, can be demonstrated in the interplay between colonial policies and linguistic description.' (Fabian, 1986: 8). This is a critical factor that makes almost all the language manuals written by such grammarians 'truncated descriptions' of artificial and reduced variants of a variety of forms of given vehicular language. Hence these language manuals are of 'doubtful linguistic value' (Fabian, 1986: 11). Therefore, African languages 'do not exist in hopeless dispersion and confusion (dispersed in space and mixed-up logically)' (Fabian, 1986: 83), and it is pure sociolinguistic fiction to assert that in most African countries, 'multilingualism is not coupled with an overarching language which is fully adapted and understood throughout the nation.' (Coulmas, 1992: 50). The multilingual make-up of Africa is well beyond the colonial and neo-colonial stereotypes.

The rise and spread of regionally-dominant and cross-border languages is largely demand-driven in the socio-economic sense, but has been helped greatly over the last four decades by rapid urbanisation and the complex social interactions resulting from this (e.g. inter-ethnic interactions and exogenous marriages), the dismal quality of government-run educational systems and the high levels of illiteracy and lack of fluency in European languages. What it shows is that the linguistic picture of Africa is not complex to the point of chaos. The classification of languages in Africa needs to take into account the real communicative networks of these regionally dominant languages, lingua francas and cross-border languages, and a number of inaccuracies and myths must be done away with, if one is to gain a genuine understandng of the real linguistic situation on the continent.

New Myths about Language and Development in Africa

Even though the nature of myths is to claim things that do not exist in fact, we are all aware that myths die hard. This makes the new myths about language and development in Africa particularly challenging, because they take us down the slippery slope of intellectualism and 'discourse (of) power', where the issues are being argued between 'unequal' individuals as it were (Tollefson, 1995: 2), since some seem to have the right to project their own practices and beliefs as universal and commonsense (also see Fairclough, 2001). And so it is that when it comes to the issue of language and development in Africa, the very people who will not sign any agreement or covenant unless it is drafted or at least translated into their mother tongue, regardless of their own competence in a particular language, are still able to argue – and with straight faces – that Africans should have no difficulty learning and working, and achieving their development goals in European languages.

On the surface, the arguments look solid and impregnable. They raise issues regarding the importance of distinguishing between 'acquired' multilingualism (i.e. acquired without formal instruction) and 'learned' multilingualism (with formal instruction). It is argued, when it comes to 'acquired multilingualism' for instance, that this type of multilingualism leads one to ask whether the African languages involved are sufficiently developed (i.e. intellectualised) to carry the energies of developing economies, and whether the people concerned have moved beyond basic interpersonal communication in their deployment of the linguistic capital inherent in these languages. In other words, does informal 'education' appropriate to the needs of endogenous development and progress in the informal economy actually happen? The obvious answer to this rhetorical question is that most development theorists, not to mention those working away in countless NGOs (non-governmental organisations) worldwide, would argue that it doesn't. But does it not happen only when 'acquired multilinguism' relates to African languages? How 'adequately developed' is the 'acquired multilingualism' that involves European languages? The evidence thus far, after 50 years of independence in most African countries, is that the adequacy of such linguistic capital, with reliance on formal education only in European languages to supply the conceptual enrichment, the skills and attitudes, needed to achieve appropriate economic development – as distinguished from World Bank or IMF impositions – is limited to no more than 20% of the population and has left the majority of Africans disempowered. Is it really necessary to deny the existence of the languages of others in order for our own language to remain dominant? Are we all to turn back to a form of linguistic and economic intuitionism?

The current orthodoxy argues that additive bilingualism (i.e. knowledge of the home language and additional language(s)) should be enriched as needed, and taken as far up the educational ladder as possible. This orthodoxy is refuted by some on the grounds that it is largely a cultural preference that is sound only in that form but lacks economic arguments. It is believed instead that the demographic distributions, plurality of languages within an economy, the necessity of economic exchange and cooperation across linguistic communities, and within and without nations, are all factors against it. Proponents of this view go so far as to say that additive bilingualism could even open the door to isolationism, the curtailing of 'normal' social aspirations, and possibly media censorship and the lauding of a form of social stoicism. They propose therefore that the educational presumption that learners perform better in their home language in the middle and higher reaches of a given education system needs to be challenged, not on linguistic, but on practical grounds, if only because the state of educational provision, formal and informal, must be taken into account before claims about the effectiveness of multilingualism in promoting appropriate development can be entertained. It would appear that the real concern here is the fear of a form of multilingual education that denies learners access at some level to one of the European languages, although time and time again advocates of multilingual education have taken care to point out that there are no sound theoretical reasons for doing so and very little chance that, at least in a democracy, the populace would acquiesce in any such attempt. Bamgbose (1991: 5), among many others, warns that whatever African countries do with their local languages, 'they will need a major world language for access to higher education, science and technology; and this same language will serve as their window on the outside world.' He stresses instead that the goal is not to ban international languages of wider communication, but to give local languages the status that they deserve, in order to provide the majority with life-long functional literacy, numeracy and management skills, and channel their entrepreneurial impulse into sustainable and long-term development solutions (see also UNDP, 2004: 63). A Decree in Senegal in 1971 went so far as to say: 'Removing French as the official language and language of instruction is neither desirable nor possible, if we do not want to be left behind in the 21st century'(Government of Senegal, 1981; my own translation).[28]

It is important not to let such ideological and political values pass for theoretical frameworks, even when they have the appearance of intellectual complexity. We need to remember that the aim of science is to produce generalisations or laws stating the causal relationships that hold between phenomena in the universe. This is an empirical pursuit that lies in part in the observation of 'raw data' and the logical character of the scientific method. If what is sought through theoretical frameworks is truth, then that truth must be independent of human whim and prejudice, for the truth of an argument must, in part, be determined by its correspondence with the facts of the world, an important criterion in the principle of verification for deciding on the truthfulness of an argument. However, the truth thus far is that no developed country has achieved its level of development on the basis of a foreign language and, most importantly, there is not very much in Africa to show for all the development programs undertaken over the last 50 years. No amount of insidious formulae of 'overseas development aid,'[29] 'structural adjustment', 'governance' and 'globalisation' will change these glaring facts. Hence, a critical look at the arguments against the use of African languages reveals that these are not always based on facts or sound theoretical or practical thinking, but short-term and short-sighted convenience, self-serving and parochial discourses of power.

What is even more disturbing (and confirms the disingenuous nature of the articles of faith we have been discussing) is that, whilst some are trying all manner of ways to convince us that multilingualism is a curse, and that mother tongue education or additive bilingualism in Africa is a form of linguistic intuition or pure fiction, others are claiming recent changes in language policies and language-in-education policies in Africa as their own. Hence, Albaugh (2007: 2) is prompted to write about a sea-change of ideas in France, brought about by 'an epistemic community', which convinced the French government that the best way to resolve the current crisis of the French language in Africa is to change the language-in-education policy. According to this view, France has replaced its long-time subjugation of local African languages with their defence, and 'Francophone' Africa is now being told that it is acceptable to use local languages in education. This new epistemic paradigm is said to be based on the belief that the international environment is a major causal factor that often influences domestic politics, sometimes to a more significant extent than local realities. As a result, the changes we are currently witnessing in language-in-education policy in Africa are achievements not really due to African leaders, but to a 'push' from an 'evidentiary community', to 'language groups demanding rights to use their languages in education', indigenous linguists and NGOs (often missionary)(Albaugh, 2007: 2). The changes are also said to be due to a 'pull' from a 'changed discourse in France in the 1990s' (Albaugh, 2007: 24), an agenda setting and strategically crafted message by well-meaning and 'Francophone group of scholars', who have decided of late to embrace the cause of African languages and promote the idea of their maintenance and development. Albaugh writes in substance:

> Tactical scholars in France advocated an innovative idea to their government, which offered leaders a new causal pathway to achieve France's perennial goal of linguistic *rayonnement*. They proposed that using local languages in the first years of education in Francophone African states actually helps children to learn French in the long run. Thus, France

could begin openly supporting the use of African languages in education without compromising its ultimate goal of French language expansion. They communicated this changed strategy through multilateral and bilateral Francophone agencies via public declarations and promises of financial support for multilingual education policies. This is a dramatic turnaround in France's long-term preference for French-only education in Africa. [...] As France communicated this new message in the 1990s, policies in most of Francophone Africa have begun to promote local languages. (Albaugh, 2006: 2)[30]

Contrary to the foregoing arguments about mother tongue education and additive bilingualism, these 'tactical scholars' are also credited with the belief that (1) 'children learn best in their first language', and (2) 'children learn a second language better if they begin in their first language.' (Albaugh, 2006: 22). The argument goes even further; in addition to economic dependency, African political leaders are said to be susceptible and responsive to theories formulated from the centre; in other words, they are susceptible and responsive to 'ideational' or 'intellectual dependency' (Albaugh, 2006: 19). If Albaugh is right, France, for instance, continues to have great influence over domestic policy outcomes in African states, which are still unable to decide what they should or should not do in terms of local languages, and have to be 'pushed' or 'pulled' into account, when it comes to issues of mother tongue education.

Albaugh's argument is essentially that African political leaders had to be shocked into action by a 'radical message' from the 'epistemic community', a message according to which the French language is in trouble, and has to be rescued by national languages. Hence, this is really about African languages serving as a pathway to educational improvement in French, a roundabout way to rescue the fortunes of the French language on the global scene, rather than a tool of linguistic and/or cultural preservation in Africa. Albaugh speaks of the French language as being transformed from 'assimilator' to 'liberator', and of the relationship between French and African languages 'evolving from Apartheid to Partnership' (Albaugh, 2006: 32), as France now promises to free Africa, and the rest of the world, from the perceived hegemony of the English language. This positive contribution by France is in contrast with what Albaugh sees as the 'indecisiveness' and 'ambivalence' of English-speaking countries regarding language-in-education policies, pointing to what she calls 'a contrasting trend' in 'Anglophone' Africa where, using the example of Ghana, the long-standing use of local languages in education is being reversed.[31]

Pervasiveness of Language Diversity beyond Africa

Fortunately, multilingualism is not unique or limited to Africa and, as the European Union has been facing up to the challenge of language diversity, it has injected some sanity into the debate and turned the issue on its head. Finally, the debate that a few years ago many people thought was relevant only to Africa is now a global debate, and, in a decade of decisive action, the European Union has achieved what Africans have failed to achieve in the area of multilingual management in five decades of prevarication.

The six founding fathers of the European Community enshrined language diversity in the Treaty of Rome by committing to the equal and balanced use of the languages of all members (Belgium, France, Italy, Luxemburg, the Netherlands and West Germany).[32] This principle has been maintained throughout the evolution of what is now known as the European Union and, with the addition of 15 new members, the number of official languages was increased to 11.[33] The latest enlargement (the addition of another 10 new members) has seen the number of working languages increased to 21.[34] In 2005, in order to communicate efficiently, member states of the European Union (representing 455 million Europeans) had to resort to 910 interpreters and 1150 translators, and the EU budget for language services increased by one third since 2004, costing well over 1.3 billion euros that year. The number of interpreters and translators will eventually have to be doubled, in order to satisfy the 420 linguistic combinations resulting from the increase in the number of working languages. With the admission of Romania and Bulgaria (announced in September 2006 and effective from January 2007), a year ahead of schedule, the European Union now has 27 member states and 23 languages. Then with the 4 states of the former Yugoslav Republic (Croatia, Bosnia, Serbia-Montenegro and Macedonia) as well as Albania, a European Union with 32 member states may have 26 languages, including Serbo-Croatian, Macedonian and Albanian, or 28, if Croatian and Bosnian are counted as two separate languages. If Montenegro and Kosovo were to be admitted as full members, this would result in a European Union of 32 members. With Switzerland, Norway and Iceland, who have not yet applied for membership in the Union, but are part of the European Association of Free Trade, the European functional space actually comprises 35 states, working with a total of 28 languages, including Icelandic and Norwegian. This still leaves aside Ukraine, Moldavia, Byelorussia, or Russia, which would complete the European picture with 38 states and 31 national languages, including Ukrainian, Byelorussian and Russian. Breton (2005: 4–5) adds that this rough linguistic picture does not take into account all the regional and

minority languages, about 20 languages of stateless peoples and three
languages of peoples without a territory.

Despite claims that the linguistic costs associated with the running of the
European Union are 'exorbitant' – they represent 3 euros per annum per
capita – Articles 22, 41, 126 and 128 of the Treaty of Rome are unambiguous
on the maintenance of the languages of member states, many of which also
refuse to compromise when it comes to respecting their linguistic and
cultural exceptions within the European Union.[35] France's *exception
culturelle* (cultural exception), for instance, is an assertion of its right to
protect its culture and language, and in particular its film industry against
Hollywood. The maintenance and promotion of this policy of linguistic
inclusion make it possible, in principle at least, for the 400,000 Maltese to
have the same language rights within the Union as the 61 million French, if
only because all documents published by the EU have to be translated into
all the languages of its member states. This language policy is a strong
disincentive against exclusionary practices, and any member-state of the
EU that has reason to believe that it is being pushed out to the periphery has
several ways to seek redress for its language. This linguistic diversity
explains the European Union's motto 'United in diversity' and its active
promotion of the use of more than one language for learning and teaching,
and in everyday life, by making available to its citizens additional
languages from its member states. Multilingualism is therefore not just
'something African', but a normal state of affairs for the majority of the
world's population, including the people living in developed countries.

Critics of the language policy of the European Union find it 'laughable,
complex and ponderous' and argue that 'It serves the interests of the more
powerful languages to keep in place a policy that manifestly cannot work
because such a policy aids language shift in their direction – primarily in
the direction of English.' (see Tonkin, 2006). This criticism is due in part to
the fact that, despite the formal policy of the European Union for the maintenance of equality between all the languages recognised as languages of
government within the borders of its member states, in practice, numerous
informal policies have the effect of promoting languages of wider communication, such as English and French. The criticism also pertains to the
question of whether the tolerance-based maintenance of *de jure* multilingualism does not ultimately lead to de facto monolingualism, as the
dominance of English in the institutions of the European Union seems to
suggest (Tonkin, 2006; Tonkin & Reagan 2003). Regardless of the criticism
levelled against it, the approach to language diversity in the European
Union allows for a discussion of language diversity, not necessarily with
new realities, not even in a new light, but – as Césaire (1956) would say –

simply because suddenly the contempt, disdain and scorn that African languages suffered are now being felt by some European languages. The debate over language diversity in the European Union has helped to lay bare the most enduring myths about some European languages that purported to be the languages of science and technology, the languages of reason, and indeed universality, and the prerequisite to civilisation, development and globalisation, as if there was some inherent capacity to these languages that was lacking in others. It is now an established fact that, on a global level, some of these languages are seen as enjoying less importance and influence than in the past, and could be dispensed with. This realisation, in some hitherto powerful language communities, more than anything else, has helped the debate become a little more sober and realistic. So, we can now ask the question that really matters: how can a people become part of a global community when, through the marginalisation of their language(s), they are practically denied the capacity to play an active role in the process of globalisation itself?

Conclusion: If You Fail to Plan, You Plan to Fail

The foregoing are the prolegomena to the sociolinguistics of development in Africa. What it shows is that language is not neutral when it comes to issues of development. It also shows that one needs to be able to separate fact from fiction, in order to fully appreciate the complexity of language diversity in Africa. If multilingualism is an enduring feature of Africa, it is not limited to Africa, and it is far from chaotic. The assumptions underlying the rhetoric behind the marginalisation of African languages are not always based on facts, and the little evidence there is, is plagued with errors or truncated in order to fit some preconceived theoretical framework or economic or political agenda. As a result, very little is known about the over-arching patterns of language use in Africa and its real sociolinguistic picture. These myths, old and new, must be corrected, in order to gain a valuable insight into multilingualism in Africa, and for the management of language diversity to succeed.

This is not about recovering some form of linguistic *status quo ante*, nor is it about the use of African languages to the exclusion of all other languages. What it is about is challenging epistemologies, policies and practices that systematically marginalise the majority of Africans. It is crucial to understand that no country can develop, whilst leaving behind its human capital. It is next to impossible to involve the majority of the people in the running of a country, unless these people are empowered, not least through a language(s) they understand. We have 50 years of exclusive promotion of

European languages in Africa to prove it. As thousands of young people coming from sub-Saharan Africa, through Mauritania, Libya, Morocco, Senegal and the Canary Islands are pressing against the European fortress of 'selective immigration',[36] developed countries now routinely require competence in their language(s) for immigration purposes, arguing that immigrants who cannot speak the language(s) of the mainstream of society become a burden. Some countries (e.g. The Netherlands) even require a basic knowledge of their laws and how their institutions function before granting citizenship to applicants. If this is perfectly understandable, then why is it so hard to understand that it is reasonable for the citizens of a country to be competent in the language of administration, education, mass media and health within their national territory? Why is it so hard to understand that a country is better run in the language(s) of the mainstream of society, as is the case in developed countries?

Language is at the beginning, in the process and at the end of development, and the individual and his/her language is at the heart. Speech communities that cannot function in the language of governance and education of their country cannot be expected to contribute to the creation and redistribution of wealth, or the creation of a space where they can strategically respond to local and global challenges and negotiate political visibility. In the Declaration of Principles of the World Summit on the Information Society, Paragraph 52 of Chapter 8 on Cultural diversity and identity, linguistic diversity and local content states that:

> Cultural diversity is the common heritage of humankind. The Information Society should be founded on and stimulate respect for cultural identity, cultural and linguistic diversity, traditions and religions, and foster dialogue among cultures and civilisations. The promotion, affirmation and preservation of diverse cultural identities and languages as reflected in relevant agreed United Nations documents including UNESCO's Universal Declaration on Cultural Diversity, will further enrich the Information Society. (WSIS, 2003)

Attempts have been made in Africa to rise to the challenge of involving the majority of the people in the process of development, through language management. Since independence, there have been a number of conferences and meetings addressing various aspects of language policy, particularly through UNESCO and the Organisation of African Unity (now African Union), in order to empower African languages (Alexander, 2005: 16, and 42–50). Initiatives that have been taken include:

(1) Article 25 of the *1963 OAU Charter* stipulating that: 'the working

languages of the Organisation and all its institutions shall be, subject to practicality, African languages, as well as English, Arabic, French and Portuguese';

(2) the translation of a UNESCO composite *History of Africa* into Swahili, Hausa and Yoruba;

(3) the *UNESCO campaigns* for education and literacy in African languages;

(4) the 1969 *Cultural Manifesto* of Algiers recommending the implementation of a translation programme of major scholarly works into African languages, the translation of major African works into major European languages, and the use of African languages as media of instruction;

(5) the 1975 *Report of the Intergovernmental Conference on Cultural Policies in Africa* (UNESCO-OAU) which recommended that member states 'promote the reorientation of the educational systems, so as to integrate values from African cultures and civilisations', because 'the school system inherited from colonisation produces people that are ill-prepared for the needs and realities of African countries; these are unemployed *[unemployable?]* people and an uprooted elite, cut off from African realities';

(6) the *African Cultural Charter*, adopted in Port Louis (Mauritius) in 1976, which called on African states to develop language policies that will ensure the introduction of African languages at all levels of education and promote cultural, social and economic development;

(7) the Declaration of Heads of States and Governments on the cultural aspects of the *Lagos Action Plan for Africa's Economic Development* (1985);

(8) the *Language Plan for Africa* of the Organisation of African Unity (1986), suggesting that Arabic, Swahili, Hausa and a Nguni-related South African language should serve as working languages of the Organisation. This plan of action encouraged every memberstate to put in place a language policy focusing on African languages as media of education at all levels, and established the following: the OAU Bureau of Languages located in Kampala, Uganda, the Centre of Linguistic and Historical Studies through Oral Tradition (CELHTO) located in Niamey, Niger, and the Regional Centre of Documentation on Oral Traditions and African Languages (CERDOTOLA) located in Yaoundé, Cameroon;

(9) the treaty for the creation of the *African Economic Community* (1991);

(10) the *Dakar Action Plan for the Promotion of Cultural Industries* (1992),

(11) the 1993 regional plan for the collection of oral traditions throughout southern Africa (Harare), calling on African states to acknowledge the

imperative for promoting African languages, in order to turn them into real instruments of socio-economic development;

(12) the 1996 *Project for a Charter of Action* for the promotion and use of African languages within the educational system (adopted on 30 August 1996 in Accra), reasserting the necessity for African governments to take specific measures for the use, preservation and protection of the cultural emancipation and socio-economic development of African populations,

(13) the *Harare Declaration* (1997), calling on all African countries to affirm multilingualism, accept European languages as an integral part of the African language repertoire, and produce language policies reflecting these realities,

(14) the 1999 *Plan of Action of the Decade on Education in Africa* (Harare), calling for the use of African languages in the first three years of education as an essential strategy to reach the objective of mother tongue education for all at primary level;

(15) the 2000 *Constituent Act of the African Union*, which reaffirms the possibility of using African languages as official and/or working languages of the African Union, on equal footing with European languages such as French, English and Portuguese. As a result, at the third summit, held in Addis Ababa in July 2004, Swahili effectively became one of the official languages and a working language of the Union;

(16) the *Cotonou Declaration on Cultural Diversity* (2001);

(17) the creation of the *African Academy of Languages* (ACALAN) in Lusaka in July 2001, with a view to enabling real African integration through African languages, and especially cross-border languages, to build relations of exchange between populations, beyond political boundaries;[37]

(18) the 2002 *Declaration of Commitment* (Dar Es Salaam), which identified the challenges that Africa needs to resolve (illiteracy, ignorance and lack of education) and recognised that 'the transformation of society requires the consideration of an educational revival at all levels, as part of a cultural renaissance, as well as the integration of the positive values and potentialities of traditional culture, the outcomes of scientific and technical culture and universally shared values';

(19) the 2003 *Dakar Action Plan* for the Promotion of the Cultures and Cultural Industries of the African, Caribbean and Pacific Group of States;

(20) the 2003 UNESCO *Convention for the Safeguarding of the Intangible Cultural Heritage*;

(21) the 2004 *Strategic Plan of the Commission of the African Union*, which puts

emphasis on the use of African languages at all levels of education, and the role of the masses in promoting African languages;

(22) the 2005 *Nairobi Declaration on Culture, Integration and African Renaissance.*

A number of themes run through these resolutions and conferences (Bamgbose, 2005a: 16). They are:

- economic and social development requires the full participation of all the African people;
- eradication of illiteracy cannot be achieved without the use of African languages;
- the potential of cross-border languages must be acknowledged and harnessed and language policies harmonised;
- lingua francas at regional and/or national levels should be adopted at least as working languages, alongside European languages;
- African languages should be developed for use in a wider range of domains, such as education, mass communication, legislature and technology;
- teaching and learning in African languages will make the transition from the home to the school more natural, and formal education available to a wider population;
- all the foregoing should be backed by national legislation, a plan of action and the necessary financial resources for implementation.

Needless to say, most of these resolutions remained a dead letter, in part because of the absence of financial resources and structures to foster the implementation of agreed policies, but also because it is not enough to issue motherhood statements on the value of multilingualism.

At a recent meeting of 16 West African countries with the European Union at a seminar aimed at launching the program of the European Fund for Development for 2008/2013 (March 6 2006 in Ouagadougou, Burkina Faso), it was agreed that the prolegomena to development lie in the areas of health, education, employment, the environment and culture, and that these are the key to achieving the development goals of the Millennium. What was glaringly missing from this programme was the role of language in all these key areas. We must commit ourselves to searching for realistic answers and refusing to indulge and limit ourselves to predicting disaster in Africa.

Linguistic policies are conceivable only when contradictions such as these, and collective hypocrisies, are acknowledged, refuted and/or resolved, and the widespread ignorance of African communicative practices are carefully researched, with a view to showing that multilingualism in Africa must be articulated and balanced for effective partnership and equitable interdependence, and that it is more an asset than a curse. It is up to the African countries that have failed themselves and their people by adopting extroverted linguistic policies to look beyond their immediate goals of economic and political expediency, in order to put together new policies that will ensure some equitable long-term returns. African languages can and must become vehicles of opportunities in education, health, the economy and governance. Only when one fails to plan, does one plan to fail.

Chapter 2
Language, Education and Development

> *Your science will be valueless, you'll find*
> *And learning will be sterile, if inviting*
> *Unless you pledge your intellect to fighting*
> *Against all enemies of all mankind.*
> Brecht (1988: 1026–1027)

> *Africa where scientific and technological discourse is conducted*
> *in the national languages as part of our cognitive preparatio*
> *for facing the challenges of the next millennium.*
> 'Vision for Africa' *–The Harare Declaration*
> (UNESCO, 2006)

Introduction: *Nam et Ipsa Scientia Potestas est*[38]

Bamgbose (1991, 2000) argues that education gets the most attention in language planning in Africa, and so it should. The role of education in promoting individual freedom and empowerment is central and takes pride of place in the struggle for development. Only through education can a community make progress, acquire and disseminate knowledge and gain an awareness of its ability to shape its own destiny. Education is therefore a resource that enables members of the community to become informed citizens, able to participate on equal terms in the betterment of their living conditions. It gives access to productive resources and remunerative activities, and is essential for increasing capacity-building through knowledge and skills transfer. Education is also constitutive of, and instrumental in, the process of development (Sen, 1999), because it goes hand in hand with economic growth. No reasonable level of social change and development can be envisaged without education. The successful implementation of development projects, for instance, depends on the capacity of members of the community to put their potential to maximum use.

Many studies have established a link between education and productivity, which is at the core of development. For example, a study conducted in 13 developing countries has shown that four years of primary education have the potential to increase the productivity of smallholding farms by

7–10% in those countries where new agricultural technical packages are being adopted, because the new techniques are more easily absorbed by the farmers who have a minimum level of literacy. Effective primary education is therefore crucial to economic performance and is indeed a prerequisite for development at a personal and national level. The social effects of primary education are also said to be quite positive and a fundamental determinant of output per worker (Easterlin, 1981).

Education is also associated with better family health and improved reproductive health and hygiene. Women who have had four years of schooling or more tend to have 30 per cent fewer children than those without education. Moreover, the mortality rate of children of educated mothers is lower than that of non-educated mothers, and children of educated parents are more likely than those of uneducated parents to attend school longer.

Although education alone is not sufficient to account for all the parameters of growth (Schultz, 1961, 1989), it makes a significant contribution to higher individual productivity and income, and thus to sustainable economic growth (Birdsall *et al.*, 1995). Moreover, when it is broadly shared, education also contributes to a more equitable distribution of incomes and socio-economic opportunities (Birdsall, 1999). It may not be an end in itself, but education is a vital part of a person's capacity to lead the kind of life they want, and deal with the issues they are confronted with, an instrument that can improve the quality of life. Better education also enhances the capacity of poor people to participate in the political process and demand or vote for governments that are more representative, responsive and accountable to them (Hamoudi & Birdsall, 2002). Most important of all, the human capital acquired through education is a critical economic asset that cannot be taken away by others. However, education can lead to growth only when it is carried out in a context of sound macro-economic planning and good governance, and this raises the issue of which language education is provided in. There is a direct link between the language of education and development, as the languages used as media of instruction are a clear indication of a country's vision for the future, and the quality of education is determined by the language-in-education policy. This explains why education is one of the pivotal areas where language policy is critical.

When one thinks of a child's formal education in the rest of the world, it is assumed that the child is educated in her mother tongue, or at least in a language she understands. Language-in-education policies in most African countries are a glaring exception to that rule, as Africa is the only continent that does not possess its own collective system of self-repoduction in this area. The African child does not see a book until she goes to school; and once there, the first book she will handle is likely to be in a language that she does not understand. Fifty years after political independence, Africa is the only continent where access to knowledge and science is negotiated only through a language other than the one the child speaks at home or in her immediate wider community. It is the only place where the language of education is largely exogenous to its own people (Ki-Zerbo, 1990: 16). And where the educational system has retained the European language as the sole medium of instruction, the system as a whole performs very poorly.

Part of the reason for this, as discussed in Chapter 1, is that colonialism deliberately undervalued African languages, as part of a conscious effort to promote the languages of the colonisers. However, the exclusive use of European languages after the end of the colonial period is the shared responsibility of the African peoples, their political class and their elite. Ki-Zerbo (1990: 9–10) notes that 'in maintaining an educational system originally conceived to please the public service left behind by the coloniser, even with a few adjustments, African countries have failed to fulfil their mission of construction of a society of initiatives, creativity and development', and he concludes that the current African educational system is 'unsuited and elitist, and continuously feeds the crisis by producing economic and social misfits, whilst ignoring entire sections of the active population, such as women, peasants, and individuals working in the informal sectors' [my translation].

Even if Edwards (1985, 1989) and Foster (1972: 593) believe that reliance upon schooling as an empowering agent is naive, because one cannot expect schools to compensate for parental, local community and societal input (Baker & Jones, 1998), schooling remains one of the most powerful institutions through which one can demonstrate one's commitment to language maintenance and development. Indeed, schools are the most important places where future generations can be empowered.

This chapter looks at the role of language and the provision of language-in-education policies in Africa against the background of language education, not just as literacy attainment, but as a critical indicator of development closely linked to other dimensions of economic performance and competitiveness. It revisits the issues raised by education in European languages and asks whether there is a case to be made in favour of mother tongue or bilingual education. What role do African languages play in the educational systems across African countries? Do African countries have a clear vision of the type of education they want? Is it possible to win the challenge of education in Africa? How best can equal access to educational opportunities be achieved?

Language and Language-in-Education Policies: The Colonial Legacy

The language-in-education policies of African countries have to be seen in their historical context. In a paper published by the UNESCO Regional Office for Education in Africa, Bamgbose (2004) provides one of the most comprehensive classifications of language-in-education policies and practices in Africa, dividing them into three categories:[39]

(1) Countries in which the colonial administration favoured the use of African languages as media of instruction in the first three or four years of education; these are typically countries that were under the British and Belgian and/or German influence.[40] Not surprisingly, these countries have had a tradition of mother-tongue education.

(2) Countries in which the colonial administration discouraged the use of African languages as media of instruction in schools; these tend to be countries that came under the influence of French, Portuguese and Spanish influence.[41] These countries happen to be the most resistant to change, even when pilot projects in mother tongue instruction have proven to be educationally sound.

(3) Countries in which there was a dual policy or whose language policy diverged from that of the colonial administration, either because they experienced a change in colonial administration (Cameroon, Namibia, Seychelles and Somalia)[42] or because of a number of different other historical reasons (Madagascar, Comoro Islands, Mauritius, Sierra Leone and Liberia). Although they were originally French colonies, the predominance of Malagasy in Madagascar, and of Ngazija or Comorien in Comoro Islands, was such that these languages were introduced in the education system at an early stage, whilst Mauritian Creole or Morisyen was neither used in education under French colonial administration nor under British colonial administration. Bucking the trend in most other British colonies, Sierra Leone did not use African languages in education, and Liberia, which was founded by the American Colonisation Society did not entertain this possibility.

Bamgbose notes that even those African countries that use African languages as media of instruction have generally been content with continuing the colonial practice of confining these languages to the lower levels of primary education, and extending their use to higher classes, even in primary school, is not perceived as a viable option. Batibo (2006: 261–263) offers a similar classification, with the addition of a fourth category, made up essentially of countries in North Africa, where Arabic is used exclusively in all high functions.[43]

Much has been written about the merits or lack thereof of colonial language-in-education policies; this chapter will not revisit this debate. Suffice it to say that the claims about the serious designs of the colonial administration to help African emancipation are dismissed by Fabian (1986: 70), who believes that 'what really counted was a growing need for skilled and (moderately) literate manpower, especially in the mining industry and its attendant services, and whatever was done for or about languages was determined first and foremost by these practical concerns'. In discussing the legacy of colonial thinking in shaping the language-in-education policies in East Africa, Roy-Campbell (2003), for his part, has shown how the continued use of European languages as media of instruction not only hinders learning, but is a waste of scarce resources. Nevertheless, the choice to retain the language of the colonial master as an official language was highly constrained by the colonial legacy, as control over the medium of education was at the centre of colonial administration. Language-in-education policies throughout Africa have remained fairly stable over the years. In 1988, the World Bank observed that, of the 15 former British colonies in their sample, 13 (87%) were still using one or more African languages in education, as against 4 out of 15 (27%) of the former French colonies (World Bank Group, 1988: 44, 154–156). Whilst some countries tried to address the issues of language policy and language-in-education policies through bold policy choices (e.g. the DRC, Guinea under Sékou Touré, Ghana, Nigeria, Tanzania, Togo and Zambia), 81.8% chose not to act, as they were afraid that the use of their own languages would undermine their development objectives and prospects (Batibo, 2006: 263). Some radical language policies were dropped altogether (e.g. Guinea) or are being stalled (e.g. Tanzania) following a regime change. As a result, there are two competing models of language-in-education policy in Africa: (1) those that maintain a European language as the sole or primary medium of education, and (2) those that use the mother tongue or a familiar lingua franca or national language as a medium of instruction, in addition to the European language. Two subcategories can be found within the latter: (a) countries where only the majority language is used (e.g. Tanzania and Botswana), and (b) countries in which several local languages are used (e.g. Namibia, Nigeria and Zambia).

These policies are not the result of public discussions about language policy, in terms of the best alternatives to the status quo, and fail to treat linguistic and language-related issues as a significant aspect of development. They assume that a foreign language is a prerequisite to good education and development and purposefully ignore the actual language practices of the majority of the people, hence creating unnecessary barriers to their participation in the process of development. When they are introduced into the school system, African languages are generally used as media of instruction in lower primary (the first three years) in a 'transitional' mode, that is to say, only to prepare the ground for the introduction of a European language. Only Botswana (with Setswana), Lesotho (with Sesotho), Uganda (with Ateso, Luganda, Lugbara, Luo, Runyankore and Runyoro), Tanzania (with KiSwahili), Somalia (with Somali), Ethiopia (with Amharic), Eritrea (with Tigrinya) and Madagascar (with Malagasy) have extended the use of mother tongues as media of instruction beyond the first three years. Their use at secondary school level is rare, with the only attested cases reported in Somalia (with Somali) and Madagascar (with Malagasy). Instead, they are generally taught as subjects in secondary schools, since they are required for entry in some humanities programmes at tertiary level (e.g. Mali, South Africa).

Looking forward, however, a new focus on African languages and their use as media of instruction is leading to their increased expansion in a range of new domains. Hence, in Kenya and Tanzania, KiSwahili has seen its use increased in legislative proceedings, the courts, radio and television and creative writing, whilst major local languages in Nigeria (with Hausa, Yoruba and Igbo) and South Africa (with Sepedi, Sesotho, Setswana, siSwati, Tshivenda, Xitsonga, isiNdebele, isiXhosa and isiZulu) have been entrenched in the respective constitutions of these countries as official languages for effective official use. In Nigeria, several houses of Assembly are taking full advantage of this provision, and in South Africa, a number of official documents are being translated into African official languages. In Ethiopia, while Amharic remains the national and official language of the country, the federal set-up has in fact resulted in linguistically-based states, each with its own official language.

After several decades of French-medium instruction, and a rather brief experiment with the introduction of local languages in primary schools from 1979 to 1981, at the start of the 2002 academic year Senegal introduced six of its national languages as media of instruction in primary schools for an initial period of six years. In 2004, 153 schools, all of them public, were involved in the experiment. Examples of successful experiments in mother-tongue instruction include pilot projects involving Bambara and Fulfude in Mali, Amharic, Hausa and Zarma in Niger, Ngbaka and Lingala in the north-west of the DRC,[44] and the well publicised Action Research Project for the Teaching of Languages in Cameroon (PROPELCA). Launched in the early 1980s by the University of Yaoundé in two private Catholic schools, with the cooperation of the Société Internationale de Linguistique (SIL), the project introduced Cameroonian languages in primary education, using a bilingual model. Seven languages were selected for the project, beginning with Ewondo, Duala, Fe'efe'e and Nso', each of which was allocated 70% of teaching time in the first year, decreasing to 30% in the third year, with the gradual introduction of French. By 1994, the project expanded to some Protestant schools and was running with nine languages in 65 schools. As the initial results of the project indicated that instruction through the mother tongue was effective and the performance in the official language was comparable to that of non-experimental classes (Tadadjeu, 1990), the project was further extended to 12 languages. Until 1998, when the Education Orientation Law finally called for public schools to use national languages as media of instruction, the experiment was limited to the private school system, because the public education authorities did not wish to be involved with the research project. In 2003, the National Action Plan for Education outlined the integration of local languages in the entire school system,[45] and by 2004, only 57% of the 287 schools involved in the project were private; the remainder were public, and many more are being added each year.

    It is not certain, however, that these developments will necessarily lead to policies of increased use of African languages. For one thing, countries like Cape Verde, Côte d'Ivoire, Mozambique and Sao Tome e Principe have remained steadfast in their refusal to use an African language as a medium of instruction at any level of the school system. Despite the number of pilot projects and the promising research findings from various experimentations, the balance remains heavily tipped in favour of European languages, and no attempt has been made to initiate innovative reforms, let alone implement the results of successful programmes in the school system. In actual fact, the picture gets complicated with fluctuations or sudden reversals in language-in-education policies in other parts of the continent, the most recent case being that Ghana. Despite an exemplary use of local languages as media of instruction over several decades, in 2001 Ghana reverted to an English-only policy from the first year of primary school. To some, the decision is not all that surprising since, on attaining independence in 1957, Ghana rejected a recommendation to use the mother tongue as a medium of instruction and opted instead for an English-medium policy from the lowest class of primary school. Although dramatic, the Ghanaian example is not an exception.

    In the DRC, Articles 4 and 17 of the new constitution (4 April 2003) have changed the language policy of this country from four official languages to only one, French. In Burundi, where the French language no longer enjoys an official status,[46] the National Council for the Defence of Democracy (CNDD), main opposition party of Burundi, felt compelled to introduce a draft bill to Parliament requesting that Article 5 of the Constitution of 13 March 2005 – which recognises Kirundi as the official language of the country – be adhered to. The CNDD tabled another in early 2006, asking that all the legal texts of the country be translated into Kirundi. In February 2006, the new President of the National Assembly requested of government ministers that all texts to be presented to parliamentarians be drafted in Kirundi. It is interesting to note that Burundi was planning to introduce English as a subject in primary school in the 2006/2007 school year.

In spite of criticisms about its failure to address aspects of status and corpus planning and effectively translate this policy into practice (Alexander, 2000; Heugh, 2003; Kamwangamalu, 2000; McLean & McCormick, 1996: 329, cited in Mazrui, 2002: 269), Bamgbose (2003: 5, 7) believes that multilingualism in South Africa is supported by the most progressive constitutional language provisions,[47] and that these genuinely attempt to address the issue of equity and opportunity for African languages. Although 9 of the 11 official languages of South Africa are African languages (isiNdebele, isiXhosa, isiZulu, Sepedi, Sesotho, Setswana, siSwati, Tshivenda and Xitsonga), English is the dominant language in the county, despite the recommendations of the 1997 Language-in-education policy (Department of Education, 2007) to use the pupils' mother tongues as the medium of instruction for as long as possible, in order to promote 'additive bilingualism', and the requirement of *Curriculum 2005* (Department of Education, 2005) that pupils learn through their mother tongue. In rural areas, where black schools are relatively homogeneous linguistically and where there are very limited opportunities to acquire and/or use English outside the classroom, English is the official language of instruction from at least the beginning of the 4th grade (Heugh, 2002: 185). In urban centres, where the schools are linguistically heterogeneous, English is introduced as a medium of instruction even earlier – from grade 1 – to accommodate the wide range of languages present in the classroom. According to the National Centre for Curriculum Research and Development (NCCRD), where there have been changes in response to changing demographics, these have generally been to extend the use of English as the medium of instruction (NCCRD, 2000). Few schools have tried to encourage English-speaking pupils to acquire a local language. Instead, they have all tended to facilitate the shift from local languages, including Afrikaans, towards English (De Klerk, 2002; NCCRD, 2000; Probyn *et al.*, 2002), in part because the teachers are not proficient in the local languages and cannot use them to communicate with the pupils. Even where the teachers can communicate with the pupils in the pupils' mother tongue, English/mother tongue code-switching is used to communicate (Heugh, 2002); or they conduct the lesson in the pupils' mother tongue, with chunks of English being read from the textbook (Probyn, 2001). The number of students studying African languages at universities has declined sharply; and not a single student has qualified as a teacher of Xhosa from the University of Cape Town in the past two years. There is a shortage of text-books and set books in indigenous languages, and a lack of research into subjects such as normal child development in African languages (Smith & Fortein, 2005).

Although Zambia is also moving to teaching initial literacy in a 'familiar language', rather than in English, in grades 1 and 2 (a total of seven languages are used as media of instruction in Zambian schools), with a pilot programme called *New Breakthrough to Literacy* (NBTL), also known as the Molteno Approach,[48] it still uses English as the sole medium of instruc-tion in primary school. This is in breach of a policy to introduce an African language medium in the first four years of primary school and despite the proclaimed right of 40 or more children in a class to demand instruction in their mother tongue. Instead, the official languages (i.e. ciBemba, ciNyanja, ciTonga, Kikaonde, Lunda, Luvale and Silozi) are taught only as subjects in schools. Again, this is not surprising, given the colonial context of language policy in the country. Indeed, when, in 1963, the then Northern Rhodesia Government asked UNESCO to study the educational system and find ways to improve it, the Radford Report (after the name of its author) recom-mended that English be adopted as the sole medium of instruction from primary school.[49] In November 1966, the Education Act and the statutory instrument No. 312 called for the implementation of the Radford recom-mendation, and English became the official medium of instruction from primary school to the University. A few years later, in a study commis-sioned by the World Bank, Kelly (1991) found that the use of English as a medium of instruction negatively affected the pupils' reading and arith-metic skills, and was 'unlikely to support good learning, especially in the critical early primary grades'. Kelly added that 'socially, it [the use of English as a medium of instruction] orientates the entire school process in a direction that only a small percentage of pupils will follow. Culturally, it undercuts the local languages and the values they embody.' In 1994, the Curriculum Development Centre of the Ministry of Education, in a paper entitled *The Structure of the New School Curriculum* (Ministry of Education, 1994), recommended the use of mother tongues or dominant local languages as media of instruction during the first four years of primary school. This recommendation was not implemented. In 1996, another policy document from the Ministry of Education entitled *Educating Our Future* was published (Ministry of Education, 1996); like all previous policy documents, it confirmed the position of English as the official medium of instruction. However, the most recent document from the Curriculum Development Centre of the Ministry of Education, published in 2000, *The Basic School Curriculum Framework*, recommended that literacy be taught in a 'familiar language' in grade 1, with English and other Zambian languages as additional language subjects (Ministry of Education, 2000). In subsequent grades, up to grade 7, the pupils are to continue learning how to read and write in Zambian languages and English. Actual practice on the ground, however, suggests that there is still a long way to go before this objective is achieved.

Is the child's major learning problem a linguistic one? And if it is, should all efforts in language-in-education policy and planning focus on mother-tongue education?

English-seeking, Not English-speaking[50]

Another aspect of the colonial legacy in the area of language and language-in-education policies is the negative attitudes the overwhelming majority of Africans have when it comes to mother-tongue education. In spite of all the available evidence on the inefficiency of education in a European language, there are practical impediments to effecting change, when it comes to mother-tongue education, because many Africans are still of the view that no meaningful education is possible in their languages beyond the early years of primary education. Attempts to use local languages in education often come up against stiff resistance from the people concerned, because they view their own language(s) as dead ends educationally and of little use in official labour markets. This, as has been shown in the previous chapter, is due in part to pre-colonial prejudice, but also to the post-colonial perception that African languages lack value. Overall, lay people, as well as the so-called elite, have been so much taken in by the myths about African languages, that they no longer believe their own language capable of intellectualisation. Only knowledge of a European language is seen as a prerequisite for higher education and socio-economic success, with slogans such as: 'If you want to get ahead, get an English head' (Williams, 1986: 514, cited by Bamgbose, 1991).

It is significant, for instance, that the Lagos State House of Assembly, after having debated the desirability of using Yoruba as a language of debate in the house, in accordance with Section 97 of 1999 Constitution of the Federal Republic of Nigeria, should have rejected the proposal (9 December 1991) on the grounds that:

> Yoruba language is not appropriate for the conduct of business of the House of Assembly, since Lagos is a cosmopolitan city. Besides, *its use is capable of demeaning and reducing the intellectual capacity of legislators* (*The Guardian*, 10 December 1999 cited in Adegbite, 2003; my italics).

It is also significant that on the eve of the 21st century, arguments should be put against the use of the mother tongue as a medium of education (see Adegbite, 2003: 190), because:

(1) children get no advantage in being taught in their mother tongue, supposedly because the mother tongue has a negative effect on intelligence-test performance of children;

(2) the mother tongue interferes negatively with learning and usage of the English language;

(3) learning in the mother tongue does not lead to educational development and does not seem to contribute to an improvement in the quality of education

(4) he language project of the Nigerian Educational Research and Development Council (NERDC) may, after all, be a colossal waste of resources.

It is therefore not surprising that many parents consider instruction in local languages as a waste of time, and would rather like to see their children fluent in a European language. Many parents, for whom sending a child to school is a major investment, believe that they send their children to school to learn the official language (English, French or Portuguese), and that a policy forcing them to learn in the local language is only a ploy seeking to dumb down their children and maintain them at the bottom of the socio-economic scale. As Fishman (1995: 60) notes, 'It is unfortunately true that very few people (including most of their own speakers) care about the impending demise of small languages'. This has led some scholars to claim that:

> Some indigenous communities object to being taught in 'their mother tongue' because schooling is perceived not as the place where knowledge is transmitted, but as a point of contact between the 'indigenous world and the white-man's world'. Non-indigenous languages (i.e. European languages) are regarded as central to that contact. (Makoni & Pennycook, 2007: 29)

However, most of the evidence available to date points to European languages being equated with the transmission of knowledge. Therefore, the objection to being taught in the mother tongue has far deeper significance that can be traced back to these arguments peddled by those they look up to as examples of modernity and success. The way people make sense of and give expression to their perception of the medium through which knowledge is transferred in Africa is predicated on these pseudo-scientific arguments. Hence the expressions of positive attitude towards European languages by individuals who have no competence in these languages and in whose lives European languages are of no real relevance (Gill, 1999) are a clear indication of how much they have been influenced by the old myths of colonial times.[51]

As a result, education in Africa is essentially seen now in terms of Western education, and it is as though being reasonably proficient in a European language is similar to being an educated person. Even the great tradition of some Muslim families who used to send their children to study in North Africa or the Middle East has now largely given way to this dominant Western trend. Hence, even in Tanzania, where well over 95% of the population speak the national language, KiSwahili, and where KiSwahili is the official medium of administration, the courts, the mass media and education throughout the primary school system, there is a burgeoning of English-medium schools called 'Academies', especially in Dar es Salaam (Rubagumya, 2003). It is argued that this is due in part to the lamentable state of government schools; but it is in fact mainly due to the fascination with the English language on the part of the elite, who are in the privileged position of being able to afford these 'Academies'.

Language and social class in South Africa have also set in train a trend whereby most Blacks move away from township and rural schools, because they are poorly resourced (83% of schools have no libraries), and into better-resourced White, Coloured or Indian schools, when their parents can afford it (Bot & Shindler, 1997: 80-81). Likewise, most teachers and students declare their preference for English as the medium of instruction (NCCRD, 2000; Probyn, 2001; Probyn *et al.*, 2002). Whilst the parents do not always believe in the notion of the use of local languages in education, the paradox lies in the fact that the very languages they are so desperate for the pupils to be proficient in, in many cases limit the pupils' opportunities for academic success. Furthermore, it is slowly becoming apparent to all that even when pupils have acquired a European language, and sometimes earned tertiary qualifications at some of the most prestigious institutions of higher education in the Western world, they have no guarantee of finding a job, let alone a decently remunerated one, in countries that have made no provisions for job creation. This is where education ties in with the economy, at the most basic level. It may not matter to have a performing education system in place, be it in local or European languages, when school or university graduates have no real prospects of finding employment, and opportunities for self-employment are stifled by various other factors. It is also argued that, at least from the perspective of governments, the reluctance to take up mother-tongue education is based on the cost factor. But what do we know about the cost of mother-tongue education?

Cost-benefit Analysis of Mother-tongue Education

Coulmas (2001) goes so far as to suggest that giving up social and cultural pride is one of the 'costs' of literacy. In other words, learning to be literate in a language other than an indigenous language is one of the prices underdeveloped countries have to pay, if they wish to build literate societies. But is the issue primarily about 'pride'? Is it about 'social' and 'cultural' values? Is it all about gaining or losing (giving up)? And supposing it is, does it have to be that way? Why do the people of Africa have to be put in a position where they are certain to lose?

In *Patriotisme linguistique* Jean-Sébastien Stehli (2006) recounts how, on 23 March 2006, the French President stormed out of a meeting of the European Council in Brussels, because the newly appointed President of the European employers' organisation (Unice), Ernest-Antoine Seillière (a French national), decided to give his speech in English, which he called the 'language of business'. In the same article, Stehli discusses the first application of the Toubon Law (*loi Toubon*) of 1994 since its adoption, resulting in General Electric Medical Systems having to pay a fine of €580,000 for not having translated the documents used by its technicians from English into French. The decision is said to have sent shivers down the spine of the Danone Group, which will now have to look over its shoulder, especially after having decided to adopt English as the official working language at its board meetings.

Japan, on the other hand, recently cancelled a plan extending English-language education into primary schools, following the widely published results of studies by the Organisation for Economic Cooperation and Development (OECD) that compared the abilities of 15-year-old children across 41 nations. Hence, it would appear that developed countries, France leading the pack, are not prepared to pay what Coulmas calls the 'social and cultural pride' price. Like France and Japan, no other developed country is prepared to consider, let alone sign, any agreement or contract of significance in any other language, including the languages they understand, unless that agreement or contract has been translated into their own language. So, who are those who, for the sake of reading and writing, are prepared– or ought to be prepared – to pay this social and cultural price that Coulmas is referring to? Is this argument applicable only to underdeveloped countries? And is it solely based on the issue of monetary cost? Is cost–benefit analysis predicated only on monetary cost? This sort of rationale assumes that African nations have to make do with what they have and cannot afford the luxury of foresight, of planning ahead and avoiding a situation that is certain to be costly to redress, socially and economically.

Chaudenson (1987: 165) outlines four models of language-in-education policies in French/African-language speaking countries:

(1) monolingual schools, where the medium of education is French only, and where African languages play no role whatsoever;
(2) monolingual schools, where the medium of education is French, but in a perspective of contrastive analysis with African languages;
(3) bilingual schools, with balanced instruction in French and African languages;
(4) monolingual schools, where African languages are the media of instruction and French is taught as a subject.

Chaudenson then hastens to point out that, on the basis of cost–benefit analysis, the first model – education in French only – is the least expensive, since most of the required infrastructure (e.g. teaching materials, teaching staff and a developed language for academic purposes) is already in place. Bamgbose (1985) also underlines the importance of having ready access to educational materials which, in the case of Africa, happen to be in European languages. Purchasing relatively inexpensive curricular materials in European languages can save scarce national resources. It would therfore appear that, above all else, economic constraints are the determining factors in favour of maintaining the status quo, even if this means spending 25% of the education budget on 12% of all pupils. Thus, when it comes to the use of African languages as media of instruction, discussions about cost immediately focus on how much more costly it will be to use African languages, rather than to use exclusively a European language in which lots of materials are already available. But this often overlooks the appropriateness and relevance, or lack thereof, of such materials for the African contexts. It seems not to matter that this sort of argument fails to address issues of social injustice, inequity and imbalance in the educational system. Is it less costly to persist in imposing ill-conceived correctives to flawed policies? After 50 years of experimentation, 80–90% of the population in most countries have yet to learn how to speak the (official) European language. What price are we prepared to put on the good health and good education of the African people? What is the price of justice, democracy and security? What is the price of a stable economy that benefits from the full participation of everyone (see Djité, 1993)?

Studies by Halaoui (2003) and Vawda and Patrinos (1999) suggest however that the volume of textbooks required in African languages is large enough to ensure that the difference in cost per unit is minimal, as against books in European languages. They also point out that this assumption fails to take into account the fact that it costs more to train teachers to use a language they are not proficient in than to train teachers to teach through the language(s) they know and speak well. While Vaillancourt and Grin (2000) agree that the use of a language of wider communication will generally be less expensive than mother-tongue education, especially with respect to language standardisation and the production of educational materials, they also point out that 'the actual activity of teaching and training would by and large cost the same, irrespective of the language in which it takes place' (Vaillancourt & Grin, 2000: 17). They further estimate that the move from the exclusive use of a European language to a bilingual education system (i.e. a European language plus an African language) would carry 'an extra cost in the 4 to 5% range' (Vaillancourt & Grin, 2000: 17); but, importantly, the mother tongue would have an edge over the European language in terms of educational outcomes (i.e. higher test scores, lower repetition and drop-out rates) and accumulation of human capital. And, as Grin (2005: 20–21) puts it 'To the extent that human capital is a predictor of labour productivity, and hence of earnings, developing a mother-tongue educational stream will eventually result in higher earnings'.

The alternative of adopting mother-tongue education is to be assessed against the option of continuing to invest in programmes, based on the exclusive use of a European language, that are certain to fail. With a success rate below 15% (Mothibeli, 2005), there is no doubt that the latter option is not worth pursuing. After all, cost is only one aspect of a much bigger challenge and ' ... makes sense only in relation with what one gets in return for the cost incurred' Grin (2005: 11). 'It follows then that even a high-cost policy can be perfectly reasonable on economic grounds, if the outcome is 'worth it'; and paying for something which is worth paying for is a quintessentially sound economic decision' (Grin, 2005: 13). For any investment to yield adequate returns, it must be a good investment. No matter how one chooses to look at it, a success rate below 15% is not a good return on investment. What is the real cost, economic or otherwise, of high attrition and repeat rates in African schools, high schools and universities? Even the World Bank (2005a: 2) now acknowledges that first-language instruction results in (1) increased access and equity, (2) improved learning outcomes, (3) reduced repetition and drop-out rates, (4) socio-cultural benefits and (5) lower overall costs.

Finally, Heugh (2005) and Grin (2005) point out that it is inappropriate and costly to ignore local languages for the sake of economic growth. Although cost–benefit analysis can help in evaluating language-planning alternatives, language is characterised by other properties (social, cultural, psychological) that are not always amenable to economic analysis. If history is a guide, medieval France for instance, had to take non-economic factors into account when it made the decision to move away from Latin as the official language of the nation; and the universalisation of education in the French language was well beyond the resources of the Republic at first, and took well over a century (until World War II) to achieve.

Another aspect of the argument about cost pertains to the publishing industry in Africa, because one of the biggest obstacles to using African languages in the classroom is the lack of books in those languages.[52] In this connection, Brock-Utne (2005: 174) notes that when it comes to the choice of language of instruction in African schools, socio-cultural politics, economic interests, sociolinguistics and education are so closely interrelated that it is difficult to sort out the arguments. And this is in part because it is an area with strong donor pressure, mainly former colonial masters (France, England and Portugal), who want to retain and strengthen their own languages, and also because there are strong economic interests from publishing companies located in these countries, who know that the use of European languages in the African educational system virtually guarantees them easy access to the African textbook market. It can be argued that the real custodians of language in Africa are textbook publishers and all the other supporting organisations (e.g. libraries, bookshops, printers), in so far as they greatly influence the educational materials available to the African child and determine the language in which she will read them. There is no doubt that for private publishers, it is more profitable to publish in European languages than in African languages, especially when these have no official status and functions in their own country. On the other hand, publishers are unlikely to extend their production of educational materials into the local languages, unless they are guaranteed a market. Given the various estimates of the number of African languages being bandied around (ranging from 1400 to 2000 languages),[53] a cautious approach is understandable on commercial grounds. If the estimates as to the numbers of African languages were true then, even taking language clusters into account, there would still be too few speakers of some of these to make publishing commercially viable.

This having been said, there are success stories in the publishing of educational materials in African languages. A case in point is the Upgrading African Languages Project (AfriLa) in Namibia. Started in 2000, this project specialises in the development of educational materials and textbooks in 6 of the 10 languages of education in the country (Rukwangali, Rumanyo, Thimbukushu, Silozi, Otjiherero and Khoekhoegowab), with the support of the German international cooperation enterprise for sustainable development (GTZ). AfriLa has already printed a total of 120,000 books, and plans to produce some 450,000 books for grades 1 to 3 to be distributed to schools. Each of the six languages develops its own materials in mathematics and environmental science, in accordance with the guidelines provided by experienced primary school teachers and officers of the National Institute of Education. The books are also translated into Setswana, Afrikaans, English and German, the other four languages used in Namibia. Projects such as AfriLa demonstrate that there are other avenues than the pessimistic and mostly misinformed scenarios, and remind us that what sounds like a simple and easy solution (i.e. the exclusive use of European language in the African educational system) is too good to be true.

No one would deny the importance of European languages and other languages of wider communication; but in view of what is happening on the ground one has to ask, as Alexander (2000) does, whether these languages are 'unattainable' for the majority of the African people. This, in view of the foregoing, is the focus of the next section.

Language-in-Education Policies in Africa: The Current State of Affairs

Language-in-education policies in Africa are largely *exogenous* to the society they seek to serve (Ki-Zerbo, 1990:16). The overwhelming majority of these children will find themselves in schools where the language of instruction is not the language(s) they know, and will struggle to make the grade. Many of them will drop out, or will be pushed out, for lack of success.[54] Accwording to the World Bank Report on Development for the period 2000/2001 (World Bank, 2001a), the illiteracy rate of those aged over 15 in 1998 was estimated to be 32% for men and 49% for women throughout sub-Saharan Africa. Less than half of the school age children are in primary school, and two-thirds of those who get the opportunity to go to school do not make it to high school. In 2005, in sub-Saharan Africa there were 23 million girls not attending school, the highest number in the world; and more than 40% of its women do not have access to basic education. Apart from countries like Zimbabwe, Kenya, Congo, South Africa and Cameroon (in that order), illiteracy affects nearly half of the male population and well over half of the female population. Some typical examples are: Angola (44% males and 72% females), Mali (48% and 62.1%), Sierra Leone (49.3% and 77.4%), Ethiopia (50.7% and 66.3%) and Senegal (50.9% and 70.3%) (Cordellier *et al.*, 2004). Across the continent, all the education indicators are in the red: low school intakes, high drop-out and repetition rates, low transition rates from primary to secondary education, even lower transition rates from secondary to tertiary education, and low intake of graduates on the job market. The inability to enter the job market is in itself an indication that those who do make it through the system are not always capable of finding a job, either because of poor planning at government level, or because they are limited in their capacity to think creatively. The basic education infrastructure is in a dilapidated state. The current state of affairs of education in sub-Saharan Africa is captured in a World Bank Report (2001b: 1), which makes the following observations:

(1)   Africa has the lowest enrolment rate of any continent at every level, and it is the only region where the numbers of children out of school are continuing to rise. The average African adult has fewer than three years of schooling, lower than the attainment for any other region. There are also growing education inequalities within Africa between income groups and between urban and rural populations.
(2)   Education trends have a direct bearing on poverty reduction efforts in sub-Saharan Africa. Africa's share of global poverty since 1987 has risen, and a growing proportion of Africans cannot meet their basic needs.
(3)   Without a quantum leap in education at the national level, Africa will miss the 2015 target of universal primary education by a margin of 55 million children.
(4)   Failing to extend the benefits of education development to the poor is likely to prove highly costly – economically, socially and politically. Accelerating education development in Africa therefore needs to be part of broader poverty reduction and rural development strategies.

At the World Education Forum, held in Dakar in April 2000 (UNESCO, 2000a), the global objectives agreed on were:

(1)   to expand and improve comprehensive early childhood care and education, especially for the most *vulnerable and disadvantaged children*;
(2)   to ensure that by 2015, all children, particularly girls, children in difficult circumstances and *those belonging to ethnic minorities*, have access to and complete free and compulsory education of good quality;
(3)   to ensure that *the learning needs* of all young people and adults *are met through equitable access* to basic and continuing education for all,

(4)   to achieve a *50% improvement in levels of adult literacy by 2015*, especially for women, and *equitable access* to basic and continuing education for all adults,

(5)   to eliminate gender disparities in primary and secondary education by 2005, and achieve gender equality in education by 2015, with a focus on encouraging the full and equal access to and achievement in basic education of good quality for girls,

(6)   to improve all aspects of the quality of education and ensure excellence of all so that recognised and measurable learning outcomes are achieved by all, especially in literacy, numeracy and essential life skills [my own italics].

Although it is clear from the various language policies implemented on the continent that some effort is being made to address these issues, one cannot help but wonder how the goals set in Dakar can be achieved in Africa when, as in many other areas of social policy, and despite the alarming state of affairs, under-funding still plagues educational systems across the continent. Indeed, real spending per student has been reduced by over 20% since the 1980s, with devastating results for the quality of education. According to the 2004 UNDP Report, many countries spend less than 6% of GDP on education (see Table 2). All the while, there is a push for universal primary education, thus increasing the number of children attending school. As a result, many children have to sit on the ground, in

Table 2 2001 Public spending on education as a percentage of GDP

Countries	*% of GDP in 2001*
Angola	2.8
Cameroon	5.4
Congo	3.2
Ethiopia	4.8
Kenya	6.2
Mali	2.8
Senegal	3.2
Sierra Leone	1.0
South Africa	5.7
Zimbabwe	10.4

Source: Adapted from UNDP (2004)

classrooms without chairs or blackboards, without books and materials, and sometimes even outdoors. In many African countries, pupils must provide their own notebooks, pens and slates, in addition to uniforms, transportation costs and meals, all things parents struggle to pay for, and in most cases cannot afford. Parents and communities are often called upon to build the entire school infrastructure, or provide housing for the teachers. Education, under those circumstances, is made a burden and perceived as one, especially when those who have gone through it and been awarded university degrees are wandering the streets, collecting dust in their shoes.

In addition, educational opportunities are unequal among individuals, as children in low-income households acquire relatively little education, compared to those in high-income households. Indeed, many studies suggest that there is a strong inverse relation between years of schooling and the probability of being poor. Only those parents who can afford it send their children to private schools or to schools overseas, even at an early age. The poor, having limited access to economic and social assets, have limited economic opportunities, and hence limited economic returns on the assets that they do have. Using data from Filmer and Pritchett (1998), Birdsall (1999) calculated the percentage of the population aged 15 to 19 who completed certain grade levels in Africa. Table 3 shows that:

(1) The initial uptake of the poorest is much lower than that of the rich minority, with a gap of 38% in Western and Central Africa and 13% in Eastern and Southern Africa.
(2) Whilst the number for both the poorest 40% and the richest 20% decline over time from the first to the ninth grade, this decline is much more pronounced for the poorest, from 40% in grade 1 to 25% in grade 5, down to 5% in grade 9 in Western and Central Africa, and from an initial uptake of 82% in grade 1 to 55% in grade 5, down to 6% in grade 9 in Eastern and Southern Africa.

Table 3 Percentage of population aged 15 to 19 who completed grade level

	Completed grade 1		Completed grade 5		Completed grade 6	
	poorest 40%	richest 20%	poorest 40%	richest 20%	poorest 40%	richest 20%
Western & Central Africa	40	78	25	65	5	23
Eastern & Southern Africa	82	95	55	84	6	30

Therefore, in its current state, schooling in Africa creates a socio-economic barrier between its own citizens, with a privileged minority that speaks a European language, and an underprivileged majority that does not and is marginalised from partaking in the basic functions of a democratic society.

As a result of the above, illiteracy still affects over half of all women and one-third of men, and over half of all children of primary school age, some 40 million of whom are out of school. And even though primary school enrolments have increased by three percentage points since the beginning of the 1990s, less than 60% of children are in school. UNESCO (2000b) estimates that 50% of school-aged children are not attending school in West and Central Africa, and one out of three children is not attending school in Eastern and Southern Africa. Instead of meeting the Millennium goal of 'enrolling all children of school age in primary schools by 2015', sub-Saharan Africa will by then be burdened with some 57 million children out of school. The overall rate of attrition is 25%, and the dropout rate is also 25% of the school age population. The performances of all sub-Saharan educational systems are among the lowest in the world, with only 60 pupils out of 100 able to complete primary school, and only 30 competent in the basic learning skills. In Burkina Faso for example, children average 2.9 years of schooling (3.5 years for boys and 2.3 years for girls). In Kenya, where school enrolment has been made free since 2003, 22% of school age children (1.7 million) are still not going to school. In Malawi, where the same policy of free enrolment has been implemented since 1994, school enrolments are still low; and of those children who attend school, only 10% can understand the school curriculum. Similarly, in Burundi, where school fees were abolished in 2005, education for all is a real struggle. According to the second Southern [and Eastern] Africa Consortium for Monitoring Educational Quality (SACMEQ II, see also Mothibeli, 2005), by grade 6 more than 55% of students in 14 Southern and Eastern African countries have not attained the minimal level of literacy required to remain in the school system. The success rate is only 14.6%.

Clearly, the colonial legacy, the prevailing language attitudes and the post-colonial practice of hanging on to failed policies play a significant part in the current state of affairs. Participants at the 2006 Biennial of the Association for the Development of Education in Africa (ADEA) believe that there are several reasons for this situation, including the poor teacher training programmes, the lack of pedagogical material and financial resources allocated to education. Other reasons include poverty, which makes it impossible for many to be able to afford to send their children to school, the prevalence of HIV/AIDS that is seriously affecting school enrolments, as well as teachers, and the language of instruction that most pupils come in contact with only in their first year of schooling. Indeed, a large body of evidence has been gathered, not only dispelling the myths about African languages and their supposed inadequacy as media of instruction, but also indicating that school performance improves when the mother tongue is used in the first three years of schooling. In 1990, The World Conference on Education for All held in Jomtien (Thailand) recognised that the language of instruction has a significant bearing on educational outcomes.

Gordon (1981: 61) is of the view that the success or failure at school is attributable to the 'intrinsic nature' of the type of language the child employs. Many scholars have argued that the exclusive use of a European language as medium of instruction is, at least in part, responsible for the illiteracy, low school enrolments, high school repeat and drop-out rates, and social inequity (Bokamba, 1991; Bokamba, 1984; Hutchinson, 1983). The dysfunction of the educational systems and the underachievement of school-aged children in Africa are widely documented, and they all suggest that educational achievement is a function of the language-in-education policies and practices. According to Obanya:

> It has always been felt by African educationists that the African child's major learning problem is linguistic. Instruction is given in a language that is not normally used in his [sic] immediate environment, a language, which neither the learner nor the teacher understands and uses well enough. (Obanya,1980: 88)

Stigmatising these practices, Roy-Campbell writes:

> One cannot overstate the damage being effected upon the psyche of African children being forced to access knowledge through a language in which they lack adequate proficiency and upon the nation which produces a majority of semi-literates who are competent neither in their own language nor in the educational language. (Roy-Campbell, 2000: 124)

Alidou and Brock-Utne (2006) found that the use of the European language limits both teachers and students in what they can say, as opposed to what they would like to say, thereby imposing an unnecessary obstacle between the students and the knowledge that they are supposed to acquire. The lack of flexibility in the language of instruction forces teachers to use inappropriate and ineffective pedagogical practices such as chorus teaching, repetition, rote-learning, code-switching and safe talk, which undermine the teachers' effort to teach and the pupils' effort to learn. Teachers tend to do most of the talking, while the pupils remain silent or passive during most of the classroom interactions. The use of a European language that the teacher does not know well also leads to the production of pathetic utterances such as: 'Please kill the blackboard for me' or 'This is called a water cow'.[55] Students in Cameroon are reported to be mixing English and French and producing phrases such *'Qu'est-ce que tu me tell-là?'* and *'Est-ce que tu see tel?'*[56] Even after learning English as a subject for four years, grade 5 pupils in African schools were not able to engage with the curriculum effectively through the medium of English (Macdonald, 1990). Macdonald and Burroughs (1991) found that, whereas the vocabulary requirements for the grade 5 textbooks were at least 5000 words when they switched to English, pupils who had been learning English as a second language for four years had an English vocabulary of 800 words at best. Probyn (2001, 2005) suggests that pupils may feel alienated from the subject content when it is not expressed in their mother tongue. Rubagumya (1994: 1) in a study of the medium of instruction in different African countries also notes that it 'acts to varying degrees as a barrier to effective learning'. Eisemon *et al.* (1989) reported that science instruction in the primary schools they surveyed in Kenya was characterised by imprecise and incoherent discourse due to the teachers' lack of mastery of the science content and competence in the English language. Many standard 6 pupils said that they found it difficult to follow instructions in English (Muthwii, 2002). Some teachers acknowledge the fact that the medium of instruction, usually a European language, constitutes a major stumbling block for pupils' understanding and academic success (NCCRD, 2000, Probyn 2001). In Burkina Faso, where most of the budget for primary schools is spent on the teaching of French (56% of the entire curriculum), Alain Sissao of the Department of Linguistics and National Languages at the University of Ouagadougou (Burkina Faso) and members of the editorial board of *Linguistique Contrastive* write in a call for conference papers: 'Only 25 of 100 pupils understand what they read in French in Burkina Faso primary schools; 20 are able to write a short essay describing a familiar situation, and not one has functional reading skills (i.e. reading a table of contents, reading instructions, etc.)' [own translation]. Sissao goes on to suggest that 'French, which is only spoken in the classroom, in the presence of the teacher, should be taught as a foreign language'. These and other examples are testimony to that fact that there can be no education and/or learning where there is no communication between the teachers and the students.

Conversely, when the language of instruction is familiar to both teachers and students, communication automatically improves and leads to better teaching and learning (Bergmann *et al.*, 2002: 66). Numerous studies have now shown that active learning does take place in programs where instruction is done in languages that are known to the teachers and students (e.g.

Burkina Faso, Ethiopia, Ghana, Mali, Malawi, Niger, Tanzania and Zambia) (see Alidou, 1997; Alidou & Mallam, 2003; Bamgbose, 2005b; Brock-Utne, 2000; Brock-Utne *et al.*, 2004; Chekaraou, 2004; Heugh, 2000; Ouédraogo, 2002). Ferguson (2000) points to several studies showing that students who learn in their own language do better in school, and refers to a school in Botswana where Prophet and Dow (1994) taught a set of science concepts to an experimental group in Setswana and to a control group in English, then tested the understanding of those concepts. It was found that the students taught in Setswana had developed a significantly better understanding of science concepts than those taught in English. Mwinsheikhe (2002) conducted a similar study in Tanzania and also found that secondary school students taught science concepts in KiSwahili performed much better than those who were taught in English. As a result, many advocate an increased use of mother tongues as media of instruction, as these are likely to promote cognitive development and improved second language learning (Heugh, 1995a). Ilboudo (2003) also found that instruction in the mother tongue leads to more effective teaching and learning of the European language as a subject. Beyond examples of successful literacy experiments in the mother tongue (Burkina Faso, Cameroon, Ethiopia, Mali, Namibia, Niger, Senegal and Tanzania) which show that initial literacy in the mother tongue can enhance learning skills, including the learning of European languages at a later stage, mother-tongue instruction in primary and secondary schools has also been shown to be a viable alternative to instruction in a European language, because it can help build on what the learners and teachers already know.

In a position paper entitled *Education in a Multilingual World*, UNESCO (2003a) defines Education for All as 'a quality education for all ... including consideration of the many varied cultural and linguistic contexts that exist in contemporary societies.' It also notes that 'research has shown that learners learn best in their mother tongue as a prelude to and complement of bilingual education approaches' (see Preface of *Education in a Multilingual World*, UNESCO, 2003a). Although cognitive development in children can also occur through languages other than the mother tongue, it is crucial that the learners become closely associated with such other languages from a young age and use them as their primary languages (Finlayson & Slabbert, 2004). UNESCO has always championed the cause of education being given to the people in the languages they know best, since the publication of its 1953 Report on the use of vernacular languages in education. Although it outlined an array of socio-cultural and economic factors militating against mother-tongue instruction (UNESCO 1953: 13–14), this report acknowledged that instruction in the mother tongue is, at least at the initial levels of education, the most efficient way to educate children (UNESCO 1953: 11). According to the Report:

> On educational grounds, we recommend that the use of the mother tongue be extended to as late a stage in education as possible. In particular, pupils should begin their schooling through the medium of the mother tongue because they understand it best and because to begin their school life in the mother tongue will make the break between the home and the school as small as possible. (UNESCO, 1953: 47–48)

This position is supported by a raft of African and international instruments, including, for Africa, the OAU *Language Plan for Action* (1986), which lays emphasis on the use of African languages as media of instruction and as working languages at all levels of government, the *Draft Charter for the Promotion of African Languages* (1996), the *Harare Declaration* (1997), and the *Asmara Declaration on African Languages and Literatures* (2000). The basic principles underlying these documents are the acceptance of multilingualism as a fact of life in Africa, and the need to empower the languages that the African people know best at all levels, as working languages, media of instruction and languages of the mass media.

Equally, several international instruments emphasise these principles, either in the form of language or human rights. Some of these are:

(1) Article 2 of the 1948 Universal Declaration of Human Rights, which lays down the basic principle against discrimination on the grounds of language: 'Everyone is entitled to all rights and freedoms set forth in this Declaration, without distinction of any kind, such as ... language';
(2) Article 1 of the UNESCO Constitution;
(3) Article 5 of the UNESCO Universal Declaration on Cultural Diversity, which states that 'All persons should therefore be able to express themselves and to create and disseminate their work in the language of their choice, and particularly in their mother tongue';
(4) the 1996 Universal Declaration of Linguistic Rights;
(5) the 1992 European Charter for Regional or Minority Languages, which came into force on 1 March 1998;
(6) Articles 2.1, 14.3(a), 14.3(f), 19.2, 19.3, 24.1, 26 and 27 of the International Covenant on Civil and Political Rights;
(7) Articles 17, 29, 30 and 40 of the Convention on the Rights of the Child;
(8) Articles 3 and 4, paragraph 4, of the United Nations Declaration on the Rights of Persons Belonging to National or Ethnic, Religious and Linguistic Minorities;

(9) Articles 1, 2(b) and 5.1(c) of the UNESCO Convention Against Discrimination in Education;
(10) Articles 28(1), (2), (3) and 30 of the ILO Convention concerning Indigenous and Tribal Peoples in Independent Countries;
(11) Articles 14, 15 and 17 of the Draft Declaration on the Rights of Indigenous Peoples;
(12) Articles 13 and 14 of the International Covenant on Economic, Social and Cultural Rights;
(13) Articles 21, 22 and 41 of the Charter of Fundamental Rights of the European Union;
(14) Article 27 of the 1966 International Covenant on Civil and Political Rights;
(15) Article 4 of the 1992 Declaration on the Rights of Persons belonging to National or Ethnic, Religious and Linguistic Minorities;
(16) Article 28 of the 1989 ILO Convention 169 concerning Indigenous and Tribal Peoples in Independent Countries;
(17) Article 5 of the 1985 Declaration on the Human Rights of Individuals who are not Nationals of the Country in which they live;
(18) Article 45 of the 1990 International Convention on the Protection of the Rights of All Migrant Workers and Members of their Families;
(19) Article 29 of the 1989 Convention on the Rights of the Child;
(20) Article 5 of the 1960 Convention against Discrimination in Education;
(21) Article 22 of the 1976 Recommendation on the Development of Adult Education;
(22) Article 9 of the 1978 Declaration on Race and Racial Prejudice;
(23) Articles 19 and 29 of the 1995 Declaration and Integrated Framework of Action on Education for Peace, Human Rights and Democracy;
(24) Article 6 of the 2001 Universal Declaration on Cultural Diversity.

But is the introduction of mother-tongue instruction in African schools a guarantee for success?

Everything is Nothing in Education without Language[57]

There is currently a school of thought in Africa that strongly believes that 'everything is nothing in education without language'. Members of this school of thought are of the view that their critics simply rehearse the same articles of faith about multilingualism in Africa and economic rationalism, while ignoring the statistics about the failure of the exclusive use of a European language as the medium of instruction. These critics have yet to grasp the incalculable human costs of the education crisis in Africa. But the tragic reality is there for those who want to see it. Claiming ignorance of the situation would be an act of disrespect, and no amount of theorising will gloss over it; quite simply, educational deprivation threatens to consign the continent to an increasingly marginal future, and the debate would be greatly enhanced if everyone partaking in it took the time to familiarise themselves with, and understand the dysfunctional nature of the education system in Africa. Ultimately, it matters little how one defines development; the fact of the matter is that no sustainable development can be achieved without language, as language is not only a *sine qua non* for communication and understanding, but also a prerequisite for any other type of learning. It is hard to deny that there is a strong positive correlation between language of instruction and achievement at school, and that the choice of the medium of instruction plays a crucial role in the learning process. Mother-tongue education therefore acknowledges not only a basic principle of the learning process; it also recognises the existing knowledge and practices of the people it seeks to serve, rather than overriding them.

This explains why, upon noticing the refusal of some major donor agencies to support mother-tongue education in Africa, whilst at the same time supporting programmes that make no provision for the transfer of knowledge and cognition from the first to the second language, Mazrui, among others (see also Heugh 1995b: 329), accused the World Bank of destroying the future of African languages in education. Mazrui writes:

> In essence, the World Bank's proposed educational configuration in Africa demonstrates the continued role of instruction in Euro-languages in creating and maintaining an economy dominated primarily by foreign economic interests and, secondarily, by a small aspiring African bourgeoisie. (Mazrui, 1997: 44)

Mazrui also argues that the process of spreading European languages, spearheaded by the World Bank and IMF, is part of a 'wider economic agenda intended to meet the labour requirements of foreign capital', and helps to constitute the 'creation and reproduction of labour hierarchy'. Heugh (1995b: 329) extends this criticism to other international financial institutions, like the US Agency for International Development (USAID) and the Overseas Development Administration (ODA).

Considering the number and extent of the various declarations, agreements and covenants listed in the previous section, one could be forgiven for thinking that this school of thought has won the argument, and that it is indeed axiomatic that 'everything is nothing in education without language.' A closer look at the European Charter for Regional or Minority Languages shows that, in the area of education, and at all levels, Article 8 stipulates that:

All parties to the said Charter undertake, within the territory in which such languages are used, according to the situation of each of these languages, and without prejudice to the teaching of the official languages of the State, to make available pre-school, primary, secondary, technical and vocational, tertiary, as well as adult and continuing education an integral part of the curriculum in the relevant regional or minority languages. The parties to the Charter also undertake to apply the necessary measures at least for those pupils whose families so request, and whose number is considered sufficient, or favour and/or encourage the application of the said measures[58] and, if by reason of the role of the State in relation to higher education institutions, these measures cannot be applied, if the public authorities have no direct competence in the field of adult education, to encourage and/or allow the provision of university or other forms of higher education in regional or minority languages or of facilities for the study of these languages as university or higher education subjects, and favour and/or encourage the offering of such languages as subjects of adult and continuing education, provide the basic and further training of the teachers required to implement those of paragraphs a to g accepted by the Party, and set up a supervisory body or bodies responsible for monitoring the measures taken and progress achieved in establishing or developing the teaching of regional or minority languages and for drawing up periodic reports of their findings, which will be made public. With regard to education and in respect of territories other than those in which the regional or minority languages are traditionally used, the Parties undertake, if the number of users of a regional or minority language justifies it, to allow, encourage or provide teaching in or of the regional or minority language at all the appropriate stages of education. (Council of Europe, 1992)

On the other hand, the Universal Declaration of Linguistic Rights of June, 1996 considers linguistic rights to be inalienable personal rights, which should be exercised in any situation. Article 25 of the Declaration states that:

All language communities are entitled to have at their disposal all the human and material resources necessary to ensure that their language is present to the extent they desire at all levels of education within their territory: properly trained teachers, appropriate teaching methods, textbooks, finance, buildings and equipment, traditional and innovative technology. (UNESCO, 1996)

Bamgbose (2001: 640) writes that 'It is unrealistic to expect all languages to be used at all levels of education' and Walter (1998) argues that, because the draft is based on the idea of 'language communities', little account is taken of the language rights of individuals, and notes that the whole declaration is drafted in terms of 'language communities' and that the right of individuals to learn languages for international intelligibility gets only an oblique mention. Walter finds the definition of 'language communities' to be rather restrictive and exclusive of 'language groups', who do not have the same rights. She also finds a problem with the lack of definition of terms such as 'territory' and 'historical' and is alarmed that a declaration, intended to safeguard linguistic rights, could be used by some governments to bulldoze small, recently- implanted groups and individuals.

More importantly, and despite all the instruments pertaining to the central role of the mother tongue, there are those who still have doubts about the relevance and effectiveness of mother-tongue instruction, especially in the African context. They point out, quite rightly, that the use of mother-tongue instruction in and by itself is not a guarantee for success. They argue that the assumption that a multiplicity of home languages can be extended sufficiently (not only theoretically, but also in terms of widespread uptake), to function successfully as media of communication has yet to be shown to be valid. The critics further make the point that, if an educational intervention can achieve the extension of mother tongues to the classroom, then it can as well achieve the ordinary goals of education. However, it is not clear whether such a system will be able to sustain the social and economic costs of such an intervention. These critics also wonder at what point the limited conceptual load artificially engineered into the indigenous home language begins to fail, in comparison with increasing proficiency in an international language, where both the concepts and the literature in which they subsist (and may even have initially been developed) are abundantly available. They further note that, without both practical commitment to indigenous language development and widespread and effective strategies for their dissemination (capacities that countries with struggling economies show few signs of developing), the notion of indigenous languages (or indigenous acquired multilingualism) as a vehicle for superior performance in appropriate (non-globalist?) development, which is by definition markedly different from traditionalist behaviour, seems idealistic, to say the least.

Language, therefore, may not be everything in education for a host of other reasons, including, but not limited to, the issue of quality. Considering all the matters raised thus far in this chapter, there is no doubt that education in Africa faces the serious challenge of quality: how to ensure better education in schools, and in literacy and early childhood development programmes. There are, of course, substantial variations in the quality of schooling in many countries, the most important of which are the urban–rural differentials, whereby good teachers tend to be concentrated in the urban areas. There are also socio-economic differentials, with poor pay in government schools leading to many teachers moving on to private schools.[59] The use of an appropriate medium of instruction being a matter of passionate debate, the wishes and priorities for a given language (European or African) will rarely be unanimous. The variety of situations therefore precludes the imposition of a single language solution for all, and each country will have to come up with a solution appropriate to its own situation. However, everyone is agreed that practically all African schools suffer from a severe lack of appropriate and quality educational materials (teachers' guides, textbooks, reference books) and sufficient training, even in the chosen and all powerful European languages, and that there is a dire need for adequate teaching techniques and curricula, backed up with sufficient financial and material resources. Everyone is also agreed that the most urgent issue when it comes to quality should be in terms of deepening and enriching the school experience in terms of lifelong learning. Therefore, the immediate practical language needs and constraints that have shaped the language-in-education policies in Africa in the past now need to be balanced against future needs and opportunities. Recent developments in Information and Communication Technologies (ICTs) now provide a pathway for accessing new knowledge articulated in the language(s) of the African child. ICTs hold the promise of bridging the digital divide, by offering the technical tools to address many of the constraints that held back African languages and the continent itself, allowing a number of myths to develop and spread. Africans received Christianity and adopted it as their own, for their own purposes and in their own way, creating their own forms (enculturation). Likewise, Africans now receive ICTs. Are they going to be able to adapt it and use it for their own purposes? These and other related issues are the focus of the following sections.

African Languages as Languages of Science and Technology: Why Not?[60]

Although it is a common assumption that English is the dominant force on the Internet, a recent UNESCO study (2005) suggests that this is gradually changing, as take up in other languages increases, especially in places like India and China. The proportion of Internet users with English as a native language has declined from 51.3% in 2000 to 32% in 2005, much more than was predicted by *Computer Economics* (Graddol, 2006: 44).[61] UNESCO emphasises the concept of 'knowledge societies', which stresses plurality and diversity, in order to bridge the digital divide and form an inclusive information society.[62] Similarly, the Bamako Declaration (2002) recommends the promotion of multilingualism and the maintenance of cultural diversity 'as the driving force for the process of developing content for local and international use.' Considering their low level of uptake in Africa today (less than 20% of the population), European languages alone are clearly not appropriate for first time computer users who have not had much formal education. Learning to use computers, whilst trying to learn a European language at the same time can be an unnecessary burden for some, and there is no reason why these languages should be a prerequisite to acquiring computer skills. Such a requirement places the majority of the African population at a considerable disadvantage. Software is first and foremost a tool. Therefore, it can be adapted to the user, just as the sacred texts of Christianity were adapted to the faithful in Africa; it is not for the user to adapt to the software. After all, it is much easier, and cheaper, to teach a computer how to translate the interfaces of an African language than it is to teach the African masses European languages.

The level of use of African languages in computing and on the Internet is hard to quantify. Although Van der Veken and de Schryver (2003) believe that the use KiSwahili, Hausa and Lingala in cyberspace is satisfactory, Diki-Kidiri and Baboya (2003) show that, of the 3000 websites they were able to access, very few used an African language as the language of communication. According to Fantognan (2005: 105–108), major findings in this area indicate that:

(1) African languages appear on the web more as topics of study than as vehicles of communication;
(2) the language of communication used to talk about African languages is almost always English;
(3) African language courses are much too rare on the web;
(4) software products or computer solutions standardising fonts for all African languages are rarely suggested on websites.

Suggestions for addressing this state of affairs include: increasing the number of bilingual and/or multilingual sites, encouraging a greater distribution of documentation on African languages, increasing the number and improving the quality of African language courses on the web, and developing and distributing software or computer solutions that facilitate the writing of African languages and their use in cyberspace.

Hence, many have turned to software localisation in African languages as a solution to their absence from cyberspace. Software localisation is the adaptation or customisation of computer software packages (user interfaces and resource files) and their associated documentation (e.g. help files and user manuals) to suit the requirements of a given, or different, language(s), and especially a target market. This usually means translating, resizing, compiling, testing and bug fixing the software and localising the materials that go with the software package (e.g. on-line user assistance and printed materials such as user manuals, installation guides, reference guides, licence agreements, and marketing/packaging materials). It may also involve source code changes, such as the re-engineering of the format and layout of screens to accommodate different language requirements, and the compilation and testing of the functionality of the localised product. Software localisation is a prerequisite to the processing of digital content in any language, because it provides the ability to type one's language on the keyboard and to access fonts that can display the characters of that language. The whole process hinges on the use of Unicode, an industry standard designed to allow computers to represent and manipulate text and symbols of any writing system in a consistent manner. Among other things, Unicode comprises a repertoire of characters, an encoding methodology, a set of standard character encodings, a set of code charts for visual reference and an enumeration of character properties such as upper and lower case.

Software localisation can have a direct impact on the individual's perception of his/her mother tongue. Indeed, many people change their perception of a language when they realise it can be used to interface with a computer program. This is why software localisation is seen as a culture-oriented solution in computing. It facilitates the uploading of local content, thus allowing communities to talk to each other in their own mother tongues. Software localisation can be carried out using open source software that does not require licensing fees.[63] A number of projects, some altruistic (?) and others guided by profit, have already been completed.[64] This is the case of the software localisation in three South African languages by translate.org.za[65] in June 2003. This effort was followed by more established software companies such as Microsoft, who released an isiZulu version early in 2006 and an Afrikaans version in July 2006. In June 2006, Microsoft Africa also announced the launch of Microsoft *Office* 12 and Microsoft *Vista* in Wolof[66] as part of the Local Language Program of Microsoft International, which began in 2004. The popular search engine Google has a program for localised versions with several African languages (e.g. the 'V-webmail' interface localised in KiSwahili). Alt-I have developed a Yoruba keyboard, and keyboard, word processing, spreadsheet and website design packages have been developed for Amharic, the official language of Ethiopia and efforts are underway to develop software packages for Somali, Oromo and Tigrinya.[67] Microsoft is also planning to translate programs into other African languages, such as Hausa and Yoruba, and although many languages are only transcribed phonetically, considerable work is under way in Burkina Faso on Mooré and Dioula (*Open Office*), in Mali on Bambara and in Benin on Fongbé, Yoruba, Mina and Dendi. Major initiatives such as these, which bring African languages into the 21st century, are certain to close the debate on whether these languages can are suited for science and technology. Digital access and literacy informs and shapes our modes of communication and thinking (see UNESCO 2003b: Preface); as such, it cannot be limited to developed countries or restricted to the elite of developing countries for the sake of perpetuating 'elite closure'[68] (Myers-Scotton, 1993). Software in African languages, by helping spread and speed up the learning of computer skills, could also reduce and ultimately break down some of the socioeconomic disparities that underlie elite closure.

Cyberspace provides a participatory means by which all languages can become real instruments of global communication[69] and, as global capital needs local languages to penetrate local markets, multinationals have an interest and a special responsibility in being linguistically aware and in localising their products in particular languages. This is particularly true now, with advances in computer processing, the ubiquitousness of broadband, new ways of using the web (web-as-a-service, architecture of participation, etc.) and Web 2.0 as it is sometimes referred to, which goes well beyond uploading and reading hyperlinked documents, and enables the user to actually do things such as buying, selling, filling in forms and booking tickets, etc.

Why this focus on local languages and software localisation when basic literacy issues have yet to be addressed? Is it enough to develop software in African languages? How many people in Africa own computers in the first place, and are able to subscribe to the Internet? Will software programmes and Internet sites in African languages necessarily lead to more Africans using computers, and will this number attain the critical mass required – both in terms of literacy and computer access – to make such an undertaking worthwhile? These are some of the crucial questions that need to be addressed through proactive and visionary language policies because, whilst linguistic diversity might be served by having web pages in various languages, few people would read them if they do not have Internet access and are not literate in their own language(s). Materials in local languages will give people an incentive to learn computer skills in their own languages only if, and when, they can read and write in their own languages. In other words, just because a page is on the web does not mean that it is used, or even 'visited'. Some developers of software localisation in African languages are already finding that web pages represent only the supply side of the equation and are not necessarily a reflection of use and demand (see UNESCO, 2005: 9). Thus, the issue of the digital divide goes much further than software localisation. If computer and Internet tools can enhance literacy in some ways, current literacy efforts in African languages, limited to elementary school and to very few countries, fall far short of the critical mass that is needed to support the development of software localisation and make it socially and economically viable and sustainable. The economic implications of the use of African languages in computer packages and in technology in general cannot be ignored, as companies will adapt technology only in those languages that make economic sense. In a globalising world, localising software in a given language has everything to do with 'making money', and unfortunately, the African languages that would benefit most from software localisation have yet to demonstrate the critical mass – in terms of literacy of the speech community – that would make economic sense to the investor.

This is where language policy comes in. European languages were introduced in Africa as media of command, not of rights, and their use in education in Africa, from the first year or after the initial stages of schooling, was predicated on the need to train a number of low-level cadres (clerks, interpreters, messengers, petty bureaucrats and primary school teachers) who would serve as intermediaries and interlocutors of the colonial administration. As Rassool (2004) remarks, education in European languages was then a potent social construct of colonial ownership, subjugation and assimilation – a displacement of national, cultural and group identity. This colonial language policy has significantly influenced the social character of many Africans, and most local languages are still under-utilised in education throughout the continent. The school remains a locus where the voices of the majority of the people are silenced, as African children continue to be taught and learn in European languages. But the purpose of sending African children to school has gone well beyond training low-level cadres for the colonial administration; why then should they continue to operate at a linguistic disadvantage? Why can't Africans enter the information age and cyberspace in their own languages, just as they have managed to find a spiritual home in the Church to live their faith within the context of their own cultures?

One Laptop per Child: A Good Reason for Hope

As is often the case when such fundamental issues are raised about African languages, questions arise about the viability and feasibility of language management in such a highly multilingual context. Some also argue that the present linguistic situation of Africa is nothing out of the ordinary. Tens of thousands of languages have historically been replaced and/or displaced, as language contact naturally leads to inter-language competition, and the fortunes of individual languages evolve, driven first and foremost by speakers and language communities, but also by imperialisms and social and economic movements (e.g. globalisation). This line of argument had to be systematically countered, until its own advocates suddenly discovered the virtues of what they call *exception culturelle*, when the English language started overtaking and overwhelming their own linguistic space and expression. And a new group of sceptics, completely oblivious to the recent history of the English language, are now gloating and celebrating the hegemony of what they believe to be the 'global language'.

A much larger question that needs to be asked is whether technology transfer has to undermine or eradicate local languages and lead to the suppression of local identities and cultures. Is development possible when the target population is not empowered, or can the African people enter the information age without becoming copies of Europeans? Everyone is now agreed that ICTs are not just about the dissemination of information; they are tools of empowerment. This means that exclusive reliance on European languages for the transmission of information and transfer of technology critical to health and wellbeing will continue to maintain the majority of the African people who are not literate in these languages at a clear disadvantage.

A recent initiative launched by faculty members at the Media Laboratory of the Massachusetts Institute of Technology is One Laptop per Child (OLPC), a non-profit organisation dedicated to research, which promises to provide inexpensive laptop computers to every child in the world and give them access to modern forms of education. It has been hailed as a technology that could revolutionise education for nearly two billion children in the developing world, and may finally end the last throes of this battle of opinions. The project was first announced by OLPC Chairman Emeritus, Nicholas Negroponte, at the World Economic Forum at Davos, Switzerland, in January 2005, and then showcased at the at the World Summit on the Information Society in Tunis, in November 2005 (McCullagh, 2005). Also known as the green or XO machine, the laptop is said to uniquely foster learning how to learn and allow children to think about thinking. Indeed, it is felt that, by moving to an electronic format such as this, a much wider body of knowledge will be made available to children than was previously possible or economically feasible with printed text books. The XO uses a slim version of the Linux operating system, a 366-megahertz processor from Advanced Micro Devices Inc. and has no hard disk drive. Instead it holds 512 megabytes of flash memory, plus USB 2.0 ports, where more storage can be attached. It has a new user interface that is different from that of other computers and can run a wide range of programs, including a web browser, a word processor and a Really Simple Syndication (RSS) reader (the software that delivers weblog updates), a built-in camera and a colour display that converts to monochrome, so that it is easier to see in sunlight. Interestingly, 90% of the underlying programming code was put together from technologies that exist in the open-source programming community. Companies such as Google Inc., Advanced Micro Devices, News Corp. and Red Hat have donated funds to the project.

The laptops will be sold to governments and issued to children by schools, whilst the schools will receive associated server equipment. They will be rugged, open source and energy efficient (a child will be able to power her own laptop manually, using a wind-up crank) and priced as low as $100. Although India backed away from the project, arguing that it is 'much more urgent to build classrooms and train teachers than create eccentric toys',[70] several millions of these laptops were expected to be sent out to several countries by July 2006. As at January 2007, official OLPC launch countries included Libya, Argentina, Brazil, Nigeria, Rwanda[71] and Uruguay. In order to take part in this initiative, which is seen not just as a laptop project, but an education project, each of these countries must commit to buying a million laptops at around $100 each.[72] OLPC plans to send a specialist to each school for a month, to help teachers and students get started, and countries will get versions specific to their own languages. There is no doubt about the merit of the OLPC initiative. At the very least, it demonstrates that adapting technology to the needs of developing countries is feasible. The OLPC team declared in their Mission Statement that they 'would [...] be delighted if someone built something better, and at a lower price'. Since then, a number of similar initiatives have been announced: in April 2007, Microsoft announced that it will make software available for US$3 to poor countries that offer PCs to pupils and students (*AFP*, 20 April 2007a). In May 2007, India, which has already developed a $47 PC, announced that it was working on building a $10 computer that will be connected via the Internet to a central server, with access to *Word* or *Excel* (needless to say, a number of specialists in the field are sceptical that this can be done). Together with software localisation and terminology work carried out in a number of African languages over the last few years – e.g. the Project for the study of Alternative Education in South Africa (PRAESA), the Centre for Advanced Studies of African Society (CASAS), and the various projects of the African Academy of Languages (ACALAN).[73] Such initiatives finally promise to make it possible to meet the commitment of providing versions of this technology in languages specific to the receiving countries. In the age of software localisation, one can no longer assume that the most effective languages for true and lifelong learning for the majority of children in the developing world are those inherited from colonisation. A revolution in education in developing countries will occur only when we are able to obviate the setting up of another white elephant project on a global scale through a reduction of the digital gap between rich and poor, alleviate and ultimately eliminate the linguistic hegemony of the rich over the poor. An Information Society for All Based on Shared Knowledge is what the World Summit on the Information Society (Geneva, 12 December 2003) articulates in its Declaration of Principles, which reads thus:

1. We, the representatives of the peoples of the world, [...] declare our common desire and commitment to build a people-centred, inclusive and development-oriented Information Society, where everyone can create, access, utilise and share information and knowledge, enabling individuals, communities and peoples to achieve their full potential in promoting their sustainable development and improving their quality of life, premised on the purposes and principles of the Charter of the United Nations and respecting fully and upholding the Universal Declaration of Human Rights.

2. Our challenge is to harness the potential of information and communication technology to promote the development goals of the Millennium Declaration, namely the eradication of extreme poverty and hunger; achievement of universal primary education; promotion of gender equality and empowerment of women; reduction of child mortality; improvement of maternal health; to combat HIV/AIDS, malaria and other diseases; ensuring environmental sustainability; and development of global partnerships for development for the attainment of a more peaceful, just and prosperous world. We also reiterate our commitment to the achievement of sustainable development and agreed development goals, as contained in the Johannesburg Declaration and Plan of Implementation and the Monterrey Consensus, and other outcomes of relevant United Nations Summits. (WSIS, 2003)

Although this may have sounded more like a programme than a practical outcome, the creative innovations we have just discussed show a willingness to face up to this challenge. It is now up to African governments and private enterprise to improve on these initiatives by ensuring not only that all school children have access to a computer, but also that they can do so in their mother tongue(s). These innovations now make ownership of new technologies possible in African languages, and further shatter the myth of 'languages of technology and science', whilst bolstering the case for linguistic plurality in information technology.

Conclusion: Looking into the Future, Learning from the Past

In as much as language-in-education policies in Africa arch back to colonialism, contemporary views pertaining to mother-tongue instruction do not exist in a historical vacuum, and date back a long way. The passion of the debate was as fierce back then as it is today. There were voices in the new Republic of 18th century France that called for linguistic federalism and argued for instruction in some of the 'dialects' and 'idioms', as the best way to spread republican ideas quickly and most efficiently (Brunot, 1967: 29, 80–83; Grillo, 1989: 36). A report of the Committee of Public Instruction (December 1792) proposed, for instance, that children be allowed to learn to read and write in French and in German, in German-speaking areas of France (Grillo, 1989: 36), and that 'other parts of the curriculum be in French and the local language at the same time' (Brunot, 1967: 136). There was also considerable opposition from the Catholic Church, when it was decided to make French the language of liturgy. For the Church, language loyalty was a matter of faith (*Qui perd sa langue, perd sa foi*),[74] and the Bishop of Rennes wrote a letter to Grégoire, the initiator of this measure, in which he asked:

> If church services are to be translated into French, what of the Bretons whose language is even older than the Greeks, or the Picards, or the Auvergnats, the Gascons and the Basques, the Provençals, do they not have the same right to desire our liturgy in their language or jargon? (cited in Brunot, 1967: 378–9)

The Church succeeded in repudiating the attack on Latin for well over a century.

Students of language and history may find it significant therefore that, at the 7th Language and Development Conference in Addis Ababa in October 2005, Bamgbose declared:

> For meaningful development to take place, emphasis needs to be put on education and mass participation in economic processes. Again, if the

majority of the population is to be reached, the country's indigenous languages need to be used for learning and teaching, and in many other domains. While a global language, such as English, is a useful tool in development, community development programmes cannot be success- fully implemented unless they are presented in a language that the people concerned understand well. (Bamgbose, personal communication)

Development requires a critical mass of knowledgeable and informed people. In fifty years, no one can provide evidence that education in an exogenous language has made it possible to secure the hands and the brains capable of giving Africa some degree of self-sufficiency in any sector. There are no two ways about it. Development will not take root without the involvement of the African masses, and the African masses will not be able to partake in development activities through a European language that they do not understand. It will prove difficult indeed to attain any educa- tional goal until the basic issue of the language of instruction is resolved. Hence, whether we like it or not, language issues, and particularly language-in-education issues, will continue to be at the heart of the educa- tion/development nexus and current debate about the best way to achieve sustainable development.

Birdsall (1999) reminds us that education is an asset; and that the low and unequal accumulation of this asset can and has reduced growth and exacerbated socio-economic inequality, through high levels of schooling for a minority of the people, and very low levels of schooling for the majority. Part of the answer to the current dilemma lies in being able to agree on what education is for, and what sort of society African countries would rather have. Clearly, education will not enhance growth and reduce inequality until it is broadly shared, and the African elite is far too few in number to drag the rest of the people along with them; instead, they run the very real risk of being pulled under by the weight of increasing poverty and growing misery. Although in and by itself education and mother-tongue education will not lead to growth and social wellbeing, there is no doubt that education can play a significant role in empowering people. Therefore, every development effort, if it is to succeed, must be geared to understanding, promoting and taking full advantage of the prevailing dominant patterns of language use of each and every country, as well as the vision its people aspire to. People will not come to recognise their own predicament just because someone else points it out to them; they will come to take cognizance of it through their own experiences, facilitated by the consciousness-raising process that education provides. And that is why economic development cannot be pursued independently of socio-political and cultural realities.

There is no denying that carving out a larger role for local languages in education is fraught with problems. However, to the extent that schools play a central role in the socialisation of the future citizen and embody the values of the dominant group, it is through schooling that African languages can regain their rightful place. It is no secret that the languages that are used as media of instruction acquire a higher status and are developed through research, terminology development and publishing. Conversely, those that are only offered as subjects for a few years, or not offered at all, do not get the same attention.

There is also a fixation about limiting mother-tongue education to the first three or four years of primary school; but the secondary and tertiary levels of education have a crucial role to play in developing and enhancing the status of African languages. University research in African languages and practice in teaching in these languages, in particular, can go a long way to dispel the widespread myths about the inherent inadequacy of African languages to be used in education, and especially in the areas of science and technology. ICTs will go a long way in disproving many of these myths. However, new technologies, no matter how promising, will not deliver a panacea in and by themselves. African children will need to know how to read and write in their mother tongues, before they can make use of and take full advantage of any new technology, and African villages will need to have access to basic infrastructure, such as electricity, to power all these fantastic innovations. It is not enough to wish for every village on the continent to be connected to the telephone and the Internet by 2015; the reality at the moment is that major cities face difficulties in guaranteeing sufficient power supply, and suffer blackouts on a regular basis. Nevertheless, as the world finds the capacity to move away from a monolithic definition of development conceived in the North and imposed on the South through the Bretton Woods institutions, Africans can no longer afford to wait on the world to change, or for others to change the world for them. They must seize on these new opportunities to approach education and development from a different angle, their own angle, and they must become active participants in the search for practical solutions to empower themselves, improve their skills and know-how, and boost their productivity.

What these recent developments in ICTs show is that multilingualism is a way of life, not a problem to be solved. The challenge African countries face is to find a way of managing their realities, complex as they may be, in the area of education, and make education a lever of development. As they say in the Congo: 'You can teach, educate and train people much more efficiently if you do so in the language they speak.[75]

Chapter 3
Language, Health and Development

> *The Africa Health Strategy is important for Africa as we recognise that Africa carries the heaviest burden of disease and therefore needs a comprehensive, integrated approach to health challenges combined with a minimum package of interventions both at the primary health care level and the health system as whole (sic). We also believe that national health plans should include social protection systems for the vulnerable groups.*
> The African Union (2007)

> *We are told everything about how Africans die, but nothing about how they live.*
> Mankell (2003)

Introduction

All men – and women – are not born equal in terms of health, and no one will be surprised to learn that less than 35% of the African population have access to basic health services, in part because the system is largely privatised and thus mostly used by those who can afford it (UNDP Report, 2003).[76] A serious health gap exists between the rich and poor, urban and rural populations, the educated and the illiterate, and between men and women. Most people will attribute this to the overwhelming situation of poverty, the unavailability and/or state of disintegration of the health care delivery systems. Health, just like education, is a fundamental component of development, vital to a nation's growth and stability. Like education, health is much more than an outcome of development; it is a crucial means to achieving it. Poor health is more than a consequence of low income; it is also one of its fundamental causes (Bloom & Canning, 2000). Indeed, a healthier population is critical to reducing poverty and improving living standards (WHO, 2006). According to Bloom and Canning (2000), good health not only promotes school attendance and enhances cognitive function, but healthier people tend to have stronger incentives to invest in developing their skills. Recent economic analysis indicates that health status, as measured by life expectancy, is a significant predictor of economic growth (WHO, 1999, 2005a), and that health improvements make the economy stronger and alleviate poverty. Better health is therefore essential to achieving higher income, and health and income improvements are mutually reinforcing, whereas poor health can seriously inhibit growth (Bloom & Canning, 2000). In 2000, the Committee on Economic, Social and Cultural Rights of the United Nations Economic and Social Council adopted a resolution recognising health as 'a fundamental human right, essential to the exercise of all other rights' (CESCR, 2000). In the same year, three of the eight millennium development goals to be achieved by 2015 and adopted by 189 countries in the context of a United Nations Declaration (September 2000) focused on health. These are: reducing infant mortality, improving maternal health, and fighting HIV/AIDS, malaria, tuberculosis and other diseases.

It is therefore understandable that one of the five recommendations contained in the *Strategic Orientations for WHO Action in the African Region: 2005–2009* seeks to 'strengthen health policies and systems to *improve the capacity for delivering essential health care at local level'* (WHO, 2005b; my italics. Governments in African countries, like all governments around the world, are duty-bound to ensure that everyone has equal and universal access to basic health services. But, although health issues are clearly visible in Africa, and although it is generally acknowledged that, in the face of the current health crisis, African countries need to organise multi-dimensional responses to mobilise the broadest range of players (governments, civil society, local communities and foreign aid sources), in the prevention of diseases, there is a relative dearth of sociolinguistic studies in the area of health. As a result, language and communication problems often do not feature in the list of priorities for rebuilding the health sector in Africa. This chapter looks at communication efficiency in the provision of health care on the African continent, and the place and role of local languages in this process. Can empowerment through local languages contribute to best practices in facilitating access to, and the administration and management of health care in Africa?

Health and Health Care in Africa: Facts and Figures

While humankind is making remarkable technical and scientific progress in medicine, poverty and ill-health are well established and deepening in many African countries. This creates fertile grounds for the spread of diseases and increasing the vulnerability of the African population to these diseases, as health care delivery systems have broken down to a point where access to, and availability of basic health services is almost non-existent. Hence, with only 11% of the world population, Africa now has about 25% of the global burden of disease.[77] According to the UNDP Poverty Report in 2000, partly because of the impact of AIDS, life expectancy in

Botswana, Kenya, Malawi, Mozambique, Namibia, Rwanda, South Africa, Zambia and Zimbabwe is expected to decline by an average of 17 years in the early part of the 21st century; so much so that, by 2010, the continent will have 40 million orphans (UNDP, 2000a). All the lowest-ranking countries in the Human Development Report of 2004 by quality of life, including life expectancy and education, are located in Africa.[78] Furthermore, the Food and Agriculture Organisation (FAO) reports that 850 million people now suffer from malnutrition in this part of the world, and around 25,000 people, most of whom are children, die every day, due to the lack of food, or from diseases directly related to malnutrition (World Bank, 2006b). The United Nations Children's Fund (UNICEF) estimates that over 35% of children under the age of 5 suffer from stunted growth in countries like Burkina Faso, Burundi, the Democratic Republic of Congo, Eritrea, Ethiopia, Equatorial Guinea, Madagascar, Mali, Niger, Nigeria, the Central African Republic, Tanzania and Zambia. As a result, 11 million children, most under the age of 5, die every year, and more than 6 million others suffer from preventable diseases such as malaria, diarrhoea and pneumonia (overall, a child dies every 30 seconds in Africa). In fact, 90% of all malaria cases are to be found in sub-Saharan Africa, where 3000 children under the age of 5 die every day (i.e. 150,000 every month) – from malaria. According to Gallup and Sachs (2001), malaria alone is estimated to be slowing African economic growth by up to 1.3% per year. Africa's infant mortality rate is nearly 15 times that of the developed world and was averaging 174 deaths per 1000 live births in 2003. Niger, with its remarkable fecundity rate of 8 children per woman, the highest rate in the world, had an infant mortality rate of around 250 per 1000 (before the age of 5). In Côte d'Ivoire, 62% of children under the age of 5 suffer from malaria, and 74 children under the age of 1 die every day from it – a total of 27,000 per year (Yao, 2006a).

Infant mortality rates are directly linked to the maternal mortality rates, which also increased from 870 per 100,000 live births to an estimated 1000 per 100,000, between 1990 and 2003. Of the 13 countries in the world with the highest maternal mortality rates, exceeding 500 deaths per 100,000 live births, 12 are located in sub-Saharan Africa (World Bank, 2001b: 182).[79] At a seminar on maternal mortality organised in March, 2006 by the Association of Women in the Media Against AIDS and for the Promotion of Reproductive Health in Côte d'Ivoire (CFMS/SR–CI), the Minister of Health revealed that 3 pregnant women died every 2 hours in Côte d'Ivoire (i.e. 36 women per day) from complications directly related to their pregnancy, or while they were giving birth. Some of the common causes leading to these deaths are a lack of prenatal consultations and family planning, and the unavailability of maternity beds in medical centres.

Of greatest concern at present is the AIDS pandemic because, like no other disease, AIDS is prevalent among the economic elite and strikes people in the most productive age groups. A disproportionate number of those who are falling ill and dying of AIDS are relatively well educated, urban, white-collar workers, whose mortality rate is 70% higher than that of the general adult population (World Bank, 2001b). One can only shudder at the thought that the teacher mortality rate is set to double over the next 10 years, before gradually declining thereafter (UNDP, 2000b). Partly because of the state of shambles into which the health care system has been plunged, AIDS in this part of the world is essentially 100% fatal. Whilst, according to the Joint United Nations Programme on HIV/AIDS (UNAIDS), the AIDS pandemic claimed the lives of 2 million to 2.5 million adults and children in sub-Saharan Africa in 2003, and an estimated 3 million Africans were newly infected with HIV over the same period of time, it was revealed in 2006 that the total number of people suffering from HIV/AIDS in Africa had increased from 25 million in 2003 to 25.8 million in 2005, with 2.8 million (65%) new infections and 2.1 million deaths (72%) – leaving behind 13 million AIDS orphans (also see UNAIDS, 2006).[80] Even countries that showed earlier successes in reducing new infections (e.g. Uganda) have either slowed or are now experiencing increasing infection rates. According to UNICEF, 8 out of 10 of the children orphaned by AIDS are from Africa. The Programme also warned that it is very likely that most, if not all, of these people will die over the following decade (UNAIDS, 2004). In fact, any apparent stabilisation in the spread of the disease is essentially due to an increase in mortality, rather than a genuine decrease in infection rates. Overall, adult mortality rates have already trebled in Africa, in comparison to the world average, and this mainly because of the AIDS pandemic.

The 20 countries with the highest HIV prevalence rates in the world were all located in sub-Saharan Africa (UNDP, 2000a). Despite the recent declines in national HIV prevalence in Kenya and Zimbabwe, exceptionally high levels of infection continue in the southern part of continent. The South African Development Community (SADC) reported that 1.2 million deaths from AIDS in 2005 were from Southern Africa, where HIV prevalence rates approaching 40% (UNAIDS, 2004) can be found in countries like Swaziland (33.4%), Botswana (24.1%), Lesotho (23.2%), Zimbabwe (20%), Namibia (19.6%), South Africa (30.2% in 2005, 18.8%, or 5.5 million, of whom are adults), and Zambia, Mozambique and Malawi whose rates of prevalence varied between 14.1 and 17%. In these countries, the number of school teachers dying from AIDS was greater than the number of graduates out of teacher training Colleges. Botswana, for example,had a teacher mortality rate of 3% a year in 2000 (UNDP, 2002)). In Kwa-Zulu-Natal

(South Africa), over a third of pregnant women were found to be HIV positive (UNDP & UNDF, 2002). Even the health care sector is not immune from this scourge, as 20% of student nurses were found to be HIV positive. Feeley (2006) documented an annual death rate of 3.5% for nurses in Lusaka and 2.8% in the Kasama district in Zambia and concluded that these death rates may well account for the country's nurse vacancy rate of 37%. A sharp rise in HIV prevalence was also found among pregnant women in Cameroon (11% of young women aged between 20 and 24 from 1998 to 2000).

Women bear the brunt of the spread of HIV/AIDS, especially among uneducated girls. In Swaziland, from 4% in 1992, HIV prevalence among pregnant women attending antenatal clinics rose to 43% in 2004 (see UNAIDS, 2006). According to a UNICEF Report entitled *L'Enfance en péril* (UNICEF, 2005), 60% of women in sub-Saharan Africa – 75% of whom are young girls between the ages of 15 and 24 – are HIV positive. The report attributes this dramatic increase in HIV infections to poverty, inequalities between men and women, often leading to violence against women, and prostitution. At the end of 2005, UNAIDS reported that women made up 77% of all those who were HIV positive in sub-Saharan Africa.[81] Even more alarming is the well-known fact that many more people, HIV positive men and women, are walking the streets unaware of their serological status.

Clearly, the AIDS pandemic in sub-Saharan Africa is much more than a medical problem. It has severe and long-term economic consequences, which require more than medical interventions. Indeed, it is believed that treating an AIDS patient for one year is about as expensive as educating 10 primary school students for the same period (Over, 1992). Economic theory predicts that AIDS has a significant macro-economic impact on growth, as it affects all aspects of the economy (health, agriculture, transport, mining, education, water, the manufacturing sector, etc.), including the labour supply through increased mortality and morbidity. This is compounded by loss of skills in key areas of the labour market (lost time due to illness, deaths, recruitment and training of workers, labour turnover), and causes enormous and almost unaffordable expenditures for medical care, drugs and funeral expenses (Over, 1992; Ainsworth & Over, 1998). Estimates suggest that AIDS has already reduced average national economic growth rates by 2–4% a year across Africa. According to Bonnel (2000), HIV/AIDS has slowed income growth in Africa, and could account for an annual loss equivalent to 2.6% of GDP. Arndt and Lewis (2000, 2001) estimate that, by 2010, South Africa's GDP per capita will be some 8% lower, and consumption per capita 12% lower than would otherwise have been the case without the HIV/AIDS pandemic.

These figures come on top of other 'neglected diseases' such as malaria (60% of the global burden) and tuberculosis (27% of the global burden), diseases that have no economic interest for most pharmaceutical multinationals. Malaria increased dramatically all across Africa in 2006 (17.6%) and is endemic in countries like Angola, where 20,000 people die from this disease every year. Stagnant water and the absence of basic hygiene combine to make cholera a lethal disease that killed 3095 people from February 2006 to May 2007 (see *AFP*, 2007d). In May 2006, Angola faced the worst cholera epidemic of its history, with 1300 deaths, 35,775 cases of infections and millions of people at risk of being infected, within a space of three months (MSF, 2006). In the meningitis (Neisseria Meningitis) belt of Africa, from Senegal in the west to Ethiopia in the east, the epidemic has affected some 250,000 people, 25,000 of whom lost their lives, between 1995 and 1997. From January to 21 March 2007, there were 15,595 cases of meningitis, in Burkina Faso (4958 cases), Uganda (2961 cases), the DRC (730 cases) and Sudan (6946 cases); 1670 of these were fatal (see WHO, 2007). In Zambia, measles is one of the five major causes of childhood illnesses, contributing about 70% of mortality and morbidity in children under the age of 5. Even though these other diseases kill some 53 million people every year – for instance, malaria alone is reported to kill between 1.5 and 2.7 million people a year, whilst tuberculosis kills 5000 people a day – those who suffer from such diseases have no resources to meet the cost of the medication they need. Hence, infectious diseases continue to emerge and re-emerge and spread to new foci, as in the case of marburg in Angola, ebola in the DRC and Buruli ulcus, human African trypanosomiasis (HAT) and polio in a number of other countries

Although Africa's small human capital predates the AIDS pandemic, it is apparent that the combined impact of HIV/AIDS and other communicable diseases worsens the dearth of human capital in Africa. This seriously affects the rate of growth and productivity of the continent, reducing the capacity of the educational system to train the next generation. Clearly, health status plays a significant role in economic growth (also see *Commission on Macroeconomics and Health*, 2001). How is development going to be possible in the face of such major health challenges? [82]

Development without Health?

The health profile of sub-Saharan Africa reflects its current socioeconomic context (see Chapter 4 for a detailed discussion of that context). Although health is not the only influence on economic growth, it is one of the most potent, and the conditions of extreme poverty under which the majority of the African people currently live simply do not enable them to access essential health care services, as diseases and poverty feed on one another. The lack of health services and the increase of preventable and curable diseases and HIV/AIDS are therefore serious threats to Africa's development.

Although there were significant increases in the health care infrastructure and in the numbers of health professionals employed in the public sector in many countries across the African continent, cutbacks in health budgets and privatisation of health services in the 1980s and 1990s have severely compromised, if not ruined, previous advances in health care in Africa and weakened the continent's capacity to cope with the growing health crisis (Colgan, 2002). As governments were forced to sacrifice social needs to meet macro-economic goals in the 1980s, the implementation of market-led growth policies undermined health care systems, and the continent now holds the world record for the least spending in the health sector (less than 1% of the global health care expenditure).[83] The available data show that in the 42 poorest countries in Africa, spending on health care fell by 50% in the 1980s (ICCAF, 1993: 17). In Nigeria for instance, per capita expenditure on health fell by 75% between 1980 and 1987 (ICCAF, 1993: 19). Health expenditure averages 8% of the total national budget of African countries, in spite of a pledge to allocate 15% of their national budgets to health (African Union, 2001). According to the African Development Indicators, 2005 health expenditure averaged only US$13 per head in sub-Saharan Africa, excluding South Africa, and was below US$10 per head in 16 countries; this, against the background of an estimated average of US$33 spent per person per year on health in the 57 countries with severe shortages of health workers (see WHO, 2006). The Chairperson of the African Union Commission observed that progress on this commitment revealed that 4 countries are allocating less than 5% of their budgets to health, whilst 25 others are allocating only 5–10%, and another 13 countries between 11 and 14% (Konaré, 2005: 5).[84] This drop in health care expenditure resulted in the disintegration of the health care systems, with hundreds of public hospitals and medical facilities being closed. Those that remained opened lacked essential medical supplies, and were severely under-staffed. Selected national health accounts indicators, measured by level of per capita expenditure on health, show that per capita government expenditure on health at international dollar rate was generally less than US$150 in 2002, except for Botswana, Mauritius, Namibia, South Africa and Tunisia.[85] And, according to a World Health Report (WHO, 2002) in 2002 per capita government expenditure on health at international dollar rate was less than US$50 for 34 countries (see Table 6 of the Annex of the *World Health Report*,

2005a: 200–203). Table 4 is an extract of a summary table of public spending on health care in 2001, in 11 sub-Saharan African countries.

Meanwhile, the WHO was announcing that an additional 4 million health professionals would be required in 57 countries, 35 of which are located in sub-Saharan Africa, 38 countries (more than 75% of the countries concerned) were well short of the WHO's minimum standard of 20 doctors per 100,000 population, and 13 of these countries had 5 or fewer doctors per 100,000 population. Furthermore, approximately 17 countries in sub-Saharan Africa did not have even half of the WHO's minimum standard of 100 nurses per 100,000 population (Amnesty International News for Health Professionals, 2004). As a result, most health facilities operate at less than 50% of the required workforce and whilst,

life expectancy has been increasing everywhere else in the world, it has been falling dramatically in many African countries over the past two decades (OAU, 2002a), averaging only 47 years across Africa. According to the United Nation's 2004 Human Development Report, life expectancy has dropped even further in some parts of Africa (UNDP, 2004). In Zambia, life expectancy initially increased from 43 years to 51 years between 1962 and 1982, but declined to 38 years between 1985 and 1999 (World Bank, 2001b) and to only 33.1 years in Zimbabwe.

Table 4 Public spending on health care (percentage of GDNPP 2001) in 11 sub-Saharan African countries in 2001

Countries	*% of GDP in 2001*
Angola	2.8
Cameroon	1.2
Congo	1.4
Ethiopia	1.4
Kenya	1.7
Mali	1.7
Senegal	2.8
Sierra Leone	2.6
South Africa	3.6
The DRC	1.5
Zimbabwe	2.8

Source: UNDP (2004)

Severe cost-cutting and under-investment in the health sector over the years have also led to an exodus of disgruntled, overworked and under-paid health professionals to wealthy countries like Australia, Canada, the United Kingdom and the United States.[86] Hence, in addition to already-battered health care systems, Africa is now confronted with a significant brain drain in the health sector, further undermining health care service delivery and seriously inhibiting the continent's ability to provide essential life-saving treatments in every area of health care. Some blame this state of affairs on developed countries, which they accuse of the 'shameless loot-ing' or 'plundering' of Africa for doctors and nurses to alleviate their hospital waiting lists, whilst at the same time putting up barbed wire to contain illegal immigration and restrict legal immigration.[87] Overall, nearly one-third of Africa's intellectual resources live in developed countries. Between 1960 and 1975, some 1800 highly qualified Africans left the conti-nent for Europe and the United States. This number increased to 4000 between 1975 and 1984, then to 12,000 a year in 1990s and is estimated to have been well over 23,000 a year in 2000.[88] These figures do not include those university students who do not return to their countries of origin after graduation (7% for Egypt, 8% for South Africa and 26% for Ghana). According to Abdelkader Messahel, Algerian Deputy Minister for African and Maghreb Affairs, at least 50,000 African professionals moved to Europe every year, and more than 4 million African experts have perma-nently settled there. Another 4 million are spread in other parts of the developed world (*La Tribune*, Algiers, 20 March 2006). The WHO estimates that 1 in 4 doctors trained in Africa works in a developed country, leaving the continent to manage with only 3 to 4% of the health workforce (see UNAIDS, 2006; WHO, 2006). This situation has particularly affected coun-tries like Angola, Congo, Guinea Bissau, Liberia, Mozambique, Rwanda and Sierra Leone, which all endured the cruelty of war in the 1990s and have lost some 40% of their medical staff. For every Liberian doctor working in his country, another two work in developed countries. Like-wise, countries like Kenya, Tanzania and Zimbabwe, which have experi-enced economic stagnation for a decade or so, have lost more than half of their medical staff. According to UNAIDS, 'In 1999, Ghana certified 320 new nursing graduates and lost 320 nurses through emigration. The following year, it lost twice that many' (UNAIDS, 2006: 189). Zambia has lost well over 50% of its medical personnel to the brain drain – only 50 of the 600 doctors trained in Zambia between 1978 and 1999 are still working in the country. As a result, Zambia has to make do with 600 doctors for a popu-lation of 11 million inhabitants, or 1 doctor for 14,000 people, whereas 16,000 Zambian nurses are currently working in the United Kingdom, which boasts 1 doctor for 600 people (Oxfam, 2006; World Health Report, 2005b). Kenya retains only 10% of the doctors it trains, and 34% of Zimbabwe nurses are employed overseas. Tanzania, Malawi, Mozambique, Ethiopia, Sierra Leone and Niger have three or fewer doctors per 100,000 people. Even South Africa, which has much better health care facilities, estimates that at least 3,500 of its 26,000 practising doctors live overseas. According to Nicholas Sarkozy,[89] Benin has many more doctors practising in France than in Benin (*Jeune Afrique*, 2006b). The United Kingdom is believed to have recruited at least 3000 nurses a year since 2001 from countries such as Kenya, Ghana, South Africa, Uganda and Zambia. In 2002–2003, almost half of the new nurses registering to work in Britain were recruited overseas, and the number of work permits issued to nurses from 2000 to 2005 rose from 14,000 to more than 27,000. In 2005 alone, some 2825 work permits for health and medical personnel were issued in South Africa, 1510 were issued in Zimbabwe and 850 in Ghana and Nigeria. In 2002, 5334 doctors trained in African medical schools were practising in the United States, where there are more than 200 doctors for 100,000 people. According to the US Immigration and Naturalisation Service, in 2002 alone immigrants with medicine and health-related occupations included 64 individuals from Kenya, 181 from Nigeria, 212 from South Africa, 15 from Uganda, 11 from Zambia and 31 from Zimbabwe.[90] The situation is expected to get worse, with Australia suffering from a lack of doctors in 65% of its rural areas and targeting overseas doctors (*ABC Radio News*, broadcast of 17 May 2007; Weaver, 2007), the United Kingdom experiencing a shortfall of 25,000 medical doctors and 35,000 nurses by 2008, whilst the United States needs to find a million nurses within the next three years.[91]

This brain drain, due in part to a demand for health professionals in developed countries, where an increased amount of care is required, but also due to to a desire by these professionals to leave their countries in search of a better professional life, is crippling sub-Saharan Africa's health care system. Such a shortage of health professionals, when it occurs in developed countries, is often the subject of enquiries and numerous educational and immigration strategies to actively seek and find appropriate solutions, for it can make or break a government. However, in African countries like Côte d'Ivoire, where some 1200 qualified medical doctors are unemployed, successive governments do not seem to be overly concerned, even though the country has only one doctor for every 12,486 patient population and is believed to be in need of at least 8050 doctors (estimates dating back to 1998!).[92] Instead, the doctors are exploited in the public and private hospitals, where they get paid anywhere between US$5 and US$10 for the graveyard shift (*Fraternité Matin*, 2006).[93]

The flight of medical staff from Africa is made even worse by the new scourge of counterfeit medicines. It is estimated that 50% of all medicines on the African market are believed to be counterfeit, and most of them are sold at 'outdoor pharmacies' when they are past their use-by date. These medicines, which have an unparalleled success in terms of sales, are wreaking havoc on the health of the poor, with an increasing number of people suffering from renal failure, rupture of intestinal wall, irregular cardiac rhythm and various types of hepatitis.[94]

There is no doubt therefore that health services across the African continent face problems of performance, due to severe shortcomings in the availability and management of human, financial and technological resources, and a lack of substantial investment in capacity building, in terms of infrastructure and human capital. But, to paraphrase the famous Swedish writer Henning Mankell, we have just discussed everything about how Africans die, but nothing about how they live.

Concerns about the state of health care services and their impact on the process of development have seen a number of international (non-governmental) organisations, like the World Alliance for Breastfeeding Action (WABA), the International Baby Food Action Network (IBFAN Africa) and Sidaction, swing into action in Africa, spurring local communities of researchers, healers and associations to organise and fight the scourge of HIV/AIDS and other diseases on the continent, in partnership with UNAIDS and the WHO. A survey carried out by Sidaction[95] (January to April 2004) found that 181 local associations and community groups are at the forefront of best practice in facilitating access to, and administration and management of, antiretroviral drugs for the treatment of HIV/AIDS in Africa. These local associations and community groups have been created to make up for gaps in a public health system that is completely overwhelmed, especially by the AIDS crisis. In Côte d'Ivoire alone (see Table 5), there are no less than 60 such organisations working in the area of health (and other related areas), trying to relieve the burden of the government health facilities.[96]

To be sure, not all of these organisations are actually active on the ground. Many are the result of what the local press calls the 'politics of hunger'; in other words, they have been created essentially to extract money from local politicians and international aid donors, and exist only in name. This fact was confirmed after several attempts to locate some of the organisations to discuss their communication and information dissemination strategies, especially in rural areas. I sent and re-sent hundreds of emails across Africa, over a period of a year and a half (January 2005 to August 2006), to organisations claiming to work in the health sector. Many

Table 5 Local organisations and associations working in the area of health in Côte d'Ivoire[97]

Acronym	Full name	Activities
2 IE 2000	Ivorian Institute Hope 2000	Health in rural areas
ADC	Community Development Authority	Health and Social aid
ADSR	Association for Rural Socio-sanitary Development	Rural development, health
AFAF SI	African Women's Association against AIDS	AIDS awareness
AFPA	Women's Association for the Development of Alépé	Rural development, education, health
AI	Act International	Health, social aid, sustainable development, conflict, action against hunger
AIBEF	Ivorian Association for Family Well being	Family planning
AINA	Ivorian Association for Cleaning and Sanitation	Health, environment
AMS	Friends of Health	Health
ARK	Korhogo Rural Centre	Rural development, health, women, literacy
ASD	Africa Health and Development	Health, development
AVDA	Association of Volunteers for the Development of Agriculture in the Rural Areas	Health, development
CASES	Health and Social Studies Centre	Health, training
CBI	International White Cross	Health, education, training
CBI	Ivorian Blue Cross	Health, humanitarian
CFMS/SR – CI	Association of Women in the Media Against AIDS and for the Promotion of Reproductive Health in Côte d'Ivoire	Women's health (AIDS)
CIC	Côte d'Ivoire Charity	Health, training, literacy
CIP	Côte d'Ivoire Prosperity	Community health, training and development
COMECI	Medical contribution of Côte d'Ivoire	Medical
COMUPASC	Committee for the Promotion of Health Mutuals and Community Health Agents	Community health

Table 5 – *continued*

Acronym	Full name	Activities
COSCI	Group of AIDS NGOs of Côte d'Ivoire	Health (AIDS)
CRAS	Rural Health Centre	Health and development
CRCI	Red Cross of Côte d'Ivoire	Community health, humanitarian aid
CTP	Solidarity for Toddlers	Health and social aid for children
Défi 2000	Challenge 2000	Fight against drugs, health
ECODEV	Integrated Approach to Development	Health, fight against poverty
EHCI	Humanitarian Space of Côte d'Ivoire for Senior Citizens	Senior citizen health
FED	Women and Development	Literacy, health
FIA	Inter-African Fouagnon	Education, health, re-insertion of homeless children
FIDICI	Ivorian Women for Integrated Development in Côte d'Ivoire	Health, education, aid to poor women
FIR	Ivorian Women of the Rural Sector	Health, agriculture, commerce
FISA	International Foundation of Aid and Friendship	Health, training, social aid
GBH	Biblical Group for Hospitals	Physical and spiritual health
ISD	Information on AIDS and Drugs	Drugs, AIDS
ULES – CI	United Youth for the Fight and Mutual Aid against AIDS in Côte d'Ivoire	Health
LIEPSC	International League for the Study and Promotion of Community Health	Health, environment
MAFIM-CI	Aid Movement for the Unmarried Mothers of Côte d'Ivoire	Social aid
MAG	Angel Gabriel Mission	Health for the poor
MI	Maternal Initiatives	Health
MPT	Doctors For All	Health
MSI-CI	International Social Medicine of Côte d'Ivoire	Health
NOSIC	No Smoking International Club	Fight against nicotinism
OCOVIE	Community Organisation for Life	Health, social aid, environment
OIJS	International NGO, Youth Help	Health assistance, education for homeless children

Table 5 – *continued*

Acronym	Full name	Activities
ONEF	National Organisation for the Child, the Woman and the Family	Social health
OSK	Objective Health Korhogo	Health
PRODESOC	Social and Community Development Programme	Health, education, social aid, development
PROSODEC	Programme of Solidarity for Economic and Community Development	Health, agriculture, environment
RAM-CI	Rural Medical Aid of Côte d'Ivoire	Health
RENOSCI	National Network of Health NGOs of Côte d'Ivoire	Health network
RSP	NGO Health Plus Follow-up	Health (AIDS)
Ruban Bleu	Blue Ribbon	Aid for children in difficulty and AIDS orphans
SAMEN-CI	Health for Mother and Child in Côte d'Ivoire	Health
SED	Health, Environment, Development	Health and development, environment
SEMEPHA	Pharmaceutical Medical Aid Service	Health, training
SFEM	Woman's smile	Women's health and social aid
SNV	Natural Health and Life	Health
SOS Famille	SOS Family	Health, social aid, rural development
SOS VS	SOS Sexual Violence	Health
UCED	Christian Union of God's children	Health, social aid
Un Amour de Commune	Un Amour de Commune	Education, training, health

of these messages, the large majority in fact (95%), have remained unanswered. The few responses received provided the names and contact details of other individuals within the organisations, supposedly in charge of the communication strategy, only for those individuals to remain silent. Those who attempted to respond to the question were evasive when it came to the specific local language(s) used in their information campaigns (spoken or written). Some referred to using 'simple language'; which, in most cases turned out to mean 'plain English or French'. Visits to some local organisations proved fruitless in more ways than one: (1) many had only a post office box and no registered address; some are run from the homes of the President or Secretary General of the organisation; (2) almost all, with the notable exception of the Ivorian Association for Family Well Being (AIBEF) seemed to treat information pertaining to their communication strategy like industrial secrets.[98] But even when the individuals speaking for an organisation were forthcoming and provided information on their communication strategy, as was the case for a Regional Coordinator in Southern Africa, it often read as follows:

> You cannot say which languages because there are many different languages. In South Africa there are about 11 main languages. In Tanzania there are about 153 different tribes speaking different languages. At some stage someone has to teach or inform in these languages although there are two main languages in Tanzania.[99]

Despite all this, it is apparent that some of these organisations and associations attempt to use local languages whenever and wherever possible, in order to facilitate communication in the delivery of basic health services. They make widespread use of posters in their information campaigns, and sometimes have their messages carried on radio broadcasts in different local languages. Indeed, this is the preferred and most accessible method of information dissemination, as many families own a radio, even though they may not always afford a battery. Radio programmes are often built around performing arts and advertising, usually in the regional lingua franca.

But even when local languages are used, another problem arises. Some radio programmes (e.g. radio drama to convey information about reproductive health, family planning and HIV/sexually transmissible disease prevention) and health leaflets have been criticised for being too explicit in their coverage of health issues, especially reproductive health, when, in the name of straight talk, they show no cultural and linguistic sensitivity to the people they aim to help.[100] Open discussion of private parts and direct reference to the genitalia (e.g. sex organs, such as the 'penis' and the 'vagina') and intimate behaviour (e.g. having an erection, having sex, use of condom when having sex), which is normally taboo in some cultures and languages, are all of a sudden brought out in the open to the shame and strong disapproval of the target speech communities. Local and/or international organisations and associations working in this area prefer this approach because of what they perceive as the tendency of most patient populations to resort to metaphors when talking to or about people with diseases such as AIDS – diseases that they would rather not refer to by name (directly or openly). The aim of this approach is threefold: (1) to create language that allows the community to abide by its cultural norms (taboos, etc.); (2) to create language that allows the community to cope with reality and (3) to create language that shows sensitivity and avoids stigmatising the disease and particularly those who are struck down by it. This tendency is borne out by research in the field, which also reveals a degree of ignorance and foolhardiness on the part of some sections of the patient populations, who sometimes fail to take a disease like AIDS seriously, until it is too late. In Côte d'Ivoire and other French-speaking countries for instance, the French acronym for AIDS (SIDA) is turned into the expression '*Syndrome Inventé pour Décourager les Amoureux*' (Syndrome Invented to Discourage Lovers), which clearly suggest a certain degree of ignorance and downright irresponsibility. According to Hampton (1990: 5), individuals suffering from AIDS are referred to as 'clients'. In Uganda, an AIDS support organisation (TASO) found that the word AIDS was never used, and HIV positive or individuals with full-blown AIDS were referred to as 'body positive'. Mutembei *et al.* (2002: 7–11) found the same process in train in the Kagera region north-west of Tanzania (west of Lake Victoria), a community with high prevalence of HIV infection. Here AIDS was variously referred to as *Endwala enkulu* (old sickness), *Eza bilebi* (modern disease) and through the religious and judgemental attitude as *Nosingwa* (you are guilty), *Jaji* (judge) or *Zawadi ya uasherati* (gift of promiscuity) and, as the disease became synonymous with death, *Malaika ontole* (receive me Angel), *Byona busha* (all is in vain), and even *Skadi* (Scud missile) or *Gadafi* (after Colonel Gaddafi of Libya), and so on. Sometimes the English acronym AIDS is turned into a stark warning as in *Angalia Isikupate Dawa Sina* (Make sure you don't get it, I don't have a cure!).

Workers of various non-governmental organisations, local and/or international, must deal with these realities in the first instance, while at the same time working out the best way to spread accurate and objective information on prevention and treatment in languages that the patient populations understand, and through which they can best appropriate the information and practices of efficient prevention and treatment. But non-governmental organisations, associations and community groups cannot replace the public health system, and cannot be expected to carry the burden of finding the best solution. Responsibility for bridging the language and communication gap in Africa lies, first and foremost, with African governments. Those governments need to understand, beyond the issues of infrastructure and staffing in the health care system, the extent to which the language used in medical encounters is critical to a successful outcome for patient populations, and must ensure that the average citizen has access to health information in a language s/he understands. But in the meantime, how do people access health information in Africa, and how is health generally administered? What is the general pattern of doctor/

patient communication? Will it be possible to re-build the health systems of Africa without the local languages? These are some of the questions that the next section attempts to answer.

Health without Local Languages?

The foregoing clearly suggests that the current health and health care systems cry out for change, radical change. Given the enormity of Africa's health problems and the shortage of resources for the sector, the overriding challenge has to be the building of equitable health care systems, with a view to delivering health care services to the poor and achieving an integrated approach to service quality, in order to strengthen human resources in Africa. A massive, multi-pronged prevention and information campaign will also have to be put in place, and the community will have to be involved in health promotion and disease prevention. Many more information packages will need to be put out in order to raise awareness, spread information and educate the masses on various critical issues such as condom use, counselling, mother-to-child transmission of diseases, and treatment and care. Whilst no one would want to suggest that finding a balanced solution to the language situation will solve all the health care problems in sub-Saharan Africa, the importance of such communication and information dissemination as a primary health care intervention tool cannot be overstated. 'Medical speech' is already difficult to understand, even when communicating with medical staff in the same language. So packaging medical information in a supposedly 'simple (European) language'[101] that the patients do not understand, as is still being done as a matter of course in many countries, can only further frustrate the best intentions in the world, and continue the wastage of scarce resources. Cameron and Williams write:

> Although we may think that the primary tools of medicine are technological, the most fundamental tool, upon which all use of technology depends, is that of language. Language allows patients and care-providers to make their intentions known, a crucial step in the process of identifying a problem, investigating how long it has existed, exploring what meaning this problem may have, and setting in action a treatment strategy. Thus if problems in linguistic encoding interfere with this process, there may be important consequences. (Cameron & Williams, 1997: 419)

The deteriorating health situation in Africa has increased the patient population's need for health information that they can understand. In situations of crisis (e.g. experiencing great pain and suffering), patients will tend to resort to the language they are most fluent in, usually their mother tongue or the regional lingua franca, but most certainly not to a European language that they struggle to speak under normal circumstances. This is particularly true for the elderly, for patients from the rural areas and especially for rural women (when the health matter pertains to private parts and intimate behaviour), who are largely illiterate in European languages.

Information dissemination is a complex, varied, long and tedious process. A small proportion of the patient population in Africa can read in a European language and/or their local language and may get simple information written in such a language. However, it is an open secret that 50 years on, most people in Africa are illiterate in European languages and depend on word-of-mouth from community development workers, if there are any, when it comes to critical health issues. Effective communication is a two-way process. This means that doctor/patient interactions and dissemination of health-related information to the patient population cannot be a one-way process. Communication itself is a tool of empowerment. People must understand what the real message of the communication process is, if they are to act on it. Participation is the essential condition for development to happen. Therefore, printing materials, putting together educational videos or broadcasting health-related information on the radio or television in European languages, beyond satisfying the ego of those who put out such materials, is not achieving much in terms of making a difference for the target population. A popular slogan of the FAO in the late 1980s was, 'There is no development without communication' (Balit, 1988).

Unobstructed communication between doctor and patient or between development worker and the community in which she works is crucial for the successful provision and maintenance of health care and promotes both the quality and course of treatment. Conversely, problematic doctor/patient or development worker/community communication is unlikely to promote patients' well being. Adequate health care can be provided if and when the medical staff, or those seeking to spread information on health care, are able to communicate or be used as a bilingual resource when dealing with patients from other cultural and/or linguistic backgrounds (Bischoff *et al.*, 2003: 504). The aim is quite simple: make valuable health information accessible to the majority of the people and help them understand essential health instructions and medical prescriptions.

When they are not able to communicate successfully with their patients, doctors may not always inform these patients adequately, not because they do not want to, but because they do not have the linguistic tools to do so. This means that patients are not given information in a form or manner they can understand and, in most cases, they do not understand the forms they sign (e.g. admission forms or consent forms for surgical procedures) or the implication of signing such forms. It also means that, because they lack the language skills to do so, patients do not ask for, and are often not adequately provided with, information about a prognosis, the effects of medication, and the outcome of tests. In other words, other than being aware that they are ill, patients undergo all sorts of treatments in and out of hospitals, without knowing specifically what is wrong with them, or how to ensure that the rest of their family (e.g. the spouse or the unborn child) is protected from contracting the same disease (also see Herselman, 1996: 165). Yet, no one in their right mind would dispute the right of patients, even poor patients from Africa, to understand their doctor's instructions, so that they can actively and efficiently deal with their conditions (Thompson & Pledger, 1993).

It is in this sense that language is put forward here as a key component in the delivery of health services: therapy, drug prescription, health information and education, etc. (see also Pugh, 1996; Drennan, 1998; Ainsworth-Vaughn, 2001; Fleischman, 2001; Youdelman & Perkins, 2002). In other words, routine procedures, let alone life-saving ones, can be severely compromised, if there is a breakdown in communication between the medical staff and the patient. Ong *et al.* (1995: 903) suggest that 'While sophisticated techniques may be used for medical diagnosis and treatment, inter-personal communication is the primary tool by which the physician and patient exchange information'. Simply put, the absence of a common language can lead to miscommunication, which can have dramatic effects. When doctors and patients speak different languages, the former often have difficulty providing a diagnosis or prognosis that the latter can understand. This inability of doctors to speak the language(s) of the patients or of patients to understand the language of doctors is problematic, because it means that patients cannot adequately explain their symptoms to the doctors, and the unfamiliar terminology coming from the doctor can confuse patients. Needless to say, the lack of effective communication between doctors and patients has negative implications for the diagnosis and treatment of patients. A wrong diagnosis or prognosis, caused by a language gap, can lead to a misunderstanding of symptoms and inappropriate prescription or surgery, all of which can have major negative outcomes. Unfortunately, major negative outcomes due to language gaps are rather the rule than the exception in the health care systems of Africa. And since most services in Africa are (officially) run in European languages, it is reasonable to assume that the majority of the African people have been denied access to essential and adequate health services for decades, on account of their not speaking a European language. It is fortunate, however, that doctor/patient interactions are managed by people, and that, essentially, local languages remain the principle media through which such interactions take place. Personal communications with a small sample of medical doctors (47) practising in six different African countries from March 2005 to June 2006 reveal that one of the first things the doctors try to establish after the usual exchange of greetings is whether both parties share a language (European or local) in which the diagnosis can effectively and successfully take place. Patients would rather have the diagnosis carried out in a language in which they are proficient (this may very well be a European language). Even then, doctors always try to use lay terms to explain symptoms, because they know that patients would ask them to do so if they were to use a medical term. The doctors underscored the need for a certain level of competence in a language, in order to be able to change registers and express the medical jargon in lay terms. Therefore, even when doctors share a common local language with their patients, they tend to refrain from using it, for fear of inaccuracies creeping into the diagnosis. Hence, in at least 7 of every 10 patients, doctors choose to look for an interpreter – mostly a relative or friend of the patient, or sometimes a nurse, with all the risks pertaining thereto. The work of these ad hoc interpreters, who are not professional interpreters and are not familiar with the medical jargon, has to be watched closely and corrected either by the doctor or the patient when the interpreters do not understand some terms or expressions in the doctor/patient exchange. In this regard, a number of doctors in this small sample (17 doctors, or 36.17%) complained about the lack of cooperation of some patients in terms of the language of communication. These doctors had gone to great lengths to find interpreters, only to discover that the patients knew the official language, at least well enough to correct the interpreter, but had chosen not to use it. A small section of the sample (5 doctors, 10.63%) raised the issue of the domain of the communication exchange (i.e. a hospital) and argued that, in their role as medical doctors, they are expected to speak the official language, which happens to be a European language, and not a variety of local languages. However, they realised that the language gap can make things worse for a patient, and were prepared to accommodate some patients, especially the elderly and the very young. All the medical doctors in this small sample agreed that they found out more about the patient's condition and were much more certain about their diagnosis and prognosis when they were able to communicate with the patient in a language they were both proficient in.

Saohatse (1997: 165; see also Saohatse 1998, 2000) suggests that 'showing willingness to speak the patient's language, however badly, gives the patient more confidence'. Indeed, when a doctor speaks no local language, patients do not feel that they can relate to them and are not particularly willing to explain their health problems fully, especially when severe pain gets in the way. Furthermore, knowledge of the patient's language not only saves time and money, it also enables the doctor to avoid the possible difficulties that may arise with interpreting. Grainger *et al.* (1990: 193), who have analysed the language used by nurses during routine activities in hospitals (doctor/patient communication) and nursing homes, make similar observations, and some studies report that doctors have developed a 'working vocabulary' or 'language of exchange', consisting of concepts that they use regularly.[102] Makoni (1998), looked at interactions between Xhosa-speaking black nurses and English-speaking white residents in a nursing home in Cape Town, and concluded that the nurses needed to enhance their capacity to communicate with the residents in the language that the latter understand best. Ferreira and Makoni (2002: 21–42) also found that most medical doctors (largely white) have problems in diagnosing dementia in black patients, because of a failure to take into account more nuanced analyses of the narratives and found that the labels used to describe the disease showed a considerable amount of variation, depending on the nature of the interpersonal relations between the descriptor and the person described. In another study of the language problems at Chris Hani Baragwanath Hospital in South Africa, Saohatse (1998) also found a huge communication problem within the hospital, and suggests that interpreters be hired to overcome this problem, or that nurses be paid more for their interpreting services. She notes that the voice of the non-European-speaking patient can get lost or distorted through the process of non-professional interpreting services because, although interpreting can be a bridge to communication, poor interpreting can increase the barrier to communication. What is more, the process of looking for *ad hoc* interpreters can at times be a source of delays in the treatment of patients, causing doctors to become agitated and patients distraught, especially when the situation requires urgent intervention.[103]

In Malawi, Kamwendo (2004) investigated language use and barriers to communication at the Mzuzu Central Hospital, in the multilingual Northern region of the country, where the majority of patients came from Mzimba, a predominantly Tumbuka-speaking district. Tumbuka is the second most widely used language in Malawi, after ciChewa/ciNyanja. English, the official language of the country, and the language required of the medical staff by the Medical Council of Malawi, is not a significant medium of doctor/patient interactions. Kamwendo writes that the language gap is most pronounced between the expatriate medical staff (non-Malawian medical and dental practitioners from as far afield as China) and the patients, and goes so far as to suggest that medicine cannot be effectively practised in Malawi through the medium of English. Most medical practitioners have to rely on the ad hoc services of interpreters; services often provided by nurses and other support staff, without appropriate training and who are not rewarded for such services[104] Whilst noting that local realities need to be considered in formulating solutions to a language problem, Kamwendo recommends that medical staff be offered language courses for medical purposes in the regional lingua franca, Tumbuka, and that the health literature and other written messages at the hospital be translated into Tumbuka and/or other local languages. Kamwendo also recommends that full time professional interpreters be recruited, and refresher courses taught on how to make appropriate use of interpreters. He also recommends an introduction to interpreting as a component of the professional training of the medical staff.

The provision of interpreting services in multilingual hospital contexts confirms the centrality of the language factor in health service delivery. The role of the interpreter is to provide a clear channel of communication between the medical staff and the patient population. Even in developed countries like the United States, Executive Order No. 13166 of August 2000[105] calls for the improvement of access to health services for people with limited proficiency in English (Youdelman & Perkins, 2002). Pugh and Jones (1999) and Lo Bianco (1987) document similar resolutions in the United Kingdom and in Australia. In all of these countries, professional interpreting services are available for any patient who may need them, because it is acknowledged that language competence in the official language may decrease or completely disappear in traumatic and emotionally-charged situations. There is anecdotal evidence of some elderly patients reverting to their mother tongue in times of crisis or due to the nature of their illness (e.g. aphasia, Alzheimer's disease). Although in the minority, such patients still deserve to be looked after. Surely, such care cannot be denied when the lives of the majority of the population are at stake, as is the case in sub-Saharan Africa.

The use of interpreters to facilitate doctor/patient interactions in societies where the immigrant population is a minority is indeed a very good way to plug the language gap. Beyond the medical context, interpreters are also used in the courts and for immigration matters. But medical doctors and nurses, as well as lawyers and civil servants in Africa, are mostly locally trained, admittedly in a European language. Most, if not all of them are proficient in a local language, if only their mother tongue, and/or the language of the mainstream (usually the regional lingua franca). Therefore, although interpreting will always be useful in some situations, it would be illogical to suggest interpreting as a global and lasting solution in this context. Interpreting is resorted to in developed countries, in order to accommodate a minority. But asking that the minority put measures in place to accommodate the majority in developing countries is not only impractical and uneconomical, it borders on the farcical, especially when mother-tongue education or at least education in the regional lingua franca could go a long way towards closing this sort of communication gap.

South-East Asian countries (except Singapore to a certain extent) have shown the way here. In Cambodia, Laos, Malaysia, Thailand and Vietnam, mother-tongue education is available right up to university level. Doctors and nurses, lawyers and civil servants are trained in the dominant local language[106] as a matter of course, and may learn a European language as part of further training or specialisation; but they are definitely not trained in languages that the patient or target population cannot understand in the first place. And yet, some of these countries (e.g. Lao PDR) have not even compiled a proper unilingual dictionary in their own national (and official) language for reference.[107] To be sure, these countries need not have the same level of concern as African countries about a brain drain of their medical staff, or any other (highly) educated individuals in society. This, in the final analysis, is the fundamental issue that needs to be resolved in the African context. Should development be based on the active participation of the end users? Is development what suits the elite or is it the implementation of solutions that put people first? What use is it to train doctors in languages the patient population do not understand, only to lose them to developed countries afterwards?

Conclusion

The Heads of State and Government of the African Union have adopted a raft of declarations and resolutions on the health sector, even if most of these are ignored by member countries. Some of the most recent resolutions pertaining to health are:

(1)   The Abuja Declaration of Roll Back Malaria in Africa, 2000;
(2)   The NEPAD document as presented in October 2001;
(3)   The Abuja Declaration on HIV/AIDS, TB and Other Infectious Diseases, 2001;
(4)   The Maputo Declaration on Malaria, HIV/AIDS, TB and Other Infectious Diseases, 2003.

None of these documents singles out language as a critical health-related issue and, as a result, all the commitments contained in the documents depend on European languages for their implementation. We can all hope and pray that this policy option works, but we all know in advance what the outcome is most likely to be in the next decade or two.

No country can guarantee its citizens good health, but most countries that want to grow and develop, create the conditions under which accessing efficient health services is possible for all, because the ability of the people to contribute to economic development depends in large part on their physical well-being. Furthermore, even in fairly homogeneous speech communities, it is not possible for doctors and patients, or any group of persons for that matter, to communicate with total accuracy. Hence, the delivery of efficient health care services in Africa constitutes a great challenge, not least of which is the re-building of health infrastructure. Health care services in Africa also need major re-investment in the training of health professionals.

But health care provision in this multilingual context is guaranteed to continue to struggle to achieve efficiency and contribute to growth and development, if it cannot be provided in a linguistically accessible manner to the client base that matters most: the majority of the people. Most studies in this area show that the use (generally) of a regional lingua franca is as an important communication bridge, even in the hospital context. Trying instead to do so exclusively in a European language can be not only fruitless, especially in the context of the current health crisis, but considering that the availability of health information material is severely limited, in most cases (economically) wasteful. There is no doubt that the health challenges Africa faces today will to some degree be alleviated if the majority of the patient population can be provided with information they understand, about how best to prevent the spread of diseases and treat them. The results of the research done thus far in this area suggest that language does have an impact on health care outcomes (Brach *et al.*, 2005; Cohen *et al.*, 2005; Ku & Flores, 2005) that, in the case of Africa, much remains to be done in terms of the management of health care in this multilingual setting, and that multilingualism itself can help narrow the language gap in the provision of health care services.

Chapter 4

Language, the Economy and Development

> *No society can surely be flourishing and happy, of which the*
> *far greater part of the members are poor and miserable.*
> Smith (1776: 79)

> *A democratic Africa where development is not construed in narrow*
> *economic goals but instead in terms of a culturally valued way of*
> *living together, and within a broader context of justice, fairness and*
> *equity for all; respect for linguistic rights and human rights,*
> *including those of minorities.*
> 'Vision for Africa' *–The Harare Declaration*
> (UNESCO, 2006)

Introduction

The lag in the productive capacity of Africa is clearly illustrated by the depth and extent of the economic condition of the continent. Fifty years after colonisation began to come to an end, it is apparent that the imposition of the languages of the former colonisers in the crucial area of the economy does not meet local needs. As most African countries are wallowing in ignorance and poverty, and the continent is virtually and literally at the epicentre of a human tragedy, Africa is still perceived as a 'basket case'. Whilst it can be argued that the expansion of European languages in Africa is due in part to economic opportunity for the locals, the economic consequences of this expansion are far from transparent. What is certain is that, 50 years on, there has not been any real Francisation, Anglicisation or Lusophonisation of the machinery of the economy for all, and the creation of a language deficit has deepened the exclusion of the majority of the people. And yet, most of the political leadership and the economists shun the debate about the relevance of language(s) to the economy, and almost all the economic studies and reports published by business and finance institutions at national and international levels make no mention of the place and role of language(s) in the process of development.[108] Economic rationalists, for whom developed countries have considerable language uniformity, ignore and/or dismiss the possibility of resorting to the local languages.

In the meantime, all the development indicators for Africa are in the red. Despite various rounds of debt reduction and forgiveness, Africa is the only region in the world that will not be able to achieve the goals set for the Millennium.[109] This state of affairs has come about, in part, because development is often viewed from the position of the 'donor countries' and the local elite. But as a number of international initiatives are again being launched to lift Africa from the doldrums of poverty, hunger and disease, the fundamental questions remain: how can the competitive capacity of African countries be increased, when there is no real investment in human capital? How can the productive engagement of the masses in the economy be objectively integrated in the development process? Can policies mobilising and revitalising multilingualism have positive implications for the economy? Can development policies succeed in a linguistic vacuum?

The aim of this chapter is to outline the case for multilingualism as an underpinning, functional and communicative tool, fundamental to sustainable and long-term endogenous development. It looks at how speech communities exercise control over their language(s), deciding which language(s) will be the media of economic activity, and how they empower themselves in gaining access to a significant share of the symbolic and capital resources of their countries through language. It examines whether there are lessons for the formal economy to be learnt from language use in the informal economy.[110] It argues that socio-political rights and obligations should follow from, and be defined by, practices of language(s) that characterise speech communities in their everyday language interactions. The chapter opens with a description of the unfavourable macro-economic environment, especially in the face of increasing global competition, with a view to showing that there needs to be a trade-off between economic policies and social policies (one aspect of which is language policy) in order to reduce poverty and inequality.

Facts and Figures: The Paradox of Poverty in the Midst of Plenty

The economic situation of Africa in the 21st century is a contrasted picture of gloom and quiet optimism. The facts speak for themselves: with the majority of the world's poorest states, the highest illiteracy rate and the highest foreign debt burden, Africa suffers from persistently low rates of growth and a vicious circle in which low growth contributes to poverty, whilst poverty and inequality contribute to low growth. With a population anticipated to reach 1 billion by 2007,[111] Africa has the greatest number of people (an estimated 46.3% of the total population) living in absolute misery or on less than US$1 a day, with no education, no regular employment, no fixed income, no adequate accommodation, no health care, no access to drinking water, no education and not enough food. If current trends continue, this figure will increase to 431 million in 2015 (UNDP, 2005). From 1981 to 2001, the number of Africans living in poverty doubled from 164 million to 314 million. From 1980 to 2000, the African continent managed a compound growth in per capita GDP of only 0.02% and contributed only 1% of the world's gross national product and 2% of world trade, as it has 35 of the 50 least developed countries in the world, and 24 of the 32 countries with the lowest levels of human development. In 2000, some 186 million people (34% of the total population), suffered from extreme famine in at least 18 countries – see the United Nations Food and Agriculture Organisation's *World Food Report 2000* (FAO, 2001). Although a net exporter of food in the 1960s, Africa now imports one-third of its grain, whilst the African farmer must pay two to six times more than the world market price for the cost of conventional fertilisers. Africa's public debt is estimated at US$2200 billion and, according to the United Nations Conference on Trade and Development (UNCTAD), had to pay US$550 billion in debt reimbursement between 1970 and 2002, when it received a total of only $US540 billion in loans during the same period. In 2002, the Heavily Indebted Poor Countries (HIPC) paid out $US30 billion to service their debts to the international financial institutions, or about $US100 million a day, whilst they received only $US17 billion in public aid to development.

All of this has been exacerbated by the economic downturns of the 1980s and 1990s when, under pressure from the World Bank and the IMF, many countries gave up on investing in and reforming social policies (such as educational and health), thereby undermining their own future income-earning ability. According to the World Bank (1980: 67–68) the aims of structural adjustment loans were:

- to ensure that current account deficits of many developing countries do not become so large as to jeopardise seriously the implementation of current investment programs;
- to maintain growth and facilitate balance of payments adjustment, and ultimately strengthen these balance of payments;
- to help countries reduce their current account deficit to more manageable proportions.

The main features of adjustment lending by the IMF and the World Bank over this period were in the direction of macro adjustment, namely fiscal adjustment, getting the prices right, trade liberalisation and movement towards free markets and away from state intervention. Hence, development aid came with strings attached, such as the need to model one's development on that of the donor country and the obligation to pay back the loans, come what may, to the detriment of health and education budgets and for other essential social services. As a result, spending in the areas of education and health declined, since overall government spending also declined. The damaging impact of the structural adjustment years has denied the majority of the people access to basic services (Stiglitz, 2002; Ziegler, 2002, 2005). In March 2007, an internal report of the IMF's Independent Evaluation Office again stated that the policies and actions of the IMF in sub-Saharan Africa are ambiguous and confused.

Although they have dramatically altered the structure of the economies of many African countries for decades, IMF and World Bank economic reforms have failed to reduce poverty and inequality in a perceptible way. Poverty and inequality remain deeply entrenched on the continent, and the proportion of poor has actually increased. Even in the one or two countries said to have performed well under structural adjustment programs (e.g. Ghana, Uganda and Zimbabwe), growth alone, modest as it was (5.66% in the best case), made little difference to the poor and failed to translate into a reduction of poverty. Market reforms did not help those who had no assets to start with, and were therefore not in a position to take advantage of the potential benefits of less distorted markets. Needless to say, as these reforms failed to address the underlying structural problems of the economy, growth in productivity and income were inhibited, and the needs of a large proportion of the population were not addressed.

Structural adjustment lending also sought to privatise state enterprises, to reform inefficient financial systems, improve the efficiency of tax collection and public spending, reform and downsize the civil service and control corruption. The World Bank itself acknowledges that little progress was made on any of these fronts. Using structural adjustment loans as a tool to put external pressure on African governments in the running of their economy has not proven to be effective, and a combination of a number of these measures has not raised the growth potential of any of the recipient countries. In 2005, for instance, the list of the top 16 Most Corrupt Countries in the world, compiled by Transparency International, included 9 African countries, namely: Angola, Chad, Côte d'Ivoire, the Democratic Republic of the Congo, Equatorial Guinea, Kenya, Nigeria, Sudan and Somalia. One of these countries – Côte d'Ivoire – has been a repeat recipient of adjustment loans. Significantly, some of the intensive adjustment loan recipients, including Ghana and Uganda, also became recipients of debt relief under the Heavily Indebted Poor Countries (HIPC) initiative, an admission perhaps that adjustment loans did not achieve the aims of bringing growth to these countries. Hence, in March 2006, in response to a request by the G8, the World Bank, following in the steps of the International Monetary Fund (IMF), approved the cancellation of US$37 billion dollars of debt belonging to the poorest 17 countries in the world, 13 of which are African countries, namely Benin, Burkina Faso, Ethiopia, Ghana, Madagascar, Mali, Mozambique, Niger, Uganda, Rwanda, Senegal, Tanzania and Zambia (the other four were: Bolivia, Guyana, Honduras and Nicaragua).[112] Mauritania was added to this group in July 2006. Another group of 20 countries, mainly from Africa, will also benefit from a similar measure once they have met all the criteria of the HIPC initiative. The African Development Bank followed suit in April 2006, cancelling US$8.54 billion dollars of debt for 13 African countries, namely Benin, Burkina Faso, Ethiopia, Ghana, Madagascar, Mali, Mozambique, Niger, Rwanda, Senegal, Tanzania, Uganda and Zambia.[113] By May 2006, the Independent Evaluation Group of the World Bank was reporting that in half of the countries benefiting from a World Bank/IMF plan for debt alleviation in the poorest countries of world, the amount of debt had not only increased, but had risen back to its original level. Eight of these countries were in Africa: Burkina Faso, Ethiopia, Ghana, Mali, Mauritania, Rwanda, Tanzania and Uganda.

Easterly (2002), among others, suggests that the strategic interests of some powerful rich nations probably affect the number of loans a country receives (the famous 'friends of the donor' hypothesis). For instance, American and French influences are said to be particularly salient in the World Bank and the IMF, especially when Michel Camdessus was Managing Director of the latter (Kapur et al., 1997). Voting patterns of poor African countries on issues of strategic significance for powerful rich nations in large international organisations, such as the United Nations, are also suspected to play a significant role in the attribution of loans (Barro & Lee, 2002). When the results of the structural adjustment measures are compared to their objectives, in order to determine their success against the ex-ante benchmarks imposed by the IMF and the World Bank and against the expectations they created, the conclusions are mixed at best, and in most cases, are not particularly favourable (Killick et al., 1998; Przeworski & Vreeland, 2000; Barro & Lee, 2002). Easterly (2002) suggests that structural adjustment lending does not necessary translate into structural adjustment policies. Indeed, none of the top 20 recipients of adjustment lending from 1980 to 1999 was able to achieve reasonable growth, and about half the adjustment loan recipients showed severe distortions, regardless of the number of cumulative adjustment loans (Easterly, 2002). Côte d'Ivoire and Ghana, for example, received 26 adjustment loans between 1980 and 1999, which suggests that new loans had to be given because earlier loans were not effective at generating the growth necessary to service debt. Nevertheless, these intensive recipients of adjustment loans had the same near-zero per capita growth rate, the same current account deficit, the same inflation rate and real interest rate as other developing countries that received fewer or no adjustment loans. This finding is confirmed by a World Bank study of African cases, which concludes 'that the 10 countries in our sample all received large amounts of aid, including conditional loans, yet ended up with vastly different policies suggests that aid is not a primary determinant of policy' (Devarajan *et al.*, 2001: 2). In the best cases, there was no respectable growth. Uganda for instance, with 20 adjustment loans, had erratic growth, high inflation and black market premiums. Ghana, with 26 adjustment loans, had recurrent problems with inflation, and Côte d'Ivoire, also with 26 adjustment loans, had negative growth, high current accounts deficits, and an overvalued real exchange rate until the 1994 devaluation of its currency (the Franc CFA). Zambia, which received 18 adjustment loans, had sharply negative growth, large current account and budget deficits, high inflation, massive real overvaluation, a negative real interest rate and a high black market premium. Even when there was limited improvement in some policy indicators, the degree of improvement was modest at best, and often offset by other policy indicators that made the overall situation worse. Although it can be argued that these results do not prove that adjustment lending was ineffective in promoting good macro-economic policies and good growth outcomes, the opposite is much harder to argue for, and it is highly questionable why the IMF and the World Bank continued to make new loans to poor performers that clearly failed to deliver. A recent World Bank statement about structural adjustment admits that 'the performance of adjustment operations has been mixed, especially during the 1980s' (World Bank, 2002: 101–111). Easterly (2002) argues, that whilst structural adjustment was understandably a multi-stage process that required multiple loans to be disbursed, one would have expected at the same time to see some improvement after a certain threshold in adjustment lending was passed. The failure of governments to follow through with the conditions of the loans cannot be raised here, since the IMF and the World Bank were under no obligation to keep giving new resources, 26 times over, to those who were in clear breach of the conditions required to achieve the outcome sought in providing the adjustment lending. Indeed, even if more than one loan was needed to achieve specific structural adjustment goals, it is hard to see why 20 to 26 loans would have been necessary in the cases of Uganda (20), Senegal (21), Ghana (26) and Côte d'Ivoire (26).

As a result, the continent is now worse off, in absolute terms, than it was four and a half decades ago, when many countries were granted independence. It is also beset by social exclusion and by wars. Poverty here goes well beyond income poverty; for many, it means having to walk more than one mile everyday simply to collect water and firewood, and suffering from preventable diseases. Economies of scale have prospered and grown exponentially, but their prosperity has not trickled down. It looks as though all that the 'free market' and 'international trade' aim to do for the impoverished world is to raise them up from nothing to a state of abject poverty. But there is no fatalism to the poverty trap. On the bright side, the enormous African energy potential remains virtually untapped. Currently only 7% of the energy potential is being used, and 21 of the continent's 54 countries could profitably produce hydropower. And although Africa accounts for only 1.3% of the world's installed solar facilities (only 4 countries have begun to exploit geothermal sources), it also has a large geothermal and solar energy potential (OECD Development Centre and African Development Bank, 2004). According to the 2005 Report of the African Development Bank on development in Africa (ADB, 2005), the continent achieved an average of 4.4% of real GDP growth in 2003 and 5.1% on 2004. This equates to 2.8% of GDP growth per capita, the best increase in GDP growth for Africa since 1996, whilst inflation reached historical lows of 7.9%. Even though growth slowed in West Africa because of political turmoil in Côte d'Ivoire and a weak performance in Nigeria (down to 3.7% in 2004), Central Africa had a real GDP increase of 14.4%, East Africa recorded the second highest real GDP growth in 2004, and North Africa was expected to continue to have a strong economic performance through to 2005–2006. Overall, growth prospects in Africa were looking up (OECD & ADB, 2005). These encouraging results can be explained by a number of internal and external factors: the improvement of the terms of trade, the increase in the volume of exports due in part to demand from the Asian markets, debt relief, as well as better macro-economic policies and reform programs, and the promotion of small and medium-sized enterprises. In 2006, economic performance in sub-Saharan Africa was in the order of 5.8%, better than the 5.5% of 2005, and even the least developed countries achieved a growth rate of 5.9% in 2004, their strongest growth rate in the last two decades.[114] The UNCTAD points out that this growth, export-oriented as it is, has yet to translate into real improvement in the day-to-day living conditions of the majority of the people, most of whom still live on less than US$1 a day. This is in part because it fails to create jobs and improve the productive capacities of poor countries, and is therefore insufficient to meet the objectives of reducing poverty on the African continent by half by 2015. African economies generally show a tendency to stagnation of productivity, and a serious inability to compete effectively in the global economy. Only Algeria, Egypt, Libya, Morocco, Tunisia and Mauritius are on track for achieving the goal of halving the proportion of people living below $US 1 per day by 2015. Half a century after they were granted independence, African countries are still far too dependent on raw materials, and yet their exports are too limited to have a real impact on the wellbeing of their people.[115] They cannot take advantage of trade and investment opportunities without first bringing into the economic and political mainstream the actors of change: women and the working masses. In other words, reliable and effective aid remains essential for most African countries, to help them meet their basic and long-term development needs.

It is also worth noting that, in addition to some of the richest mineral and energetic reserves in the world (e.g. gold, diamond, uranium and titanium), raw materials, large empty spaces and its peoples, Africa is now a major player on the crude oil market. The UNCTAD estimates the continent's total oil reserves to 80 billion barrels, or 8% of the world's crude reserves (UNCTAD, 2001), which is set to reach 13% by 2020, with Nigeria, Libya, Angola and Equatorial Guinea as the region's leading oil producers. Although 70% of Africa's oil reserves and production is currently concentrated in the Gulf of Guinea (stretching from Côte d'Ivoire to Angola), a region likely to become the world's leading deep-water offshore production centre, with estimated reserves of 24 billion barrels, all regions of Africa are net crude oil exporters, with the exception of East Africa.[116] New oilfields are being discovered every year, as the traditional producers, Algeria, Libya, Nigeria, Gabon, Egypt, Tunisia and Angola have been joined by Equatorial Guinea, Sudan, Chad, São Tomé e Príncipe, Mauritania and Côte d'Ivoire, increasing Africa's production by 40 % between 1990 and 2004, and by 36% in 10 years, compared with 16% for the rest of the world. A return to democracy in the DRC, whose reserves were estimated to be some 1.5 billion barrels in 2002, could also see that country become a major player in the near future. The reserves estimated at 53.3 billion barrels in 1980 have increased to a stock of 135.1 billion barrels in 2005, lifting Africa's share in world production from 8% to 11.1% within that period. Considering its current output of 10 million barrels a day, these reserves can last for 38 years. This production is forecast to increase by 50 % in 2010; by which time one out of every three barrels of oil produced in the world will originate from Africa, and by 2015, 25% of all American oil imports will come from Africa. With a total output of more than 4 million barrels a day, sub-Saharan Africa already produces as much as Iran, Venezuela and Mexico combined. Sudan, which started exporting oil three years ago, now outputs 186,000 barrels a day, 60% of which is exported to China, whilst Nigeria, the continent's leading exporter of crude oil, is set to increase daily output from 2.2 to 3 million barrels, rising to 4.42 million by

2020. Angola, which emerged from 15 years of civil war in 2002, is now at the centre of the oil boom and has become the second producer of crude oil in Africa. Its output has increased from 722,000 barrels a day in 2001 to 930,000 in 2005. In 2006, Angola was China's most important supplier of oil, ahead of Saudi Arabia; it received US$30 billion from oil exports in that year and achieved a growth of 17.6% in its GDP. Angola's oil output is expected to reach 3.28 million barrels a day by 2020. Mauritania, a country where oil was not discovered until 2001, exported 950,000 barrels of oil to China in March 2006 from the Chinguetti Field, 80 kilometres outside of the capital Nouakchott. This was followed by a further 1.9 million barrels in April 2006. In 2006 alone, the production of crude oil from the Chinguetti Field reached 18.4 million barrels. The production of the Chinguetti Field will soon reach 75,000 per day and, together with the three other oil fields discovered thus far, the most important of which is the Tiof oil field, the production of crude oil from Mauritania should reach 200,000 barrels per day in a few years' time.[117] The output of other minor oil producers such as Equatorial Guinea, Chad and Côte d'Ivoire could more than treble. With 740,000 barrels a day, Equatorial Guinea currently holds the record (alongside Angola) for oil-prospecting permits and is on course to becoming Africa's third largest producer of crude oil, ahead of Congo and Gabon, over the next 20 years. Better known for its exports of cocoa (it is the world's top producer) and coffee (it is third in the world), Côte d'Ivoire, with its production of 100,000 barrels a day (expected to reach 135,000 barrels a day by the end of 2007), has joined this group of countries whose economy is becoming more and more dependent on oil exports. Crude oil and oil by-products represented 28% of Côte d'Ivoire's total exports in 2005 (compared to 18.5% in 2004), whilst, the share of cocoa and coffee dropped to 21.3% (against 26% in 2004) (*Jeune Afrique*, 2007).

The economic powerhouses of the world, not least the United States and China acknowledge the importance of the vast African reserves. The United States currently derives 15% of its oil supplies from Africa, as against 22% from the Persian Gulf, and, according to the United States National Intelligence Council, could be importing as much as 25% of its oil from Africa by 2015 (*People's Daily Online*, 2005). Nigeria alone is the fifth-biggest source of American oil imports, with the United States accounting for half of Nigeria's oil exports. In his *State of the Union* speech (CBS, 2006), the US President pledged that America's dependence on oil from the Middle East will be cut by 75% by 2025 through alternative sources of energy (e.g. batteries for hybrid and electric cars, hydrogen and ethanol technologies). This, for many, clearly meant that the United States will progressively source more oil from Africa.

China,[118] on the other hand, currently derives a quarter of its oil imports from Africa, with oil interests in Algeria, Angola, Sudan and even Chad, given that that country still maintains diplomatic relations with Taiwan. At the same time, China is increasing its stakes in Equatorial Guinea, Gabon, and Nigeria, whilst it receives more than half of Sudan's oil exports, accounting for 5% of its total oil imports. The China National Petroleum Corporation (CNPC) owns a 40% stake in the Greater Nile Petroleum Operating Company and pumps more than 300,000 barrels per day in Sudan, which now earns some US$2 billion in oil exports each year, half of which goes to China. China National Offshore Oil Corp (CNOOC) also announced (January 2006) a US$2.268 billion purchase of a 45% share in an oilfield offshore of Nigeria. This oilfield, called OML 130, covers an area of 1300 square km and includes the Akpo field, around 200 km offshore of Port Harcourt, discovered in the year 2000.[119] Another Chinese firm, Sinopec, is constructing a 1500 km (932 miles) pipeline to Port Sudan on the Red Sea, where China's Petroleum Engineering Construction Group is building a tanker terminal. Links between China and African countries are growing fast and making an impact on global equilibrium. In 2003, trade between Beijing and the continent amounted to US$18.5 billion – an increase of more than 50% over 2002. Between 2002 and 2003, Sino-Africa trade increased by 50% to US$18.5 billion; this is expected to grow to US$30 billion by 2006. According to the IMF, the total value of imports and exports between China and Africa was well over US$50 billion, and could reach US$100 billion by 2010. It comes as no surprise therefore that China declared 2006 the 'African year'. Some 40 African heads of states or governments, from 48 countries invited, attended the third Sino-African Forum held in Beijing from 3 to 5 November 2006, where 2500 partnership agreements in commerce, investment, training and aid were negotiated, and a new plan of action was agreed to for 2007–2009. China promises to double its financial aid to Africa within three years in addition to cancelling some of the debt already outstanding.[120]

Whilst the African Development Bank is encouraging China to continue its massive investments in Africa, and to begin looking at non-extractive industries, the G8 is expressing concerns about China's presence on the continent. It warning against a remake of the strategic and economic errors they made and calling for an International Charter for Responsible Lending (see *AFP* of 19May 2007, *Le Monde* of 19 May 2007 and *Reuters* 19 May 2007). China is criticised for its focused interest in raw materials (especially oil), for its unconditional support for undemocratic regimes, for turning a blind eye to ever-increasing corruption and for encouraging re-indebtedness. From 2005 to January 2007, the American Congress adopted no less than 27 bills against China.

History tells us that the same sort of criticism was levelled at Malaysia, when it too started investing in Africa. Although widespread diplomatic ties were not established until 1989, history also tells us that China's presence in Africa goes back to the great trade expeditions of the Ming Dynasty in the 14th century, and that Mao's China was back on the old continent during the era of decolonisation. For its part, China claims to have fulfilled its obligations through debt relief in a number of African countries.

Such criticism no doubt expresses the frustration on the part of the G8, as they see the centre of gravity of world trade and economic influence shifting, and other major players, like China and India, making it difficult for them to continue to set the rules of the game. Liberalism or the free market, when successfully practised by others, is suddenly perceived as a form of aggression and the goal posts have to be moved; but the G8 have to face up to the reality of their diminishing influence and accept that things may never be the same again. Peyrefitte (1973) sounded a warning with *When China awakes the World will Tremble.*[121] Peyrefitte (1996) also announced 20 years later that China had indeed awoken (1996). Hegemony is not eternal, and it is not certain that some of the critics always took the high moral ground when dealing with the Sudan of Omar El Bachir, the Congo of Sassou Nguesso, the former Zaïre of Mobutu Sesse Séko, the Gabon of Omar Bongo, the Cameroon of Paul Biya, the Togo of Gnassingbé Eyadema or his son successor Faure Gnassingbé or the Equatorial Guinea of General Teodoro Obiang Nguema Mbasogo. G8 countries have been known to lend money to corrupt or repressive regimes, in order to buy political allegiance. Verschave (1994, 1999, 2000, 2001a, 2001b, 2002, 2004a, 2004b; Verschave & Coret, 2005; Verschave *et al.*, 2005) and Harel (2006) have chronicled a number of such actions by successive French governments in Africa, denouncing armed intervention and political interference, election frauds, civil wars and complicity of genocide, the plundering of forests, the embezzlement of public funds, tax havens, illicit arms trafficking on the conti-nent.[122] Verschave (1999) constantly accused France of systematically pillaging French-speaking Africa and manipulating political regimes for commercial advantage since the sixties through 'linguistic influence' (*Survie*, 31 March 2005; http://www.survie-france.org/; accessed 28.6.06).

No one would want to be seen as welcoming a new form of neo-colonialism in Africa. However, it has to be said that China at least has not gone to Africa under false pretences, something that cannot be said of members of the G8, who bear the brunt of criticism for failing to keep their promises in terms of Official Development Aid. They are, for instance, reminded of their commitment to cancel the multilateral public debt of 35 of the poorest countries and to double the annual aid to Heavily Indebted Poor Countries up to US$50 billion by 2010 (2005 Summit at Gleneagles). This is because it is becoming increasingly clear that, even though charitable donations to Africa in sectors such as health, agriculture or the environment are steadily rising, and private investment in developing countries increased by 17% or US$481 billion (World Bank, 2007), the level of aid is dropping. Figures published by the OECD in April 2007 show that aid to Africa dropped by US$8 billion, (€5.9 billion) in 2006 and total Official Development Assistance (ODA) from members of the Development Assistance Committee (DAC) fell by 5.1% to US$ 103.9 billion or 0.3% of members' combined Gross National Income in 2006.[123] This figure includes US$19.2 billion of debt relief, notably exceptional relief to Iraq and Nigeria (OECD, 2007). Notable among the countries lagging behind their own target were: Italy (behind by US$8.1 billion), France (by US$7.6 billion), and Germany (by US$7 billion). In an article published in, Jeffrey Sachs (2007) notes that American aid to Africa represents less than three days of expenses of the Pentagon, or US$13 per capita per year in the United States (*Jeune Afrique*, 25 January 2007). Oxfam International (May, 2007) warns that the G8 is running the risk of not reaching its goal of debt reduction, and that this could cost 5 million lives. Indeed, Oxfam International is of the view that many of the existing trade and economic partnership agreements, bilateral and regional, between developed and African countries (covering about 30% of international trade) are inequitable and place more stringent requirements on the latter to open up their markets to exports that are heavily subsidised.

The United States and China are not the only states vying for energy resources in Africa. Recently, Korea National Oil Corporation obtained 65% oil and gas production rights in two Nigerian offshore blocks, while India's Oil and Natural Gas Corporation Videsh obtained a 25% stake. India and China both hold stakes in the Greater Nile Oil Project in Sudan and India has invested US$700 million in Sudan's oil sector. They have also been engaged in direct competition for African energy resources, as seen in October 2004 when China outbid India to buy an interest in an offshore block in Angola. It is therefore justified to speak of a paradox of poverty in the midst of plenty, because Africa is not poor. Indeed, Africa possesses adequate energy, mineral, food and human capital resources, but it has been impoverished, constantly, from the dawn of the slave trade and Europe's empire building enterprise, to the puppet governments in the twentieth and twenty first centuries. But although it is rich in minerals and oil, the distribution of these resources across the continent and across society is highly uneven, and the majority of Africans lack basic health and educational facilities. Industrialisation is in its infancy; for instance, Africa consumes only 26% of its oil; the rest is exported, whilst 77.5% of its own population has no access to electricity. Furthermore, the debt burden and the constraints placed on many countries to service this debt are such that most of the continent is still unable to invest in the crucial areas of education, health and job creation that affect the well-being of the majority of the people.

The wealth of nations in the 21st century no longer lies in the production of raw materials, but in the nations' know-how and their capacity to innovate. The Asian Tigers (and Tiger Cubs) – and especially China, India, South Korea, Singapore and Taiwan – have clearly understood this. They are currently challenging the supremacy of the United States in the area of new technologies. The number of patents taken out and articles published by the researchers in these countries has markedly increased. India for instance is now the world's second-largest producer of computer applications. The city of Bangalore, in the south of India is being referred to as the new Silicon Valley. South Korea is beginning to overtake the United States in the production of computer chips and the design of communications software. The Republic of South Korea, like Japan, is investing 3% of its GDP in research and development (2.7% for the United States). China is specialising in biotechnologies, aerospace equipment and semi conductors and poured 1.5% of its GDP into research and development in 2005 (against only 0.6% eight years ago). The countries of South East Asia are also beginning to make their mark in this area.

One is also justified in being concerned about, and warning against, the 'resource curse', that is to say, when commodity windfalls create bad political economy, corruption and mal-administration, as Africa's riches make its economy even more export-oriented and heavily dependent on, and vulnerable to, terms of trade over which it has no control. Economic historians suggest that factor endowments predict inequality, and inequality predicts bad institutions, low human capital investment, and underdevelopment (Sokoloff & Engerman, 2000; Easterly, 2005; Birdsall & Hamoudi, 2002), as there is a strong negative association between inequality and per capita income, and as inequality also affects other development outcomes, such as institutions and schooling. It is indeed suggested that institutions are worse in resource-rich economies, and that such economies tend to be much more associated with worse institutions than those that are not (Isham *et al.*, 2005; La Porta *et al.*, 1998, 1999; Woolcock *et al.*, 2001). In this context, knowledge of European languages serves to further facilitate the entrenchment of the kind of extractive economic structures in which the majority of the African people come second best.

New Initiatives to Combat Poverty

New initiatives, led by the UN, the G8 and the UK's Commission for Africa, were launched in 2005 to mobilise international support for the fight against poverty and disease in Africa. The Report on the Millennium Development Goals (UNDP, 2006), lauded as the most comprehensive and cost-effective strategy ever for combating global poverty, hunger and disease, called for 'a decade of bold actions' and 'ambitious national development strategies'. The aim is to cut extreme poverty in half, reduce child mortality by two-thirds, and radically improve the lives of at least one billion people in Africa by 2015. The Report proposes targeted actions and investments in essential public services such as health, education and infrastructure to make poor communities less vulnerable to the hardships of disease, hunger and environmental degradation. It calls for a major overhaul of the international development system, which is found to be inefficient, as only about 30% of international aid actually reaches those in need. It is believed that the Millennium Development Goals can be achieved with an investment of just 0.5% of the incomes of industrialised nations, well within the international aid targets that have already been set; in other words, an investment figure of US$135 billion in 2006, rising to US$195 billion in 2015 – only 0.44% and 0.54% of the GDP of industrialised nations, and less than the target of 0.7% these countries had already committed themselves to at the United Nations Financing for Development Conference in Monterrey in 2002.[124] The report makes 10 core recommendations, including some macroeconomic remedies, such as the cancellation of the debt of African nations and the re-examination of and improvements to the terms of international trade, without which African countries have no chance of competing on the global market.

Everyone is agreed that, without urgent action, the goals of the United Nations' 2000 Millennium Summit will not be met by 2015. Hence, on 12 January 2005, the then Chancellor of the Exchequer, Mr Gordon Brown, was proposing a 'New Marshall Plan' for Africa and a public aid envelope of $US 100 billion'.[125] Gordon Brown was also advocating the cancellation of the $US 80 billion owed by the heavily indebted poor countries to the international financial institutions.[126] Professor Jeffrey Sachs, who led the team that drafted the Report on the Millennium Development Goals, openly criticised the Bush administration's preferred option 'Trade, not aid'[127] and point out that (1) international trade is not the miracle solution for development, and (2) trade liberalisation is not the only option. At the start of the 2005 G8 Summit in Davos, Tony Blair, the British Prime Minister, invited the United States to 'join the agenda of the rest of the world' on this and other pressing issues, such as greenhouse gas emissions(Friends of the Earth, 2004). And, on 6 February, 2005, at the close of the G7 summit in London, Gordon Brown was able to announce that Finance Ministers from this group of industrialised nations were willing to provide 100% debt relief to the HIPCs[128] and that the IMF would examine a proposal to re-evaluate its gold supplies to finance debt relief when it met in April 2005.

It is in the context of these new initiatives to lift Africa out of the poverty that Thabo Mbeki of South Africa, Abdelaziz Bouteflika of Algeria and Olusegun Obasanjo of Nigeria, Hosni Moubarak of Egypt and Abdoulaye Wade of Senegal set up the New Partnership for African Development (NEPAD), a regional organisation to intercede between the affluent West and Africa. Launched in July 2001, NEPAD received the blessings of the G8 at the Kananaskis (Canada) and Evian (France) Summits in 2002 and 2003. NEPAD is defined as 'a vision and a strategic framework for Africa's renewal' and aims to raise the annual growth rates of African countries to 7% across the board during the first 15 years, and to halve poverty in Africa by 2015, in 'partnership' with international financial and economic institutions such as the IMF, the World Bank and the World Trade Organisation (WTO). NEPAD has ten priorities: (1) good public governance, (2) good governance of the private economy, (3) infrastructure, (4) education, (5) health, (6) new information and communication technologies (NICT), (7) agriculture, (8) environment, (9) energy and (10) access to the markets of the developed countries. It is expected that these priorities will help shape a series of key projects aimed at stimulating regional and integrated development, building economies of scale and harmonising industries at a continental level. NEPAD believes that poverty in Africa is a result of 'exclusion' and 'marginalisation' from globalisation, but still aims to help along the policies of globalisation in Africa by offering African countries incentives to comply with democratic governance, peace building, respect for human rights and sound economic policies that will give confidence to investors (OAU, 2002b).

Critics of NEPAD believe that this new partnership is nothing but globalisation by stealth, because it fails the test of a genuine social project (Pretoria & Patel, 2004; IAI, 2003) and does not offer a critical analysis of the structural adjustment policies implemented by the IMF from the 1980s. These critics are of the view that NEPAD seeks to carry on the same policies of globalisation, based on the same failed economic principles of the past 30 years, namely privatisation, integration into the global market, elimination of trade barriers, liberalisation of all sectors of the economy. These are the neo-liberal prescriptions of the institutions of Bretton Woods, the WTO and European Union that have proven a dismal failure and destroyed the socio-economic fabric of African countries, while reinforcing their technological and financial dependency vis-à-vis multinational enterprises from the developed nations. It is also argued that NEPAD remains focused on 1970-style projects of prestige and wants to continue, for instance, to promote intensive and entrepreneurial agriculture with irrigation, when food security is of most concern in the Sahel. Six years after its creation, NEPAD has failed to attract foreign investments in Africa. In July 2005, one of its founding members, President Abdoulaye Wade of Senegal, declared that the organisation was full of the 'bureaucrats' who waste scarce resources (Spilpunt, 2007).[129]

Of most serious concern is the fact that mass poverty in Africa is not coincidental to globalisation, but an intrinsic feature of it, a direct consequence of African political leaders choosing to pursue the goals of globalisation, even though they know very little about the workings of the international economic system. It is widely acknowledged that poverty in Africa and other parts of the world is due to vulnerability and dependency upon global financial markets, where the rules are set by and for those who do not intend to adhere to them. So the question is: why would African countries want to persist in going down the same path as the developed world, when economists in these countries are now saying that the growth of the developed world over the last few decades is neither sustainable nor desirable, socially or ecologically? Why choose to promote the policies of globalisation when the developed countries are looking for ways to put the brakes on their growth rate? Is it not possible to build an efficient society that does not produce millions of tons of grain just to burn them or dump them on other less fortunate economies? Considering that Africa is the only region that will not be able to achieve the goals set out for the Millennium, is it not time to start looking for solutions from within?[130] But what is globalisation, and what does it mean for Africa?

Globalisation in Africa: Can the Majority be Globalised?

David Ricardo expounded the Principle of Comparative Advantage more than 200 years ago, explaining why no country can ever be so disadvantaged that it cannot benefit from international trade (Ricardo, 1817). In other words, no matter how poor, countries around the world would be even worse off if they did not partake in international trade. Africa has been integrated into the global economy for centuries, mainly as a supplier of cheap labour and raw materials for the economically powerful. According to Obstfeld and Taylor (cited in Bruthiaux, 2003: 85), the global integration of capital markets dates back to the late 19th century when, aided by technological advances such as the steam engine, international trade in goods and human beings (slavery) led to the growth of financial networks across the industrialising world, from 7% in 1870 to just under 20% in 1914. This phase of globalisation came to an end with World War 1, and the pound sterling floundered in 1925. The demise of the Bretton Woods monetary arrangements followed in the early 1970s, when the American dollar went into receivership in 1971. This period was dominated by the British, who were in control of almost 80% of the total foreign investment, far in excess of the share of the United States in 1995 (a mere 22%). Following more than 15 years of worldwide depression and war, the free trade principle was pursued again from 1947 with the creation of the General Agreement on Tariffs and Trade (GATT). Progress accelerated sharply in the late 1950s, with the creation of the European Free Trade Association (EFTA),[131] the European Economic Community (EEC)[132] and a succession of other free trade areas.

Globalisation is an economic process centred upon increasing integration of economies and societies, through the flow of goods, services, capital and people. In other words, the aim of globalisation is to free the market from state controls. Today globalisation, at its simplest, means the cross-border movement of people, capital, companies and ideas. Economists characterise it as the gradual integration of the world economy, in particular in the free flow of goods and services and especially capital. It is their firm belief that globalisation leads to faster growth and the reduction of poverty in Africa. The protagonists of globalisation argue that although the current picture is rather bleak, we fail to note that the absolute number of people living on less than $US1 a day has in fact declined by some 200 million individuals since 1980 (Schaefer, 2003). Although David Ricardo did not believe that this would lead to super profits for multinationals, the principle he put forward has proven to be very robust over time and is today the foundation for the view that free trade is beneficial. But is it really?

Current patterns of globalisation differ from earlier ones; and all the evidence points to the fact that Africa remains a marginal player in the globalisation of capital. Today's capital flows to Africa are well below the levels reached at the beginning of the 20th century. In 2000, for instance, only 1% out of a total 81% of US direct investments flowed to Africa (Graham, 2000; cited in Bruthiaux, 2003: 86). Foreign direct investment for 2001 declined to less than its 2000 levels, and the magnitude of this decline ranges from 59% in high-income countries to only 14% in Africa (Bruthiaux, 2003: 86).

The World Bank, the International Monetary Fund and the United Nations have all produced countless econometric studies arguing in favour of globalisation and its advantages in terms of income equalisation, economic growth, improvement in the standard of living (reduction of infant mortality, better health and increase in life expectancy), democratisation and good governance. In short, illusions have been produced, appropriated, valorised and exchanged, yet, everywhere in Africa, one is faced with the evidence of economic inequality and social degradation, and there can be no words at any time of human existence to gloss over the glaring fact: the economic disempowerment of the have-nots. And although no one would want to go so far as to point to globalisation as the cause of deep poverty and destructive inequality, it is clearly not the solution either, as there are more and more voices pointing out the perverse nature of the economic concepts used. Indeed, in those places (e.g. China) where globalisation is reducing poverty, it is also associated with rising inequality, planting the seeds of future problems. Critics of globalisation suggest that aid to development is often in stark contradiction with the discourse of solidarity that goes along with it, when the aid comes attached with constraints that aim to force African countries to adopt solutions that have nothing to do with their real needs. When a development agency from a developed country insists that the contract for a project it has agreed to fund must be awarded to a company from that country, rather than to some Chinese firm that can do an equally good job, but at a much lower cost, one has to ask who is really benefiting from the aid, and who is really helping whom. Opponents of globalisation also argue that the market free from state controls increases the gap between rich and poor not only at state level, but also internationally, and makes life insecure for most people, causing widespread lay-offs and immeasurable environmental damage. There is no doubt that globalisation of the economy contributed to the informalisation of the workforce in many countries (Standing, 1999), because global competition tends to erode employment relations by encouraging companies to hire workers at low wages, with few benefits, and because global market integration reduces the competitiveness of many informal businesses or self-employed producers, by flooding domestic markets with cheap imports. Global markets, by their very nature, are inequitable and generate inequality. This, in turn, inhibits growth in developing countries, where markets and governments are weak, and often leads to injustice and inequality, which undermine good public policy and collective decision-making. Globalisation is therefore seen as dis-equalising, because it reflects the market power and interests of the rich. The current rules (e.g. the trade regime, international migration and international property rights) all favour the interests of powerful rich countries and hurt the poor.

But globalisation is only one aspect of the global economy. More important than globalisation is market integration, which means the removal of barriers to trade. And, ideally, market integration should provide African countries with an opportunity to reduce costs for domestic producers, and combat the monopolistic power of oligopolies and cartels by eliminating national protection from external competition and byincreasing economic welfare. Unfortunately, it now appears that the champions of unfettered market access and integration are the first ones to engage in erecting trade barriers to protect selected industries in their own economy (e.g. large subsidies for agriculture in the United States and Europe, the car and foot-wear industries and some sectors of agriculture in Australia and Japan). [133] The European Union will have spent 35% of its US$156 billion budget in subsidies in 2007. In 2006 alone, OECD countries distributed nearly US$350 billion of subsidies to their farmers, for production and export (OECD, 2006). This means that agricultural products from developed countries cost a third of the price of products produced locally. The United States and Europe subsidise their cotton farmers to the tune of US$25 billion, and the American Farm Bill is soon to increase cotton subsidies from 60 to 65%. In this area alone, it is estimated that the losses suffered by West-African cotton producers are in the order of 30% of their income, or US$26 to US$504 million a year. This may explain the fall in cotton production in this part of the world to 4.4% in 2006-2007. In 2005, cotton companies in Burkina Faso lost €61 million as a direct result of the subsidies distributed to cotton farmers in developed countries. In 2006 they were on the verge of complete collapse, as many companies trading in cotton became insolvent and were unable to pay farmers who had sold them their entire production. Over 2 million people in Burkina Faso live off the cotton sector, which generates 60% of that country's public income. In his 2007 award-winning book, Orsenna (2006) suggests that, without cotton, countries like Mali and Burkina Faso may as well be wiped off the world's geo-economic map. He quotes the President of Mali, Amani Toumani Touré who says: 'Cotton represents half of our export income and directly feeds a third of our popu-lation, or 3 million and a half men and women! And perhaps an additional 15 million people in neighbouring countries! How can you expect us to give up growing cotton?' However, it is not at all certain that the end of agricul-tural subsidies to farmers in developed countries will necessarily see a resurgence of production in Africa, especially in the cotton sector. Indeed, Orsenna does not blame this situation on American subsidies to cotton farmers alone,[134] but the 'white apprentice sorcerers' of development and Africa's inability to invest in 'intelligence' (i.e. funding research) and influ-ence what is happening in this most crucial sector. As a result, Africa cuts herself off from the 'noises and silences' and the 'rhythms' of humanity's push forward.[135]

Furthermore, whilst developed countries maintain low average trade barriers amongst themselves as part of various free trade agreements, their highest trade barriers tend to apply to the goods that Africa exports (e.g. textiles and agriculture products). The World Bank and Oxfam estimate that trade barriers by developed countries cost Africa US$100 billion a year, or twice the amount the continent receives in official development assistance. The former Director-General of the World Trade Organisation (WTO), Michael Moore, estimates that removing all tariff and non-tariff barriers could result in gains of US$182 billion in the services sector, US$162 billion in the manufacturing sector and US$32 billion in agriculture for Africa. It is therefore apparent that the industrialised nations that committed themselves to energising the round of trade talks, launched in Doha, Qatar, in September 2001, with the aim of slashing subsidies, tariffs and other barriers to global commerce, are only paying lip-service to using trade to help poor nations. How can subsidies offered by the American government to its producers of cotton be explained in terms of the doctrine of free exchange? It is also significant that the final negotiations ended up being conducted by the giants of agribusiness, namely the United States, the European Union, Japan, Australia, India and Brazil, and that the poor nations were not represented at these discussions,[136] leaving their hope for a better future to rest on the magnanimity of others. And, just like the previous round of acrimonious negotiations in Hong Kong in 2005, the Doha round of trade liberalisation talks held in July 2006 in Geneva should have collapsed, owing to the deep differences between the European Union and the United States on market access and trade-distorting domestic subsidies for farmers, and the unwillingness of both sides to make significant and ground-breaking concessions. This raises a number of questions. Are there countries that are more 'globalisable' than others? Is globalisation anything else than the Westernisation of the world economy?

Concerns about globalisation are quite simply that this process is not really about a fair and just process of economic integration, but rather about economic agglomeration, in which the big get bigger and the small get smaller in terms of both size and per capita income. Indeed, it is difficult to ignore evidence of the increasing systemic inequalities and dislocations that accompany globalised capitalism. Hence, it comes as no surprise that the request of the Trade Commissioner of the European Union (EU), Mr Karl Falkenberg, for an opening up of African markets, the reduction of customs tariffs and a liberalisation of trade laws in Kenya, arguing that this is 'fundamental for African development' (TWN Africa, 2005), was turned down (18 January 2005). These issues and those pertaining to cotton[137] led to the failure of the WTO Summit in Cancún (Mexico) in September 2003.

Every year, African producers of cotton lose $US 1 billion due to export subsidies paid to European and American farmers. Furthermore, the EU presented the African, Caribbean and Pacific States (ACP) with a reform (on 14 January 2005) to take effect in July 2005, aiming to reduce the guaranteed price of sugar by 33%, as well as a reduction of exports from the ACP countries representing some US$55 million, in exchange for a preferential access to the EU market and a promotion for the diversification of their economies, in order to reduce their dependency on raw materials. But the economies of some ACP would be seriously affected by such reforms; Mauritius, for example, gets 20% of its energy from the by-products of sugar cane and the livelihood of one-third of the population is directly or indirectly tied to the sugar industry. When one-sided, and without fair and just rules, globalisation can increase the cost of competition for poor countries, especially in the areas of trade, finance and technology, leading to economic disempowerment.

Debates about globalisation are not about, and rarely mention, the place and/or role of local/African languages, except as a potential barrier to trade. Such debates tend to focus on purely economic variables, and essentially take place outside and without any concerns about the medium in which trade is carried out, in part because it is assumed that everyone in Africa speaks a European language, and at the very least English, and also because, when it comes to trade, the focus is on the overall level of output (i.e. Gross Domestic Product). No one realises that the language(s) of local consumers, producers, workers and investors also play a significant role as an input into the bigger, macroeconomic picture. All the facts and figures, as discussed above, fail to call into question the current 'business as usual' approach of the push for globalisation. But how do we globalise the majority of the people? Is globalisation only for the elite?

Language and the Economy

Robbins (1935: 16–17) argues that economics exists as a discipline, because of scarcity; but if 'scarcity' is at the core of economic theorising, then how relevant is economics to the field of multilingualism? We can find a possible answer in Grin *et al.* (2003) who argue that linguistic diversity is profitable even within an economic welfare-based paradigm and that: ' ... the usefulness of an economic perspective on language probably is not so much that it helps to understand language-related processes *as such* ... ' (Grin, 2003: 5; italics in the original). In Grin's view, 'the chief usefulness of language economics is derived from its capacity to formulate, evaluate and compare policy options regarding language, and hence to assist in

decision-making'. 'Economic tools do not replace political debate or contri-
butions from other disciplines', and 'this alone indicates that the endeavour must be interdisciplinary' (Grin, 2003: 5). Grin adds that 'the
application of basic economic concepts [to language?] suggests that society
is likely to be best off not when it tries to eliminate diversity, nor when it
attempts to embrace limitless diversity' (Grin 2003: 39). Grin (2003: 15)
notes that studies in the areas of multilingualism and the economy or the
economics of language date back to the mid 1960s and can be grouped into
three main orientations. These are:

(1) *Empirical studies*, which viewed language mainly as an ethnic attribute,
    with socio-economic consequences. These studies were used to
    analyse income differentials between ethnic and language groups in
    the United States and Canada (Fogel, 1966; Grin 1997; Grin & Sfreddo,
    1998; Raynaud *et al.*, 1969).
(2) *Studies in languages as human capital*, which looked at the acquisition of
    language skills as a source of economic advantage (Chiswick & Miller,
    2002; Chiswick & Repetto, 2001; Dávilo & Mora, 2000; Dustmann,
    1994; Dustmann & van Soest, 2001; Grenier, 1984).
(3) *Economic studies* of languages, not only as elements of identity or valu-
    able communication skills, but as a set of linguistic attributes that influ-
    ence the socio-economic status of individuals (Vaillancourt, 1980, 1996).

As can be seen, all three orientations focus on industrialised nations and
stress the role of language as a determinant of labour income, or economic
incentives as the principal determinant for language choices (Nettle, 2000).
In part because of such studies, when social and economic issues are
debated in relation to language in developing countries, if at all, the debates
are often in terms of the rights (and not always the obligations) that accrue
to the mastery of European languages, and pertain only to official, public
and formal arenas. But language practices in Africa, and everywhere in the
world for that matter, do not solely occur in formal and public domains,
and local languages in Africa are closely connected to generation of capital,
as they are part and parcel of the development and promotion of a survival
(literally and figuratively) from the market hegemony of European
languages.

Some believe that language is what defines a nation naturally and that
'diversity is negatively correlated with macroeconomic welfare' (Pool,
1972).[138] Coulmas (1992: 25) adds that, if it is agreed that language is an
asset, multiplicity of languages is deemed not to be conducive to social
wealth. Rather, 'the inverse connection seems to suggest itself and has been
interpreted as a causal rather than merely an accidental correlation [...]',

hence, 'it is ruled out that a high level of socio-economic development is compatible with linguistic fragmentation'. The gist of this argument is that multilingualism hurts growth and development. Laitin writes in this connection that:

> ... Correlation analysis involving all countries of the world suggests that there is a positive statistical relationship between societies with diverse speech communities and low level economic development ... Scholars who provide policy advice accept these results and argue that *economic development* presupposes the settlement of the language question and therefore *depends upon agreement on a single national language*. (Laitin, 1992: 53–4; my italics)

Choi (2002) goes so far as to suggest that a monolingual trading regime would be the most economically efficient. The undergirding assumption of these statements is that monolingualism in the official language should be the norm, and if one wants everything to be done much more efficiently and be better off financially, one should speak the official language. In other words, the prospects for development are much more likely if everyone can get on with the job and become literate and functional in a European lang-uage (some will say, preferably in English!). Therefore, only the languages of the economically powerful can give access to material wealth. Hence, in multilingual contexts, economic forces have been used as justification for, and contributed to, the disempowerment of language communities, as language is largely seen as an optimising economic tool that one learns for nothing else but its utility value, and multilingualism is perceived as an expensive proposition, especially in Africa, even though very few studies have been carried out on this specific issue (Chiswick *et al.*, 2000).

For Laitin, the argument according to which 'changes in language diver-sity' (and engineering of monolingualism) can lead to improvement in the economic fortunes of developing countries is 'scientifically suspect', since the data based on the socio-economic indicators from 40 African countries show no obvious statistical relationship between language diversity and economic growth (Laitin, 1992: 54). This argument is all the more 'suspect', as it seeks to ignore multilingual societies in developed countries (e.g. Belgium, Spain and Switzerland) – see Chapter 1. Coulmas (1992: 25) adds that this view is essentially 'based on *the high degree of coincidence* of virtual and [more importantly] *perceived* monolingualism and economic develop-ment observed in the industrialised world', but not on science.

The basic structure of economic theory looks at individual economic units such as consumers, producers, workers and investors (micro-economics) and aggregate economic quantities, such as the overall level of output or Gross Domestic Product (GDP), unemployment, general price levels or inflation and interest rates (macroeconomics). Students of language have always argued that language is much more pervasive to human experience than the object of study of micro- and macroeconomics. Economics has limitations when it comes to the study of human behaviour, for there is something about language behaviour that is not quantifiable, but which is still considered valuable. The evidence in Africa at least is unequivocal: the economic experiments of nearly half a century have failed, maybe not because of the exclusive use of European languages in the formal economy, but most certainly partly because the actors of change have not been allowed to participate in the formulation and implementation of development policies. The literature on economic growth and development suggests that the best way to tackle such issues is through significant investment in human capital (as well as re-distributive policies and quality institutions). The use of local languages in the process of development will contribute to such an investment, at least in terms of participation levels and empowerment, making it possible for Africans to understand and make informed decisions on the merits of development projects and thereby increasing the efficiency of such development projects. Effective and efficient linguistic communication can serve only to establish and reinforce economically beneficial relationships; language is the vehicle for the transfer of knowledge, but this transfer is conditional upon the efficiency of communication.

In this particular regard, the Report on the Millennium Development Goals (UNDP, 2006: 38, 102, 139) has the added merit of making direct, positive reference to multilingualism as a contributing factor to, and a key ingredient in creating a favourable context for sustainable long term-term endogenous development and acknowledges that economic development can occur through languages other than those of developed nations. This is the point illustrated in the next section, which looks at the informal economy and the language practice(s) of the masses to create their own economic space.

The Informal Economy

One cannot really perceive the full structural vitality of the African economy until one delves into the informal economy. The phrase 'informal sector' was first coined in the early 1970s (Hart, 1973) to describe the range of subsistence activities of the urban poor. However, the most quoted definition of the term is that of the International Labour Organisation's Kenya Report (ILO, 1972: 6), in which informal activities are defined as 'a way of doing things', characterised by ease of entry, reliance on indigenous resources, family ownership of enterprises, small scale of operation, labour intensive and adapted technology, skills acquired outside of the formal school system, and unregulated and competitive markets. This definition has evolved over the years, as has the character of the phenomenon itself (see Charmes, 2000: 1–2, for the 'International Definition of the Informal Sector' as adopted by the 15th International Conference of Labour Statisticians in 1993), shifting the focus from the characteristics of enterprises (i.e. not legally regulated) to the nature of employment (i.e. relationships that are not regulated, stable or protected). Informal activities encompass different types of economic activity (trading, collecting, service provision and manufacturing), different employment relations (the self-employed, paid and unpaid workers and disguised wage workers) and activities with different economic potential (survivalist activities and small successful enterprises). In Africa, the informal economy concerns small entrepreneurs that no traditional bank is prepared to help, but who find the answer to their financial needs through micro-finance institutions, and the 'tontines'.[139] According to a study on 'The Informal Sector in sub-Saharan Africa',[140] covering 13 predominantly English-speaking sub-Saharan countries, whilst there was a decline or stagnation in formal employment opportunities in this part of the world, there was a significant increase in informal sector activities, and 'an important contribution by the informal economy to a country's GDP' (Xaba et al., 2002: iii). Chen (2001) estimates that the informal economy represents 78% of non-agricultural employment, 61% of urban employment and 93% new job creation.

Although the growth of the informal economy in Africa may in part be attributed to heavy internal migration from rural areas to urban centres, the informal economy also tends to flourish in times of economic crisis – East Asia, Russia, Latin America and South Africa during 1997–1999, Turkey and Argentina in 2000–2001 (see also Tokman 1992). This is because, despite all the clichés and prejudice, no human being can afford to be unemployed – especially in Africa, where there is no social safety net. During the Asian economic crisis, millions of people in the Asian Tiger countries tried to find jobs or create work in the informal economy. The same happened in Africa during the decades of structural adjustment[141] and currency devaluation,[142] and in the former Soviet Union and in Central and Eastern Europe during the economic transition, when government-owned companies were privatised and private and public enterprises downsized or closed, retrenching millions of workers who could not find alternative formal jobs. Because of the peso crisis of 1994–1995 in Mexico, for example, the informal economy has swelled considerably, up by 13%

during the year of the crisis alone. It is also argued that globalisation of the economy contributed to the informalisation of the workforce in many countries (Standing, 1999), because global competition tends to erode employment relations by encouraging companies to hire workers at low wages, with few benefits, and because global market integration reduces the competitiveness of many informal businesses or self-employed producers, by flooding domestic markets with cheap imports. According to a report of the ILO (2002: 22), there are several potential negative economic impacts of globalisation on the formal economy. Some of these are: unemployment, loss of livelihood, loss of marketing outlets, drop in real wages coupled with a rise in the cost of living, lack of public services, decline in health services, rise in health care costs and in malnutrition, decline in education services and rise in school dropouts. In such circumstances, the informal economy acts as a giant safety valve for the poor, preventing even greater hardship and social explosion.

In Africa, self-employment comprises 60 to 70% of informal employment, outside agriculture. Informal wage employment is also significant, comprising 30 to 40% of informal employment, outside agriculture. The informal economy represents over 80% of the active urban population, particularly in sub-Saharan Africa. It is estimated that it contributes 43% of GDP in Africa and 45 to 60% of non-agricultural GDP, and is responsible for 93% of new jobs. In Senegal, where the role model in Senegal is no longer the civil servant, but the small business entrepreneur, it represents 70% of GDP. But Senegal is not alone. The results of a recent three-year study of the economic capitals of 7 such countries in sub-Saharan Africa (Cotonou in Benin, Ouagadougou in Burkina Faso, Abidjan in Côte d'Ivoire, Bamako in Mali, Niamey in Niger, Dakar in Senegal and Lomé in Togo) show that an average of 2.7 million people or 76% of jobs in these cities are involved in the informal economy and generate US$9 billion, or the equivalent of the combined GDPs of Senegal and Mali (Afristat & DIAL, 2003). In Côte d'Ivoire, 75% of small business entrepreneurs operate in the informal economy and generate some US$6,810,000 per year. All the available data suggest that, in almost all cases, the informal economy plays a far more significant role in the economies of African countries than the formal economy does, as is reflected in its share in the GDP of these countries.

But make no mistake; the informal economy is not confined to Africa. New Delhi, Mumbai, Mexico, Lima, New York City, Madrid, Paris, London, Toronto and Rome all have their share of pushcart vendors, street vendors, industrial outworkers and home-workers, off-site data processors, and more.[143] It is estimated that there are 2.3 to 13.1 million 'African micro-entrepreneurs' (note the euphemism ...) in the United States, with no access to credit. In European OECD countries, the average is 18%, with 48 million workers in the informal economy. In Italy alone, the informal labour force is estimated at 30 to 48% of the official labour force. What most workers in the informal economy have in common is the lack of formal recognition and protection, and the realisation that informal production costs less and rewards more. They are also noted for their enterprising spirit, efficiency, creativity and resilience. Generally, businesses in the informal economy are not public limited companies, with a pool of shareholders listed on a stock exchange, but are, for the most part, owned by the family; shareholders, when there are any, are often family members (e.g. fathers and sons, husbands and wives, mothers and daughters, uncles and nephews).

Whilst some will simply say that the informal economy undermines state control and revenues and hinders the modernisation of the economy, it is of such importance that many local and national governments are now trying to make the informal economy an entry point into the formal economy – in part, with a view to increasing their tax base. This is certainly what is happening with Durban Unicity, which, in 2000, developed a policy on the informal economy and invested into infrastructure such as markets, stalls of drinking water, electricity and garbage removal for the activities of those involved in the informal economy. The city's strategy is to allocate specially demarcated sites where trade can occur, and traders then pay rent for the use of stalls and services. The policy states: 'the formal and informal parts of the economy are mutually interdependent. The good health of one depends on the good health of the other' (Spurr, 2001). In 1996, there were an estimated 20,000 traders working in the Durban metropolitan area. In 1998, black households spent approximately R500 million in this sector (Spurr, 2001). In Egypt, where nearly a fifth of business activities take place in the informal economy, arrangements are afoot for owners of small enterprises in the informal economy to have access to credit in their local post offices, and 10% of all public procurement is being set aside for them.

What the foregoing clearly shows is that the distinction between the formal and informal economy is political, not economic, and the sheer size and continuing growth of the informal sector in Africa is a great challenge to the key neo-liberal assumption that it will decline as economies liberalise and grow. It also shows that poverty is not a congenital condition, nor is it an issue of lack of skills. It is merely a symptom of dysfunctional societal conditions that can be reversed.

Whilst it is not being suggested here that making a living as a street vendor is what people should be aspiring to, in order to lift themselves out of the dungeons of poverty and disease, all the data point to an increase in the activities of the informal economy, concurrently with a decline or stagnation in the growth of formal employment in Africa. So, although most people involved in the informal economy do not always earn a decent living and may not have the skills to build and run good businesses, the point here is that they can become active participants, and thereby contribute to a thriving system, when the language used is a language they can understand. Being able to read and write in the de facto language(s) of the market, which may not be the official languages, will help these people improve their skills in setting up and running efficient businesses. Of more interest to us at this stage are the patterns of communication and the linguistic repertoires of people involved in the informal economy. Although the research on the informal economy says nothing about language, the obvious question is how does it manage to exist at all? Are commercial transactions in the informal economy carried out in European languages? Are European languages that are said to be so crucial to the survival of developing countries necessary for this sector to work? If not, how do people in the informal economy manage to do business? What languages are good for the business of the masses? And is there any way that these communicative patterns can be replicated in the formal domains of education and health, and at the microeconomic level in Africa?

The Language(s) of the Informal Economy: An Argument for Localisation

Noting that there has been widespread language shift among the indigenous communities of the United States and Canada, Palmer (1997: 265) argues that this was most likely caused by what he calls 'the language of work' in addition to other external factors such as government or educational programs and intergenerational transfer (Fishman, 1991).The language-of-work hypothesis states that 'In a minority language community, if the national or regional language is used as the language of work for virtually all the 'jobs' of the community that language will, within a few generations, replace the minority language as language of the home as well' (Palmer, 1997: 264). Palmer suggests that a change in work structure of the dominant society has a direct bearing on language, without ever being a central focus; and this is the case because:

> The citizen of today in every developed country is typically an employee. He works for one of the institutions. He looks to them for his livelihood. He looks to them for his opportunities. He looks to them for access to status and function in society, as wells as for personal fulfilment and achievement (Palmer, 1997: 266).

The language of the workplace in North America and in most of the rest of the world tends to be a common, written, official language. It is the sole language of government, business and education. More importantly, indigenous communities in developed countries 'have largely lost their land base or no longer find traditional means of support practical or adequate, [and their] participation in the wage-based economy has become very important for meeting needs up and down the hierarchy' (Palmer, 1997: 273).

We find the language-of-work hypothesis interesting, not so much because it reflects what is happening in the case of language(s) used in the informal economy in Africa, but because it highlights a fundamental difference. Indeed, evidence from language practices in the informal economy in Africa is in stark contrast with some of the certainties we hear or read about whenever the use of local languages is contemplated. The same economic forces that were expected to help spread European languages in Africa have given a boost to African languages of wider communication at local, regional or national or cross-national levels, as well as to non-standard (nativised) varieties of European languages, especially in the urban areas (Djité, 1989). The language-of-work hypothesis is also interesting, because it shows that language does not exist independently from human beings and what they do.

Most research reports on the informal economy, on its efficiency and contribution to the overall wellbeing of people in African economies, are silent on the language(s) used in everyday interactions and transactions. Yet, people must and do communicate somehow, as they struggle to eke out a living. A large body of sociolinguistic research from the early 1990s sheds some light on the linguistic inner workings of the market place in Benin, Cameroon, the Republic of Congo, Côte d'Ivoire, Mali, the Democratic Republic of Congo, Niger and even in the province of Canton in China (Calvet, 1985) and tells us much more about the relationship between multilingualism and the economy. The data from this body of research point to the predominance of vehicular languages or lingua francas at the market place. Even in the relatively structured economies of Tunisia, Algeria, Morocco, Egypt, Kenya and Botswana, the informal economy represents a third of the GDP (Charbi, 2007b). Without the informal economy, there would hardly be a viable source of income and survival for the masses in Africa. This sociolinguistic evidence suggests that some of the pre-colonial language practices that sustained large and powerful kingdoms and empires survived colonisation and, in many cases, developed and spread during colonial administration (e.g. Dyula and Hausa in West Africa, and KiSwahili in East Africa).

We also know that one essential characteristic in carrying out business in the informal economy is 'bargaining'. Whether one really needs a product or not, and especially when one needs it, whether affordability is an issue or not, and especially when it is, bargaining is a necessary ritual. It has both a socialising and a pragmatic function, for it matters not whether the buyer can afford to pay the price the seller is asking for. He who simply pays the price asked for is perceived either as having missed the whole point of the exercise or as patronising. And it is best not to try to bargain in the official language, especially if one is a local, since the official language is associated with higher socio-economic status and therefore attracts higher prices. The potential buyer and seller come into the interaction ready to linguistically and strategically outdo (or outbid) one another. What matters is whether either the buyer or the seller can speak the language of the other, because speaking the language of the interlocutor gives one the edge. Whether the transaction is successfully concluded or not does not really matter sometimes, as both the buyer and the seller will have enjoyed the verbal tussle.

This sort of linguistic practice empowers those involved in the informal economy in more ways than one. The question here is not about what they _need to do_ with their languages, but what it is they _actually do_ with them. Most people engaged in a commercial activity in Africa are not university graduates. In fact, most of them have not even completed high school, through no fault of their own, but partly because the education system is poorly equipped to help them, linguistically biased and highly selective. Hence, they communicate mostly in the languages their customers understand best – in the local languages or, increasingly, non-standard forms of European languages, such as popular French, Nouchi, Pidgin languages. Indeed, a report by the International Labour Office (ILO, 2006) published in October 2006 confirms that unemployment amongst the 15 to 24 years old in sub-Saharan Africa (45% of Africa's labour force) has seen many young people turn to the informal sector to earn a living.[144] In addition to dealing in everyday consumer goods, these languages have opened up a niche for the production of goods, many of them cultural goods, such as music, that are prized by an ever-growing section of society (e.g. the youth that makes up 60% of the population in most African countries), and given access to economic opportunities that would otherwise be out of reach for a sizeable proportion of the majority of people. Whilst millionaires in the formal economy in Africa often tend to be politicians or senior public servants, who embezzle public funds, genuine self-made millionaires, such as the 'Mama Benz' (so called because they drive Mercedes Benz) and the Mozambican _'commerciantes'_, travel from Nigeria to Sierra Leone or from the Southern Mozambican province of Gaza to South Africa, Malawi and

Zimbabwe for business transactions carried out in various local languages, and create and continue to build their wealth without speaking a word of the languages of the formal economy. But that is not all; women, the elderly and rural inhabitants all take part in these systems centred around economies generated by and in local languages, and speakers move into, between, and across various sociolinguistic domains defined by different practices they have to abide by, and exhibit multiple and varied language skills from their repertoire of languages. Local languages therefore generate economic value, in the true sense of the word.

If the formal economy shows Africa as void of economic life and promise, the informal economy and the language use patterns that enable the very existence of this type of activity shows a much more vibrant, yet linguistically streamlined Africa, an Africa of people who toil to take charge of their socio-economic and linguistic survival and that has nothing to do with the caricature of the one that descriptive linguists have for so long tried to sell to the rest of the world. Patterns of language use in the informal economy are testimony to the ability of Africans to register their dynamism, even at the margin, their capacity to resist everything – be it colonisation, the single party, dictatorship, debt, poverty, wars – and seize on every parcel of freedom offered to them.

A true cost–benefit analysis of multilingualism would therefore seriously be distorted if it did not take into account an analysis of its impact on the informal economy and the impact of the informal economy on the daily lives of the majority of the people in Africa, as well as on the economic viability of most African countries. The data on the informal economy suggest that economic development in Africa is not only about international trade. Although it represents only about 10% at the moment, there is such a thing as regional trade (south–south as opposed to north–south), and effective regional integration can boost this fragmented regional trade. Whether formal or informal, such regional trade will require communication in the production and provision of services, and regional/cross border language(s) will have an economic impact on the nature and cost of such regional trade. A simple example of this would be the way language(s) used on the labels of basic goods or equipment, whether imported or produced locally, can seriously affect lives, as well as current and sustainable efficiency (Djité, 1993).

At the African Growth and Opportunity Act (AGOA) Investment Forum of 7 July 2006, Paul Wolfowitz, President of the World Bank, made the point that infrastructure investments in Africa must be regional, as African countries have much to gain from developing south-to-south commercial exchanges and help in the creation of an internal market where they can sell and buy their own products (*Fraternité Matin*, 14 July 2006).[145] Were this to occur, who is to say that a prosperous internal regional market cannot be based around KiSwahili in large areas of Central and Eastern Africa, Hausa and Dyula in large areas of Western Africa, or IsiZulu and Xhosa in large areas of Southern Africa? The UNCTAD (2006) Report is also pleading for a reduction of the gap between the informal and formal sectors of the economy in the developing and especially the least developed countries, although the pleas of this organisation are not being heard by the prevailing dogma. An argument for the promotion of local languages and localisation was also made by Microsoft Africa when, in June 2006, they announced the launch of Microsoft *Office* 12 and Microsoft *Vista* in Wolof, a language of wider communication in Senegal, as part of the local language program of Microsoft International, which began in 2004, in the wider context of having Microsoft *Windows XP* and Microsoft *Office 2003* available in some 40 languages, in order to engage governments, universities and local authorities around the world.

While they will broadly agree that economic activity in the 'informal sector' naturally goes on in terms of local languages, some will still be very sceptical at the suggestion that endogenous development in Africa should benefit from the extension of indigenous communication networks, especially in the more formal or 'formalising' sectors of the economy. Coulmas, for instance, writes that:

> The long-term dilemma for the communication economy of many Third World countries is that the chances for spreading exoglossic written languages and the chances for the coming into existence of efficient new endoglossic written languages are equally poor. (Coulmas, 1992: 216)

To his credit, Coulmas (1992: 215) acknowledges that 'the prospects for the spread of exoglossic written languages are not good, because they do not emerge in conjunction with the communicative demands and the underlying economic necessities ... ' Indeed, is spreading an exoglossic language to 90% of the population comparable to making official a language understood by over 90% of the citizens of a country? What is the scientific basis for so much pessimism? Why would Africa today not be able to do what was done in the times of the great kingdoms and empires? Is this not what King Edward III did in England in the 14th century by proclaiming English the official language of the Courts? How likely was it back then that the Northern, Midland and Southern dialect rivalry would be resolved? More importantly, what was the reason behind the King's proclamation? Quite simply, that *the people need to know the language through which they are being governed*; hence, emphasising the importance of participation of the majority in the process of development. King Edward III was able to make such a proclamation even though Anglo-Norman had been the language of ordinary interactions among the upper classes and most of the monarchs of England for some 200 years after the Norman Conquest, and English the language of the lower orders (Baugh, 1959). The use of English as a principal language of record and written documents did not start until after 1420 and this task was in the hands of a small bureaucracy of some 120 clerks. Even if one was cynical enough to suggest that this was only a shrewd ploy, and that the real aim of making the language of the peasantry official was mainly to improve compliance in paying taxes, one would be remiss not to acknowledge the visionary nature of the King's decision.

Intellectual sophistry now suggests that 'the value of a language is determined in relation to that of other languages', a criterion that is 'above all economic', in part 'through its advances on the foreign language market' (Coulmas, 1992: 77, 79, 80). Hence, Coulmas (1992: 81), using data from the IMF on reserve currencies, argues that: 'there is an almost perfect match with the great foreign languages of the world'. But like other articles of faith before it, this line of argument loses sight of at least two important facts pertaining to reserve currencies. First, central banks around the world have been dumping the US dollar as the preferred reserve currency in favour of the Euro, or at least diversifying their reserve currency base. And whilst in 2003 the proportion for both currencies was 70% for the US dollar, against 20% for the Euro; by 2005, this proportion was 66% for the US dollar, against 25% for the Euro (*The Economist*, 29 September 2005). This trend is likely to continue, and many are of the view that it is not unlikely for the Euro to overtake the US dollar as the preferred reserve currency in the not-too-distant future. Significantly, and further confirming the sophistry of the argument, the Euro is not matched with any particular European language; as it happens the Euro is the currency of a multilingual economy, the economy of the European Union. Secondly, the true value of European languages is in part proportional to the role of colonial powers in the transatlantic slave trade and colonisation, as well as the size of their empires. These languages became 'economically valuable' if not as a result of, at least following these major historical and socio-political and economic events. Indeed, the current status of European languages is due in large part to the fact that they have served as tools of imperialism and oppression throughout the world.

In any event, whilst African countries are still debating the economic merits of multilingualism, the industrialised nations of Europe have moved away from traditional defensive linguistic nationalism and embraced the linguistic richness and diversity of their multilingual and multicultural communities. Europe is not just a space of bankers and marketers; it is now a polity where the respect for cultural and linguistic diversity is enshrined in various provisions of the Treaty of Rome.*146* Still in Europe, the *Economist* (2001) points out that 22% of the budget of the WTO is spent on language services, and then refers to a failed attempt to reduce the seven working languages of the ILO to three. Some developed countries, fervent defenders of the open market economy do not hesitate to enact laws requiring the labelling of foreign products in the national language and the protection of sensitive industries (e.g. the film industry), in the name of their *'exception culturelle'*.[147]

In Australia, the 1987 National Policy on Languages institutionalised the teaching of Languages Other than English (LOTEs), including Aboriginal languages, with a specialist programme in Asian languages. Each of the six Australian states and two territories developed their own language policy, along the lines of the federal policy, and identified eight LOTEs as priorities for more extensive curriculum development and teacher training. LOTEs are introduced early in primary schooling and various incentives put in place to reward individual students and schools. Although the Asian economic downturn of 1997 and the Australian–Indonesian fallout over the East Timor independence struggle in 1999 led to the Conservative Government withdrawing all funding from this language policy in 2002, a large number of LOTEs are still being studied at primary, secondary and university levels across the country (Djité, 1994; Lo Bianco, 2002). In New South Wales, the State government's funding scheme allows for the maintenance and development of some 56 languages during and after school hours, including Community Languages, and most language minorities are guaranteed equal access to government agencies and services in their native languages throughout the Commonwealth of Austrlaia. Both the Conservative Federal Government and Opposition are proud to have Ministers on their front bench who are fluent in the languages of Australia's major trade partners, such as China, Indonesia and Japan. The Australian National Language Policy is explicitly geared not only to reducing the economic and social problems of linguistic minorities (high dropout rates, unemployment and lack of political participation) and the language bias within the political institutions of the country, hence reducing language-based inequality, but also to enticing the majority to familiarise themselves with and/or learn one or two minority language(s). This policy, also known as *Multiculturalism*, revolves around four core principles:

(1)   the value of multilingualism in enriching culture;
(2)   the contribution of multilingualism to the Australian economy;

(3)   the importance of multilingualism to social justice;
(4)   the potential for multilingualism to enhance the country's role in the
      Pacific region.

The available evidence from Africa, and the rest of the world, therefore suggests that policies aimed at the protection and promotion of multi-lingualism are well worth the cost, and that language barriers are barriers to progress. It also suggests that there is a limit to economic rationalism when it comes to language. Multilingualism is a ready resource for the facil-itation of the transfer of information and technology and know-how. Although it may be argued that the proclaimed multilingualism within the European Union, and in countries like Australia, does not necessarily translate into most people in Europe being multilingual themselves, the crucial point at this stage is that multilingualism and its benefits are recog-nised and entrenched, at least at the institutional level. Just as it took over 100 years to make French the everyday language of the majority of the French population, it may take some time yet for the majority of the people in Europe to become multilinguals. Nevertheless, the main instruments for the implementation of the process are now in place, and the early signs of interest in the younger generation of Europeans in speaking more than their national or regional language(s) are promising.

Conclusion

This chapter set out to show how a section of the African people empowers itself in gaining access to a significant share of the economy, and how speech communities exercise control over their language(s) and deciding which language(s) will be the media of economic activity, and over symbolic and capital resources of their countries through language in the area of the informal economy. The foregoing has demonstrated that, 50 years on, European languages do not meet the day-to-day communicative needs of the majority of the African people in the crucial domain of the economy. People often understand and speak more than one language, and will use the code most appropriate for successful communication when required. Even where this individual multilingualism does not always match societal multilingualism, civilised, independent and democratic nation-states take it upon themselves and strive to strike a balance in insti-tutionalising equality of languages and managing their multilingualism for the benefit of the majority, and do not purposely rig the stakes or tip the scales in favour of a minority to have all the communicative advantage and socio-economic benefits attached thereto. Such language exclusion and inequality can lead only to economic exclusion which, in turn, leads to poor economic performance, because the minority cannot by themselves drive economic growth. It is therefore in everyone's interest to encourage and support development approaches that work, and investing in multi-lingualism in Africa will help release the tremendous resources of human capital, regenerate communities and place them where they should be – at the universal table of the give and take. The language situation affects and impacts on the process of information exchange upon which the success of the economy rests. And communication facilitated in the local languages may be the key to removing the inefficiencies introduced by the selection and promotion of European languages. If African countries really want to increase per capita GDP, they will adopt policies that are most likely to achieve that result, such as the promotion of growth with equity, by taking the language(s) issue into account.

Although, on reading about the woes of Africa, one is hard-pressed to find logic or hope in some of the prescriptions coming from the developed countries, the IMF and the World Bank, the material resources, human capital, perseverance and creativity required to combat poverty and hunger in Africa are within reach. This is demonstrated in the strength of the informal economy. We now need to work out how multilingualism can be made the preferred alternative, and transfer its benefits into the formal domain. What are needed are bold and imaginative leadership, and the will and determination to harness and put these alternatives to work. Ingenuity and success often come from acknowledging that one is different and being prepared to dare to act differently. The economic futures of African countries therefore lie in their own hands, through the policies they will choose to adopt. The instruments of economic analysis are just that – instruments; these instruments cannot replace linguistic insights and political decisions; they can only complement them.

Chapter 5

Language, Governance and Development

> *The king, desiring the good governance and tranquillity of his people,*
> *and to put out and eschew the harms and mischiefs which do or may*
> *happen in this behalf by the occasions aforesaid, hath ordained and*
> *established by the assent aforesaid, that all pleas which shall be pleaded*
> *in his courts whatsoever, before any of his justices whatsoever, or in his*
> *other places, or before any of his other ministers whatsoever, or in the*
> *courts and places of any other lords whatsoever within the realm, shall*
> *be pleaded, shewed, defended, answered, debated, and judged in the*
> *English tongue, and that they be entered and enrolled in Latin.*
> *Statutes of the Realm of October 1362, I: 375–76*
> (cited in Baugh, 1959: 178)

> *A democratic Africa that seeks to enhance the active participation of all*
> *citizens in all institutions – social, economic, political, et cetera.*
> 'Vision for Africa' – *The Harare Declaration*
> (UNESCO, 2006)

Introduction

Coulmas (1992: 67) reminds us that 'The opportunities for realising the functional potential of language are not determined by economic factors alone. Other interfering factors of a political or socio-psychological nature have to be taken into account'. It appears that this is what happened on the African continent when, in 1997, the Intergovernmental Conference on Language Policies in Africa placed the topic of 'Multilingualism in Democracy' at the heart of the debate on good governance in Africa (*The Harare Declaration*). In 2001, the NEPAD blueprint emphasised that 'development is impossible in the absence of true democracy, respect for human rights, peace and good governance' (NEPAD, 2001: 17).[148] In 2005, in a study entitled *Striving for Good Governance in Africa*, the United Nations Economic Commission for Africa (UNECA) suggested that, overall, governance is getting better in Africa, because (1) political performance indicators (i.e. voter turnout, competitiveness of the political system, legitimacy of the political framework) rank higher on average, and (2) decentralisation, tax evasion and corruption indicators rank lowest (UNECA, 2005a: 3–22).

However, UNECA (2005a: 26–37) also found that there is still a prevalence of capacity deficits in governance institutions, and these are of human, material and institutional dimensions. The study stressed that these capacity gaps create an imbalance between legal formal provisions and implementation and execution, and suggests an Action Plan, before 'we can say that the capable state is the norm in Africa' (UNECA, 2005a: vi). The aims of the Action Plan lead one to wonder about the claims of improvement that are made about economic and political governance in the first place.[149] Indeed, the signs of weakness in every sector of economic, democratic and political governance suggest that the population does not understand or cannot effectively participate in the development of the African continent, because of a democratic deficit. Where the people have been granted the opportunity to exercise their right to participate, that right has often been limited to the ballot box, and they have not been empowered to get involved in the decision-making process after the votes have been counted.

Abraham Lincoln's definition of democracy as *'government of the people, for the people and by the people'* highlights the pivotal role of people in a democratic setting. In his view, the people must be able to choose from alternatives and actively participate in the decision-making process. In the context of most countries of the world, such participation can be effected only through one or more of the languages understood and used in the speech communities, for participation implies that decisions are made by the people (for example through the ballot box), or on their behalf (through Parliament) in ways that reflect their will. But 'meaningful democracy goes beyond electoralism to include the improvement of the material conditions of the people and the fulfilment of their expectations' (Jozana, 1999: 7). Although many more elections are now being organised on the continent, many citizens have lost faith in what these can achieve for them in terms of real transparency, democracy and freedom. The routine in many countries is like that of Egypt, where Hosni Moubarak has always won elections in landslides – just like Omar Bongo in Gabon and Zine Abidine in Tunisia. Even the elections in Mali, Nigeria and Senegal in 2007 were arguably tainted with a number of irregularities. The *Afrobarometer*, a non-partisan research instrument that measures the social, economic and political atmosphere in Africa (Keulder & Wiese, 2005; Bratton & Logan, 2006),[150] shows that, although most Africans prefer democracy to other types of regimes, in 2001only 45% believed that the electoral process was satisfactory. It also shows that, whilst 84% of Nigerians were satisfied with the status of democracy in their country in 2000, only 25% still held the same opinion in 2005. In other words, beyond elections, people must be able to take part in the everyday social, economic and political processes that affect their lives. This sort of participation implies that issues about which decisions are to be taken must be presented, explained and argued in a language, or in languages, that people understand. According to Starkey (2002: 9), 'Healthy democracies are composed of individuals who are able to communicate with fellow citizens and use their linguistic skills to participate actively in, for instance, associations, movements, cultural groups and political parties'. Democracy is therefore about people, *all people*, about being able to talk to one another; about issues of common concern, and about being able to actively participate in the resolutions of such issues.

But, democracy is not just about participation; it is also about representation and benefaction, which implies that (1) those representing the people hold their positions with the people's consent and realise that they owe such positions to the people, and that (2) the goal of representing the people (in parliament or government) is to look after the welfare of the people. Representation and benefaction also imply that the representatives must communicate with the people they represent; and in most countries, such communication is feasible and efficient only in the language(s) the people understand, so that they can take full advantage of their rights, first by becoming aware of such rights and second by exercising these rights if and when they choose to do so.

Together, participation, representation and benefaction make up what the Council of Europe regards as *democratic citizenship*; that is to say, the 'inclusion rather than exclusion, participation rather than marginalisation, culture and values rather than simple procedural issues ... ' (Starkey 2002: 8).

Since the independence of most African countries in the 1960s, instead of sending children to school, helping mothers get healthier and providing jobs for the poor, governments have been acting in their own interests, siphoning off resources into the hands of a corrupt and greedy few, giving priority only to the convenience of administration, largely unaccountable to those affected by their decisions. Hence, the adoption of what were then perceived as 'pragmatic' language policies, which in no insignificant way have contributed to continuing economic dependency with debts built up by irresponsible borrowing and lending, lack of full participation of the people in the conduct of the affairs of the state, educational underachievement, unemployment, poor health, short life expectancy and increased marginalisation. The list of least developed nations in the world is dominated by African countries: Angola, Benin, Burkina Faso, Burundi, Central African Republic, Chad, Congo, Côte d'Ivoire, Eritrea, Ethiopia, Gambia, Guinea, Guinea Bissau, Malawi, Mali, Mozambique, Niger, Nigeria, Rwanda, Senegal, Sierra Leone, Tanzania, Uganda and Zambia.

Although democracy was supposed to have spread across the continent in the 1990s, African politicians[151] and their followers are able to get away with social and political ills: corruption, nepotism, manipulation of electoral laws, the rigging of elections and rewriting of constitutions and the refusing to submit to Aristotle's definition of 'citizen' as one who rules and is ruled in turn (Kerber, 1997). All these undemocratic practices are due, in no small measure, to the way African politicians have managed to keep the majority of the people ignorant through their language and language-in-education policies and/or practices. The rich elites have suppressed democracy and equal rights, in order to preserve their privileges (Acemoglu, 2005; Bourguignon & Verdier, 2000), leading to unstable institutions over time, slowly but surely (Benabou, 1996; Perotti, 1996; Persson & Tabellini, 1994).

Nowhere else in the world, but in Africa, is democracy restricted to the 'elites' alone, significantly through the language of government. But the process of decision-making cannot remain the preserve of the elites; educated and uneducated people alike have a right to information pertaining to their own affairs, and deserve to engage in transactions of official government business or seek and receive public service in a language they understand.

Good governance can be defined as 'the traditions and institutions by which authority in a country is exercised *for the common good*' (Kaufmann, 2005; emphasis added). It is the opening up of the political space, respect of human rights and adherence to the rule of law. It is also predictable administration, legitimate power and responsive regulation. Good governance also means that governments have to pay special attention to the social agenda and must provide basic education and health *for all*, increase growth and improve income distribution and equity. Countries can derive a very large 'development dividend' from better governance, and improvement in governance can triple the population's income per capita, and reduce infant mortality and illiteracy (Kaufmann, 2005). Needless to say, when governance is poor, policymaking is severely compromised, and there can be no long-term development.

In view of the foregoing, this chapter aims to examine an aspect of these capacity gaps and democratic deficit: – language. It puts the issue of language forward as a political and social concept pertaining to welfare and equity, and argues that there is a need for people to understand and take an active part in governance, through the language(s) they know best. It suggests that the primary language of governance ought to be based on the most efficient way of getting the message of those representing the people through to the masses, and for the latter to be able to pass on their ideas to their representatives. Clearly, neither of these objectives can efficiently be achieved through a language that is spoken by less than 20% of the people[152] and only empowers those who have mastered it. The chapter asks the following questions: what value has a democracy that favours participation by only a minority of the citizens at the expense of the vast majority? Is good governance possible when the majority of the people cannot understand the language in which the law of the land is drafted and do not have a political voice? To what extent does a political system exclusively structured around a European language allow democratic principles to operate in Africa? Can civic information be efficiently disseminated? Can the people access basic information on the health issues that affect them most? Is there a case for good governance when the human resource base is being deprived of its basic rights and privileges?

Facts and Figures: Looking into the Mouths of the Peanut Roasters

With the most extreme form of government failures, a string of 'presidents for life', more than 107 Heads of States overthrown between 1960 and 2003 (two thirds of whom were murdered, jailed or forced into exile), and two dozen ruthless or benevolent dictators over the last 50 years, one would be tempted to say, along with the UNECA, that the continent has been to hell and back. We wish![153]

Noting that Africa is under-developed because of her lack of organisation, method and rigour, Kabou (1991: 205) writes: 'Africa in the 21st century will have to become rational or there will be no Africa to speak of'. Of most concern to Kabou are a number of attitudes, excesses, paradoxes and contradictions that underline and bring home aspects of the prevalent maladministration (embezzlement of public funds through artificial financial arrangements, forged invoices and book entries, over-billing) in many African countries over the last five decades. It is no exaggeration to say that it is quite rare in Africa to find people seeking to be anointed into public office simply because they genuinely want to serve their country and their people; generally, the aim is to help themselves and those close to them. Corruption and nepotism have not only severely undermined fledging democracies; they have reduced access to basic services for the poor, who do not have the sort of disposable income that others use for bribes (see Dumont, 1980, 1986, 1991).

As his successive governments were repeatedly accused of corrupt practices (he was in power for almost 40 years!), Félix Houphouët-Boigny,[154] the late President of Côte d'Ivoire, remarked in his typical tribal chief style that one should not seek to look into the mouth of the peanut roaster, meaning that s/he who roasts peanuts is compelled to taste them every now and then. Put differently, one cannot expect a cook not to taste the food they are cooking. Hence, Africa managed to accommodate hoards of public servants and politicians, 'hearty' eaters, committed not just to tasting, but destructively and recklessly consuming the public sustenance. This urge to plunder has given rise to blatantly corrupt and ruthless regimes that do not hesitate to redraft the country's constitution to stay in power, as was the case in Togo with the late Gnassingbé Eyadéma and the former Zaire of Mobutu Sese Seko, and still is the case in Burkina Faso (with Blaise Compaoré) and Gabon (with Omar Bongo). Through an interesting examination of the family tree of William Tolbert, Jr, the late President of Liberia assassinated by Samuel Doe in 1980, Lamb notes that:

> Tolbert's brother-in-law Frank was President of the Senate;
> his brother Stephen was Minister of Finance;
> his sister Lucia was Mayor of Bentol City;
> his son A. B. was Ambassador at large;
> his daughter Wilhelmina was his own physician;
> his daughter Christine was Deputy Minister of Education;
> his niece Tula was his own dietician;
> his three nephews were:
> (1) Assistant Minister of Presidential Affairs;
> (2) Agricultural Attaché to Rome;
> (3) Vice-Governor of National Bank;
> and his six sons-in-law were:
> (1) Minister of Defence;
> (2) Deputy Minister of Public Works;
> (3) Commissioner for Immigration, Board Member of Air Liberia;
> (4) Ambassador to Guinea;
> (5) Senator;
> (6) Mayor of Monrovia. (Lamb, 1987: 9–10)

Although this example dates back a quarter of a century now, excesses such as these unfortunately remain the rule in many African countries, not the exception. Control of public life by one family still occurs in the Gabon of the Omar Bongo, in the Togo of Faure Gnassingbé and in the Congo of Sassou Nguesso.

According to a study published by the African Union (2002), corruption represents 25% of GDP or US$148 billion of Africa's annual GDP, increasing the cost of goods by as much as 20%. Africa also remains a net exporter of capital to European countries, and the amount of funds embezzled and now held in foreign banks is reported to be well over half of the continent's external debt (*UK Commission on Africa Report*, 2005). It is estimated that 40% of the private financial wealth of Africans is invested outside the continent. No less than 9 of the 16 most seriously corrupt nations (Trans International, 2006) and 11 of the 20 most vulnerable countries in the world (*Jeune Afrique*, 2006a) are on the African continent.[155] Examples of corrupt activities can be drawn from almost every African country.[156] In *Biens mal acquis ... profitent trop souvent. La fortune des dictateurs et les complaisances occidentales* (March 2007), the Comité Catholique contre la Faim et pour le Développement (CCFD, 2007) accuses the leaders of the developed world of facilitating the depositing of embezzled funds, estimated at US$200 billion, into bank accounts in their own countries.[157] Yet, developed countries, in the name of economic and geopolitical interest, have refused to cooperate when asked to return these funds to their rightful owners.[158]

Maladministration has therefore been rife in many countries for the last five decades, when a number of indigenous Africans, some of them still in power, and most of them having forced their way into power – generally through bloody military coups d'états – presided over the pillage and plunder of their own peoples, imprisoning and murdering any opponent, while siphoning off hundreds of millions – sometimes billions – of dollars into foreign bank accounts.[159] Maladministration reached an alarming and tragic level, when the economic capital of Côte d'Ivoire, Abidjan, became a toxic waste dumping ground in August 2006, as public authorities allowed a ship named Probo Koala to dump 528 tonnes of 'slops' (i.e. industrial toxic waste) containing hydrogen sulphide (H_2S, also known as rotten egg gas), mercaptans and sodium hydroxide (E524), killing at least 15 people and intoxicating 100,000 others, many of whom had to be hospitalised (*Soir Info*, Yao, 2006b; Fadegnon 2006).[160] The government of Prime Minister Konan Banny was forced to resign. The Probo Koala, which had been at sea for 8 months, had been refused the right to dock in many countries along the Coast of Guinea, before being given the green light by the Ivorian authorities to unload its deadly cargo at the Port of Abidjan.[161]

Such incidents are a direct result not only of a growing trend in developed countries, where shady waste management operators illegally export industrial waste (including refrigerators and televisions full of harmful gases, waste oils, waste of electrical and electronic equipment, used tyres, etc.) to poor countries in containers with dubious way bills, but also of the greed of the peanut roasters, who have grown bolder and greedier, and have no regard for the welfare and safety of the people.[162] The first wave of export of toxic waste to Africa from the United States and Europe was from the mid 1980s to the early 1990s, when countries like Angola, Benin, Congo

(Brazzaville), Djibouti, Guinea-Bissau, Nigeria, Senegal, Sierra-Leone and Somalia were affected.

Indeed, the Probo Koala incident reminds one of the 5600 liters of chlorine dumped in a small village, near Douala, the economic capital of Cameroon, in 2005. The authorities tried to dissolve the chlorine at sea, when tragedy struck; a soldier was killed and a dozen others were injured in an accidental explosion. It also reminds one of the poisoning of Koko Beach (Nigeria) in May 1988, when 8000 drums of hazardous chemical waste were sent to the small port town in Nigeria, and forced many to be hospitalised for severe chemical burns, nausea, vomiting blood and partial paralysis. Citing the Basle Convention on the Control of Trans-boundary Movements of Hazardous Wastes and their Disposal (March 22 1989), Greenpeace argued that vessels transporting toxic waste should not be allowed to leave Europe in the first place. Greeenpeace points the finger at global governance and bemoans the ugly face of globalisation, that of wolves in the sheep-pen, which again and again wreaks havoc with the weak and the defenceless of this global village by turning them into dumping grounds.

To be sure, fish does not just rot from the head; it mainly rots from the guts. In other words, corruption in Africa is not just a white collar crime, it is a pervasive practice among blue collar workers as well. The *beautyful* ones are truly yet to be born,[163] and there are still a lot of white men in black skins behaving badly all over Africa,[164] from customs officers and policemen who go to work, not to enforce the law, but to make more than their monthly salary in a day, to academics who leave the classroom for the comfort of air conditioned offices, to public servants who assume that it is for the public to serve them, to semi-literates who believe that speaking a European language, no matter how badly, is the passport to economic wealth and to politicians who feel no contrition in affirming that it is their turn to 'eat'.[165]

In October 2004, Kingsley Amoako, head of the United Nations Economic Commission for Africa, told African politicians gathered in Addis Ababa that they were failing their people because of corruption, tax, dilapidated public funds and services, accountability and transparency of civil servants. As a result, 'poverty in Africa is chronic and rising' (UNECA, 2005a: 1). Based on current demographic trends, Africa needs to create 8 million new jobs every year in order to absorb the rising numbers of job seekers (UNECA, 2005a: xiii), yet unemployment and underemployment have significantly increased (10.9% in 2003), especially when viewed in conjunction with the large numbers of working poor and those who have given up trying to find decent employment. Measured unemployment in sub-Saharan Africa alone was estimated at 29.4 million in 2003, with the highest unemployment rate being in Southern Africa (31.6%). Youth unemployment is worse, with at least 21% of youths in sub-Saharan Africa unemployed (this is 63% of the total unemployment). Even though youths represents only 33% of the labour force, they are 3.5 times more likely to be unemployed than adults (ILO, 2004). The working poor (mostly engaged in the informal sector and in agriculture) account for almost 45% of the total number of the employed (ILO, 2004), whilst an estimated 110 million people considered to be employed, actually earn wages well below the poverty line and are unable to provide their families decent living conditions (UNECA, 2005a: 7). In the developed world, governments are elected or thrown out of office on issues of poor economic results, poor literacy standards and mathematics skills in schools, widespread unemployment, hospital waiting lists or interest rates. Political campaigns are not just built around an ideology and style of government, but hinge on the political parties' programmes to address the issues that are of most concern to the people: health, education, (un)employment, the economy, etc. These standards of good governance have yet to be taken on board in many African countries.

Although they will accept that internal responsibilities in the lack of good governance are undeniable, some critics of this state of affairs still point out that one should not overlook other fundamental historical and structural factors that contribute to this situation (e.g. the debt burden). It would be naive and plain wrong to suggest that there is no one in Africa with the competence, willingness and integrity to help their people out of poverty. They are those Africans who ask: who chose Joseph Mobutu (as he was called back in the 1960s) over Patrice Lumumba, and aided and abetted his underhand dealings?[166] Who supported, maintained, encouraged and tolerated Jean-Bedel Bokassa, Hissène Habré and Gnassingbé Eyadéma? Who was it who said that 'democracy is a luxury for Africans?' How can one purport to promote human dignity, when one is unwilling to let others make their own choices and decide their own destiny?

Developed nations should support the development of democracy in Africa; but far too often they have aided and abetted the transfer or confiscation of political power from the barrel of a gun, through rebel groups, coups d'états, gross human rights violations and murder of political activists and innocent civilians and corruption. An interesting example of this was still playing itself out in Côte d'Ivoire in 2006, as a result of a failed coup d'état (19 September 2002), which quickly transformed itself into a pseudo-civil war, splitting the country into two, the south being under the control of government troops. Many in the Western press, mainly French, have been quick to conclude that this was the result of inter-ethnic and religious rivalries between the northern part of the country (mostly Muslim and Dyula-speaking), and the south (mostly Christian), blissfully overlooking the fact that the main protagonists on both side of the divide are a mix of Muslims and Christians,[167] that many people originally from the north of the country currently live in the south, many having taken refuge in the relatively more peaceful south after the start of the hostilities, that north–south mixed marriages between individuals from the north and south still hold, and that Dyula, a language originally from the north of the country, continues to enjoy its status of national lingua franca. Political scientists and economists will no doubt debate the truth, or lack thereof, of this pronouncement in years to come. The Cardinal of Côte d'Ivoire, Bernard Agré, for one, believes 'This Ivorian war has the strong smell of oil.[168] For students of language interested in the remarkable spread of Dyula in Côte d'Ivoire over the last 50 years, the debate itself is of no significance, because the political squabble pitting north against south, whether real or manufactured, has not seriously damaged the status of Dyula as a national lingua franca, at least for now. Indeed, Djité and Kpli (2007) believe that a presidential address calling for peace in two or three of the main regional languages of Côte d'Ivoire, including Dyula, would be a sign of great political leadership and will go a long way in helping to appease the population and heal the rift.

Getting rid of individual politicians and regimes not doing their bidding, and installing others that do, is still the dominant practice of some developed nations in Africa, a practice that overrides the principles of democracy and good governance and that leads many to ask: who is afraid of good governance in Africa? Indeed, anyone who wishes to proclaim his or herself a democrat should not impose anything on anyone else, and should renounce making kings and unseating them at their own will. After all, independence, democracy and development go hand in hand, and come down to having control over key sectors of the national economy and security, the capacity to transform one's own raw materials, the freedom to choose and diversify one's economic partners, and the awareness and freedom to act globally for one's own economic and strategic interests, without seeking the green light from Paris, London or Washington.

The problems of governance facing Africa are therefore a great challenge, and it would be simplistic and naive to argue that democracy and good governance will be assured once a balanced language policy, acknowledging the place and role of the local languages, is adopted. The case of Somalia, where there is yet to be a state, would immediately demonstrate the flaw of this kind of rationale. A balanced management of multilingualism is still conditioned by the level and quality of education, including language education, because the crux of the matter in governance is the exclusion and marginalisation, through language, of the majority of the people. As Bertrand Barère of the *Comité du salut public* once said: 'In a democracy, to leave the citizens ignorant of the national language, unable to exercise critical judgement over [government] power, this is to betray one's country' (cited in Adamson, 2007: 7). As long as European languages continue to maintain pride of place as the languages of governance and power, ignorance will prevail for the majority of the people, depriving the country of the contribution they could otherwise have made and making it impossible to achieve a viable democracy. Good governance is first and foremost the right of a people to participate in the formulation of decisions that affect their very existence; and language is the main vehicle through which one can effect active participation in the affairs of the land. At a time when the English language is largely perceived as the dominant international language, a reminder of its rise to officialdom illustrates once again what we can learn from history.

Language and Governance in Africa: When History Shows the Way

Even 200 years after the Norman Conquest, and even though Anglo-Norman was the language of ordinary interactions among the upper classes and most of the monarchs of England, English remained the language of the lower orders (Baugh, 1959), and did not begin to spread until the 14th century, when King Edward III proclaimed it the official language of the Courts. In the text of the proclamation, the King made it plain that the people needed to know the language through which they were being governed. The full text of the Statute of Pleading, itself in French, but later translated into English, reads as follows:

Because it is often shewed to the king by the prelates, dukes, earls, barons, and all the commonalty, of *the great mischiefs which have happened to divers of the realm, because the laws, customs, and statutes of this realm be not commonly known in the same realm; for that they be pleaded, shewed, and judged in the French tongue, which is much unknown in the said realm; so that the people which do implead, or be impleaded, in the king's court, and in the courts of others, have no knowledge nor understanding of that which is said for them or against them by their serjeants and other pleaders; and that reasonably the said laws and customs shall be most quickly learned and known, and better understood in the tongue used in the said realm, and by so much every man of the said realm may the better govern himself without offending of the law*, and the better keep, save, and defend his heritage and possessions; and in divers regions and countries, where the king, the nobles, and others of the said realm have been, *good governance and full right is done to every person, because that their laws and customs be learned and used in the tongue of the country: the king, desiring the good governance and tranquillity of his people,* and to put out and eschew the harms and mischiefs which do or may happen in this behalf by the occasions aforesaid, hath ordained and established by the assent aforesaid, that all pleas which shall be pleaded in his courts whatsoever, before any of his justices whatsoever, or in his other places, or before any of his other ministers whatsoever, or in the courts and places of any other lords whatsoever within the realm, shall be pleaded, shewed, defended, answered, debated, and judged in the English tongue, and that they be entered and enrolled in Latin. (*Statutes of the Realm of October* 1362, I: 375–76, cited in Baugh, 1959: 178; my italics)

The passages in italics could very well have been written in the 21st century in any African country, that is if the African politicians had the vision of King Edward III. Indeed, *great mischiefs,* as described above, are currently happening across the continent, because *the laws, customs and statutes* of African countries *are not commonly known* by the majority of the people they have been written for, and it would make sense, for *the good governance and tranquillity of* [the] *people,* to ensure that *the said laws and customs ... be most quickly learned and known, and better understood in the tongue used* by the people. It is interesting to note that, at the time of this proclamation, the King relied essentially on a small bureaucracy of about 120 clerks who began using English as the main language of record keeping and, in so doing, contributed to its standardisation in grammar and orthography until the advent of printing (from 1476), which consolidated the process (Grillo, 1989: 155).

Good governance was also the main concern of the Ordonnance of Villers-Cottêret of 1539 in France. Article III of this Ordonnance reads:

And because such things [doubts and uncertainties] frequently occurred in connection with the interpretation of Latin words contained in the said decrees, we wish that henceforth all judgements, together with all other proceedings, whether of our sovereign courts and other subordinate and inferior courts, or accounts, inquiries, contracts, warrants, wills and any other acts and processes of justice or such as result from them, be pronounced, recorded and issued to the parties in the French mother tongue, and in no other way. (Grillo, 1989: 28)[169]

Other examples of change in language status, functions and roles include the Romans' shift from Greek to Latin, when they ruled over western and Mediterranean Europe, as well as the global shift in Europe from Latin to 'modern' European languages. Weber (1924: 289) explains in his *Wirtschaft und Gesellschaft: Grundriss der verstehenden Soziologie* that the inability of most Chinese mandarins to understand the dialects of the provinces they administered was one of the reasons why no 'rational state' could develop in China. Examples of good governance in Africa, through the use of the languages of the peoples, can be drawn from the pre-colonial kingdoms and empires, which could not resort to European languages.

History therefore teaches us that language can be the source of 'unequal relations of power' (Fairclough, 2001: 1), and that it is mistaken to claim that any language is neutral. The argument according to which development in Africa can be achieved only through a European language has essentially resulted in the crystallisation of closed oligarchies oriented mainly to self-aggrandisement, the maintenance of power and prestige and the continuation of political instability (Djité, 1988). A European language in Africa, in its standard form, is selectively spread within the elite and has not helped overcome communication problems, and those who speak and write European languages have better access to information and therefore to power, whilst the masses cannot participate actively and democratically in all aspects of their own lives, let alone in the affairs of the state. This 'elite closure' (Myers-Scotton, 1993), or linguistic stratification along the lines of European language versus African languages, coupled with the association between the European language as the language of the elite and the African languages as the languages of the masses, leads to inequity, and favours a minority over the majority of the people. Furthermore, the elite, whose status is largely dependent on their proficiency in European languages, manipulate language policy to maintain their positions of power in society, thereby denying the majority access to knowledge and know-how, and full and active participation in the exercise of power, hence depriving them of the benefits generated by all. Alexandre showed a keen understanding of what was at stake in the imposition of a so-called 'neutral and beneficial' language (Pennycook, 1994: 9), when he wrote:

> Power, it is true, is in the hands of this minority [the elite]. Herein lies one of the most remarkable sociological aspects of contemporary Africa: that the kind of class structure which seems to be emerging is based on linguistic factors. (Alexandre, 1972: 86)

Alexander confirmed this observation three decades later, when he noted:

> ... the neo-colonial language policy is an important aspect of the middle class policy of neo-colonial regimes; it empowers the few against the interests and the rights of the many and helps to create and maintain a

vicious circle of the poor majority becoming poorer and ever more marginalised and the rich few becoming ever richer and self-glorifying. (Alexander, 2003: 24)

Therefore, it is ignorant, naive, hypocritical, or all these at once, to say that, in Africa, the European language is used 'as the language of choice for official transactions, to avoid giving any one of many historically established languages priority over the others' (Walter, 1998). Pursuing a monolingual policy, especially in multilingual Africa, equates to limiting information dissemination such that important matters are kept away from the people and available only to those who are proficient in a European language. Language is a key to social advancement at the individual and the collective levels and a means by which the participation of the people in the democratic process can be facilitated or hindered (Bamgbose, 2000). The lack of knowledge of or proficiency in the official language of the state can prevent or impede socio-economic mobility. The current language policy practices in most of Africa deny individuals direct participation in public interaction and, as a result, put the brakes on an open system of governance in which those in positions of power are not accountable to the masses. This state of affairs results in the wastage of human capital by way of a depleted workforce – since the language of the workplace excludes the majority, and since even those who work have to use a language in which they are not always competent. This in turn leads to massive unemployment, reduced productivity, poverty, and underdevelopment.

Seven centuries after King Edward III's proclamation, a number of United Nations bodies and organisations (e.g. UNDP and UNECA) now define development in terms of local participation. The 2004 UNDP Human Development report, and the very concept of Human Development Index, highlights the necessity of bringing issues of language into focus; because 'Human development is first and foremost about allowing people to lead the kind of life they choose – and providing them with the tools and opportunities to make those choices'.[170] According to the 1986 United Nations Declaration on the Right to Development, the individual is at the centre of development, and all human rights, including civil and political rights, are indivisible and worthy of equal attention. Failure to observe civil and political rights, as well as cultural and social rights, constitutes an obstacle to development.

Instead, everywhere one looks, innovative knowledge, social prestige and economic advancement are linked to proficiency in a European language. In spite of the motherhood statements about the importance of local languages that are inscribed in various instruments (e.g. constitutions, official language policies, language-in-education policies), there is a gap between the letter of the law and actual practice when it comes to the use of local languages in the exercise of power. A case in point: whilst both Kirundi and French were declared the official languages of Burundi in Article 21 of the 1961 constitution and Article 3 of the 1974 constitution, Article 7 of the 1981 constitution and Article 8 of the 1992 constitution read as follows: '*La langue national est le kirundi. Les langues officielles sont le kirundi et d'autres langues déterminées par la loi*' ['The National Language is Kirundi. The Official Languages are Kirundi and other languages as specified by the Law']. In other words, the last two versions of the constitution make no mention of French. This provision was taken a step further in Article 5 of the constitution of 2005, which reads as follows:

> *La langue nationale est le kirundi. Les langues officielles sont le kirundi et toutes autres langues déterminées par la loi. Tous les textes législatifs doivent avoir leur version originale en kirundi.* [The national language is Kirundi. Official Languages are Kirundi and other languages as specified by the Law. All legislative texts must have an original version drafted in Kirundi.]

At the end of 2005, the National Council for the Defence of Democracy (CNDD), the main opposition party of Burundi, introduced a bill asking for Article 5 of the constitution of 18 March, 2005 be adhered to, and the government to ensure that all the laws of Burundi that have yet to be translated into Kirundi are finally translated into the official language of the land. Furthermore, in February 2006, in an official letter to members of the government, the President of the National Assembly requested that all government bills brought into Parliament be drafted in Kirundi. The President of the country finally responded to these requests in June 2006, promising that all draft laws and/or existing laws will be drafted and/or translated into Kirundi. That such a matter should require so many changes to the constitution of Burundi and be the subject of ongoing political debate is quite puzzling, if not revealing of the nexus between language and governance in Africa. After all, speakers of French in Burundi are estimated at only 3 to 10% of the total population, a figure that includes some 700,000 French nationals living in the country, and Kirundi is spoken by virtually the entire population of Burundi.

But it would be unfair to single out one country to illustrate the nature of the relationship between African and European languages, at least in terms of how these are dealt with by African governments. Most African countries continue to rely on exoglossic languages, including countries like Botswana, Burundi, Lesotho, Malawi, Rwanda and Swaziland that have local languages as national languages, but do not actively pursue an endoglossic policy (Heine, 1992). Some exoglossic countries, like Kenya, have adopted a bilingual policy in which the mother tongue is used as the language of instruction in the first three years of education and a European language for the higher levels of education. In these situations, the mother tongue is usually relegated to a less important role after these first three years.[171] This is in spite of estimates of speakers of European languages (English, French, Portuguese and Spanish) in any African country over the last 50 years hardly exceeding 20% and sometimes reaching as low as 5% (Bamgbose, 1971: 38–39; Heine, 1992: 27; Heugh, 1999: 75–76). In a number of cases, the politicians who hide under the cloak of the mastery of a European language, including some Heads of State, are themselves hardly proficient in the said language. On the other hand, most politicians in Africa speak at least one local language, and sometimes a lingua franca, and they use local languages as tools of mass mobilisation during political campaigns, when they need to reach the majority of the people. Only Tanzania, Ethiopia and Somalia stand out as examples of countries that have adopted a local language in almost all aspects of governance.

Nevertheless, there is growing evidence of a reversal of attitude in a number of countries. In South Africa, when the Rules Committee of the South African Parliament made a proposal that English should become the sole language of record in Parliament, in order to cut down on costs, the Multilingualism Action Group issued a Media Statement against the proposed policy, pointing out that multilingualism is one of the democratic values enshrined in the constitution, and that, as it is, the use of English excludes 'the majority of South Africans who are poor and marginalised and do not understand English'. The statement concluded as thus: 'A multilingual country with a monolingual government cannot be called a democracy' (*Multilingual Action Group*, 2003, cited in Bamgbose, 2005b).

Conclusion

The nexus between language, governance and development has been of concern to visionary leaders of nations from time immemorial. These leaders have come to the realisation that democracy means that people who make decisions must be accountable to those who are affected by these decisions and that, when people are excluded from the decision-making process, when they lack access to political institutions, they are unable to affect the policies adopted by those institutions. Capable, responsive governments are a prerequisite for good governance and development. Good governance is not just about stamping out corruption and/or nepotism; it is about governments making sure that they do not fail the most

vulnerable citizens; that they do not work against the interest of the
majority of the people. The solutions offered by King Edward III in England
in the 14th century, and François I in France two centuries later sought to
provide opportunities for participation through language empowerment.[172] In contrast, the current practices of governance in Africa, both local
and imposed from the outside, essentially seek to dis-empower the people
in order to further marginalise them. Alternatives have to be found to these
practices, if Africa is ever to achieve a reasonable level of development.

Multilingualism is neither an impediment to a viable democracy, nor is it
an obstacle to development. Many languages have already carved out a
role for themselves in society, some in transactions at the local level, others
at a state level and yet others at a national level. A number of cross-border
languages can already be used as instruments of political and economic
integration (Hyltenstam & Stroud, 2004; Omoniyi, 2004: 153–189). All that
is lacking is political will, especially at national level. In any event, a reduction of multilingualism is not likely to reduce the current state of underdevelopment in Africa.

It is encouraging though that some efforts in this regard are being made
at the continental level. Hence, a meeting of language experts endorsed by
African Ministers of Education and culture agreed that language policies
'should be construed within the broader context of democratisation in
Africa'. Accordingly, the following recommendations were made:

(1) a democratic Africa *that seeks to enhance the active participation of all citi-
     zens in all institutions* – social, economic, political, etc.;
(2) a democratic *Africa where development is not construed in narrow
     economic goals but instead in terms of culturally valued ways of living
     together;* and within a broader context of justice, fairness and equality
     for all; *respect for linguistic rights as human rights, including those of
     minorities;*
(3) in broader terms, an *Africa that acknowledges its ethno-linguistic
     pluralism and accepts this as a normal way of life and as a rich resource for
     development* and progress;
(4) a democratic Africa that seeks to promote peaceful coexistence of a
     people in *a society where pluralism does not entail replacement of one
     language or identity by another,* but instead promotes complementarity
     of functions as well as cooperation and a sense of common destiny;
(5) an Africa where *democratisation in a pluralistic context seeks to produce
     through sound and explicit language policies Africans who are able to operate
     effectively at local levels* as well as at regional and international levels;
(6) a democratic *Africa that provides the environment for the promotion and*

preservation of an African identity as well as the cultivation of a proud and confident African personality;

(7)   an *Africa where scientific and technological discourse is conducted in the national languages* as part of our cognitive preparation for facing the challenges of the next millennium (Chimhundu, 1997: 44; my italics).

The passages in italics enunciate the same principles as those of Kings François I and of Edward III before him. Chimhundu comments on these recommendations by stressing that the aim is to respond 'to the real needs of the people' and goes on to ask:

How can you fully participate in anything, or compete, or learn effectively or be creative in a language in which you are not fully proficient or literate? Above all, how can a country develop its human resource base to full potential without the languages of the people? (Chimhundu, 1997: 63)

In December 2005, the First Ordinary Session of the Conference of African Union Ministers of Culture, meeting in Nairobi (Kenya), issued a Declaration on Culture, Integration and African Renaissance, which states the following in Item 6 of its 14 recommendations:

Encourage any policy which is in favour of the development of African languages, and especially their use in education, and improve communication and the participation of all in cultural life, in accordance with the requirements of a democratic society. (AUCMC, 2005; my translation from the French)

The African Union has gone even further with an initiative of the former President of Mali, Alpha Oumar Konaré, which established an African Academy of Languages (ACALAN). The goals of ACALAN are: the revalorisation of African languages, the adoption of these languages as media of instruction and intellectualisation, the dissemination of information for active participation in the democratic process and in increased productivity and economic growth. Among other priorities, ACALAN lists (Alexander, 2005):

(1)   terminology development;
(2)   standardisation of orthographies;
(3)   literacy and continuing education in African languages;
(4)   development of high-quality and standardised teaching materials inthe major languages of communication;
(5)   making use, wherever possible, of popular media in electronic form and in print, to further spread the use of African languages in all contexts.

As mentioned in the introduction, NEPAD also considers democracy to be one of the measures that need to be put in place if Africa is to develop. NEPAD's blueprint, like most economically-inspired documents, does not explicitly refer to language. However, a successful implementation of NEPAD's programme cannot rely on monolingual language policies if it really aims to generate some form of people-oriented development. Students of language will always be puzzled by the fact that, having come to the realisation of the importance of language in governance and development, and having established all these instruments, many governments still adopt a 'business as usual' attitude.[173] The challenge in Africa has always been the ability to transform political rhetoric into action.

Fortunately, examples are beginning to emerge in Africa, showing that bringing the issue of language back to the fore of the governance and development debate in Africa is not a simple idle fancy – and has never been so!. In 2005, in order to involve the masses in the democratic process in the Democratic Republic of Congo (the DRC), the DRC and the Electoral Institute for Southern Africa produced translations of the draft constitution in four local languages: Lingala, Ciluba, Kikongo and KiSwahili. Likewise, in Côte d'Ivoire, in 2006, the relevant documents for the identification process that was to lead up to democratic and transparent elections were translated in some of the main languages of the country. In November 2006, a speech by the country's acting Prime Minister was also translated in 6 languages.[174] It is indeed through such initiatives that the majority of the people get to find the voice that the exclusive use of a European language suppresses. Democracy and good governance will not be achieved in a linguistic vacuum. Only when the people find their voice can they effectively make a contribution to the running of their own affairs and make their political representatives accountable. Economic and political accountability by the people and for the people will go a long way towards ensuring economic growth and development. According to the UNDP, poor people desire much more than increased income; they also desire:

> ... good and safe working conditions, freedom to choose jobs and livelihoods, freedom of movement and speech, liberation from oppression, violence and exploitation, security from persecution and arbitrary arrest, a satisfying family life, the assertion of cultural and religious values, adequate leisure time and satisfying forms of its use, a sense of purpose in life and work, the opportunity to join and actively participate in the activities of civil society and a sense of belonging to a community. (UNDP, 1999: 17)

Conclusion

But if my life is for rent and I don't learn to buy
Well I deserve nothing more than I get
Cos nothing I have is truly mine.
Armstrong & Armstrong (2003)

Everybody talks about a new world in the morning,
New world in the morning taking so long ...
Whittaker (1974)

Introduction

Although Africa is one of the best-endowed regions of the world, it is still the least developed. The cradle of humanity is known only for major calamities, wars, political instability, poverty, epidemics. In the late 1980s, the UNECA (1989) was already sending warning signals about the persistent and generalised decline in economic activity, social well-being and standard of living, and recommending that African governments reassess their development strategies by rejecting programmes that focus on the symptoms, rather than on the fundamental causes of the economic malaise. Noting the persistence of a number of major dysfunctions and challenges (e.g. the trade barriers imposed by developed countries, the farm subsidies, the burden of foreign debt, the dependence on exportable raw materials and the health crisis), the 2003 UNDP Human Development Report warned that sub-Saharan Africa may not achieve its poverty-reduction objectives until 2147! (UNDP, 2003; 33).[175] This message was again reinforced by Asha-Rose Migiro, the Deputy General Secretary of the United Nations, in early June 2007, in view of the moderate growth rates (5.5% in 2006, and possibly 6% in 2007). And upon its inception on the eve of the new millennium, having estimated the annual amount Africa needs to overcome poverty at US$64 billion, NEPAD was expressing the view that most of this amount will have to come from external sources such as debt relief and increased development assistance in the short and medium term, as well as from private capital contributions in the long term. Noting that unemployment (estimated at over 10%) 'is one of the greatest challenges to Africa's development', the UNECA, in its *2005 Economic Report on Africa*

(UNECA, 2005b: xiii), urges African governments to urgently address the need to 'create more employment and thus tackle the scourge of hunger, malnutrition and the overall low living standards the continent continues to witness'. More significantly, the Report states that: 'The poverty rate has remained practically stable on the continent for the past two decades, even as it declined in other developing regions. In real numbers, at least 61 million more Africans go hungry today than they did in 1990' (UNECA, 2005b: xiii). The Report goes on to say that it is not enough to have growth rates averaging 5%, when this growth is not equitably distributed in order to reduce poverty in real terms. It further admits that, in spite of some improvements in economic growth and governance over recent years, Africa is still characterised by:

- sluggish economic growth that lags behind the 7% growth rate needed to achieve the Millennium development goal of reducing poverty on the continent by 2015;
- debilitating conflicts and wars that exacerbate human deprivation, social crises and poverty;
- government systems that are still very weak;
- a health crisis that is threatening the very existence of its people.

Fifty years on, one cannot help but ask: how much longer will Africa have to depend on others to feed her own children, provide them basic health services, send them to school and find them rewarding jobs? When will all these vulnerabilities (i.e. material poverty, poor health, illiteracy, lack of education, linguistic, economic and political marginalisation) come to an end? Will the African elite alone be able to face up to these challenges and bring them under control without the input of the majority of the people?

Poverty on the sort of scale we have discussed here, in the areas of economic growth, education and health, demands a forceful response or, more specifically, capacity-building strategies that must take full account of the continent's diversity in its people and languages and must tackle exclusion. The well-being of all African people, even the poorest of the poor, has intrinsic value. It is in giving them a basic standard of living, in ensuring basic education and health services for all, through languages that can improve the delivery of such services, that Africa will begin to move towards sustained and sustainable development.

Why the Sociolinguistics of Development?

Early in the 20th century, Ferdinand de Saussure warned that outside of language 'no other subject has focused more absurd notions, more prejudices, more illusions and more fantasies ... ' He further observed that '[It] is the primary task of the linguist to denounce them, and to eradicate them as completely as possible' (de Saussure, 1916/1986: 7). Nevertheless, the mythologising of and about language, especially in Africa, has gone on unabated, in the form of pseudo-scholarly treatises, with the imprimatur of individuals, some of whom have come to be known as 'Africanists' (Chaudenson, 1989; *Fraternité Matin*, 1980; Dumont 1990).[176] It is to these Africanists that we owe the widespread assumptions on the inferiority and intrinsic lexical and structural inadequacy of African languages handed down from colonial and neo-colonial times (for 'primitive' peoples speak 'primitive' languages) and congruent with race theories (Gobineau, 1853–1855; Herrntein & Murray, 1994) that are part and parcel of the imperialist construction of political, cultural and racial hegemony (DeGraff, 2003: 391). One is therefore faced with dogmatic evidence, by way of skilful perception management (for lack of a better word), proving Bourdieu's point that 'every theory ... is a programme of perception ... ' (Bourdieu, 1980/1990: 1).

Hence the status of European languages in Africa is based on perceptions rather than on realities, and their purported spread, significance and usefulness for the African masses are inflated in terms of number of speakers, and mainly reinforced through the mass media. The subservience to these languages is presented as an asset that makes economic sense, and a strength and social norm for the educated and worldly, as these are the only languages with the adequate vocabulary to express modern scientific concepts and their most recent technological developments. If the ambivalence of the masses towards their own languages is due in part to ignorance, it is deeply rooted in these colonial and neo-colonial myths, based on articles of faith, rather than on science.

Calvet (1987) described the brutal and well-documented methods used in the 1970s to promote Russian and displace the local languages in the former Soviet Republics, mainly through the educational systems. There is virtually no student of language who would today argue that dictating language policies in the Soviet republics worked. Similarly, dictating language policies in African countries over the last 50 years has not worked; and it is amazing that some would still persist in their belief that Africa has no alternative but to acquiesce to the imposition of European languages on the continent.

The sociolinguistics of development seeks to introduce a paradigm shift in the analysis of the language situation in Africa, whereby sociolinguistic research is complemented and informed by an interdisciplinary approach that includes historical, socio-political, educational, economic and health analyses. The root causes of Africa's predicament do not all lie in economic growth, as economic growth itself does not – and will not – occur in a vacuum. The sociolinguistics of development argues that language constitutes a major factor, not only in economic growth, but also in all the other aspects of socio-economic and political structure of a polity. Language also constitutes the common thread that links all of these aspects together; so much so that, except for analytical purposes, it makes no sense to try to dissociate education from health, education from good governance, health from the state of the economy and economic growth from good governance and democracy. The sociolinguistics of development rests on the age-old linguistic principle that every language is normal, just like the processes that create language in the minds of the native speakers (Chomsky, 1966, 1975; DeGraff, 2003: 402). 'The human mind is the same in every clime; and accordingly we find nearly the same process adopted in the formation of language in every country' (Greenfield, 1830: 51f.), and 'reason is by nature equal in all men' (Descartes 1637, cited in Chomsky 1966). Thus, 'when it comes to linguistic form, Plato walks with the Macedonian swineherd, Confucius with the head-hunting savage of Assam' (Sapir, 1921: 219). Speakers of any language create vocabulary items needed to fulfil their evolving representation and communication requirements (Sapir 1921: 223). The sociolinguistics of development therefore works on the premise that Francophilia or Anglophilia is an illusory tool for nation building. It goes beyond this linguistic idealism to trace and be guided by the concept of development itself, in its most contemporaneous and widely accepted definition. For, if language is at the core of development, it still remains for those who seek to achieve it to understand what it is they are striving for.

Development, not Anglicisation, Francisation or Lusophonisation

Mazrui (2001) defines development as 'modernisation minus dependency', modernisation itself having been defined as 'change which is compatible with the present state of human knowledge, which seeks to comprehend the legacy of the past, which is sensitive to the needs of future generations, and responsive to its global context'. He goes on to suggest that 'indigenised' modernisation would include greater use of African languages in the pursuit of scientific, economic and constitutional change. Mazrui further notes that:

> No country has ascended to a first rank technological and economic power by excessive dependence on foreign languages. Japan rose to dazzling industrial heights by [sic] the Japanese language and making it the medium of its own industrialisation. Korea has approximately

scientificated [*sic*] the Korean language and made it the medium of its own technological take-off. (Mazrui, 2001: 31)

Hence, 'when two Japanese physicists meet to discuss a problem in physics, it is now possible for them to discuss it in the Japanese language;' however, 'when two African economists (let alone physicists) meet to discuss economics, even if they come from the same linguistic group in Africa, [...] they can only discuss advanced economics or physics in a European language' (Mazrui, 2001: 31). Moreover, of all the Africans who have won the Nobel Prize for literature, the only black laureate, Wole Soyinka of Nigeria, cannot write in his native tongue, Yoruba. Mazrui concludes that 'for the foreseeable future, the Nobel Prize for literature is unlikely to be awarded for brilliant use of an indigenous African language.'

Ki Zerbo (2003) also criticises this Africa that is helped by developed countries to only seek to live on imported values, as if Africa had nothing positive to offer. He sees the imposition of European languages as part and parcel of this self-destruction, for a people who give up their language are certain to lose their culture and wonders whether this slow erosion of African cultures will not result in a 'flat encephalogram' (Ki Zerbo, 2003: 160)

The importance of maintaining and even fostering linguistic pluralism in Africa is not just a matter of language rights or humanistic approach to development. It goes to the heart of the welfare of the majority of the people, the ones who can actually produce (not just consume!), and can effectively put an end to a situation of increasing dependency on the West. A politically unstable and famine-stricken Africa is of no use to itself or to anyone else (Djité, 1993). If by development we mean a technico-economic and a socio-political change, then this sort of change cannot be divorced from the people and from the realities of these people. Innovativeness and creativity can be expressed in African languages, and these languages can help speed up the process of popularising new ideas and techniques in education, the economy, health and good governance. They can be a determining factor of progress. The results of agricultural research can be put in the hands of the grassroots, who will be able to develop sophisticated skills in the adaptation of new techniques. Africa does not have to depend on hired experts to conceive and offer development strategies and exercise the right of citizenship, in lieu of the 'numerous locally more accessible authorities' (Ray, 1968: 764). What this requires, among other things, is the use of the appropriate medium of transmission of knowledge and know-how between the grassroots and the extension service personnel. Instructions for use on household and agriculture machinery, canned food such as baby milk, basic information on agricultural techniques, domestic economy, local management, preservation and marketing of traditional artefacts and basic civic instruction, are all areas that, in this way, can be affected positively and efficiently. Development does not have to be assumed to be some Western concept and/or model that can be attained only through the use of a European language. It is now widely acknowledged that developing countries should be allowed to pursue development policies, especially macro-economic policies, in a flexible manner. Such policies should be cognizant of the specific situation of each country (see UNCTAD's 2006 *Trade and Development Report*). It is significant that, whilst African countries are debating the merits of multilingualism, the rest of the world, with the European Council in the leading pack, has come full circle within a few decades, and is reclaiming societal multilingualism and richness that it brings in terms of human and cultural diversity.

Living on Borrowed Tongues?[177] A Note of Caution

The main argument throughout this book is that African speech communities will be empowered when they can live and operate in their own mother tongues, and when these mother tongues are actively promoted and used at all levels and in all functions of society. A logical corollary of this argument is that empowerment through African languages presupposes that the use of European languages are a cause of disempowerment for these speech communities. There is enough research evidence to suggest that this is indeed the case. However, these findings, and the continued push for a balanced management of multilingualism in Africa have raised questions in the minds of many, including some Africans, who express fears that raising the status of African languages could ultimately lead to the banning and subsequent marginalisation of European languages.

A cursory survey of the language repertoires of the average African suggests that the reality is much more complex. Speech communities in most of Africa, especially in the urban areas, have undergone substantial socio-economic and linguistic changes, and these have had a considerable impact on their language practices. A new generation of Africans, through no fault of its own, has grown up – and is growing up – speaking European languages more often than the previous generations of African parents and grandparents. Indeed, an increasing number of privileged individuals in this new generation (mostly children of the middle class), and their own children speak no other language than the European language passed down to them by their parents, within the home. This new generation justifiably considers the European language as their mother tongue and will not take kindly to any suggestion that it is 'living on borrowed tongues'. Who are we to tell members of this new African generation that speaks French or English as their first language(s) that they are suffering some form of disempowerment through language, and that they will have to revert to speaking an African language? The use of the European language was subsequently strengthened by the educational system and the prevailing language policies in many countries that give preference and rewards to those who have mastered the official (European) language. Hence the European language, or its simplified and popular variety, is very much part and parcel of Africa's multilingualism in the 21st century. It is an alternative that reflects the reality of the linguistic market, a response to the sociolinguistic constraints that have been placed on the African people and under which some lucky few were able to empower themselves. Therefore, language management in the 21st century and beyond will need to be cognisant of this complexity of multiple language repertoires and elusive identity.

In as much as linguistic identity is determined by historical, linguistic and psychological factors and does not mean withdrawing into oneself and rejection of the Other, balanced management of Africa's multilingualism will have to acknowledge, integrate, protect and celebrate the new Africans that some of us have become. African linguistic identity has never been affirmed through the denial of linguistic difference, and the richness of diversity must not be limited to indigenous languages. It will have to be extended to the European languages (such as French, English, Portuguese and Spanish), which were subsequently acquired, as well as their popular varieties (a form of empowerment through language), which are now spoken across the continent. Africa is not about to open up to the Other; for the Other is already part of us, in as much as we are part of the Other, and our true identity is being conquered and constructed, together with the Other. It is only as liberated individuals that we can undertake to build a new African society, capable of looking after itself.

Conclusion

Baldauf and Luke (1990) have pointed out that it is important to relate aspects of historical, social, political and economic forces to the shaping of language planning. That is what this book tries to do, by examining the place and role of language(s) in education, health, the economy and governance. In so doing, it has tried to argue that language policies cannot be made based on assumptions but, rather, should be built on the existing patterns of language use and language attitudes in the countries and communities concerned.

If one of the prolegomena to language planning in Africa is the revision of the present language classification, the other is the maintenance, development and management of its multilingualism, through a balanced and naturalistic approach to the questions of language planning and language-in-education policies. This book argues that the major patterns of actual language choice and use by the population in interethnic communication should take precedence over the obsession of a few to maintain a status quo that, in the long run, could be detrimental to everyone. The actual sociolinguistic realities, those that are to the long-term advantage of the masses, have been overlooked for too long, with disastrous educational, social, economic and political consequences. Nationism is not a gloss for forced and inadequate imposition of an international language. Attending to world affairs presupposes attending to one's own affairs first, and this is why emphasis should be placed on the most efficient ways to overcome the current state of affairs.

In making this point, it is not being suggested that social policy alone can change the economic environment or all the underlying problems that contribute to poverty and slow overall growth in Africa. What is being advocated is that the masses need to acquire the tools or assets that will give them access to the economic opportunities not otherwise available to them. The masses have to become the 'engines' that drive economic growth and development; without them, the economy will run out of puff. In Africa, the economy of many countries has already run out of puff. Hence, for the African people to be given the chance to improve their productivity implies some form of social policy. Therefore, social policy, understood as empowering the masses to increase their ability to acquire human capital (e.g. access to health services, education, land and credit), must be at the heart of any development strategy. Increasing public spending on health and education programs will go a long way in achieving this goal. Making these health and education programs available to the majority of the people in the language(s) they know best will make great (socio-economic and political) sense. Knowledge is power, but knowledge has to be acquired through language. And when the majority of the people are systematically excluded from having the opportunity to acquire knowledge, then they are indeed disempowered; and when the majority of the people in a nation are disempowered, the whole nation is disabled and relegated to the squalor of underdevelopment.

There is no doubt that the adoption of a national or official language or a medium of instruction is always a complex process that requires the balancing of political and practical considerations, and that implementing a new language policy and language-in-education policy will incur considerable costs. Paying for what is worth the cost is the choice many countries and communities around the world, including the European Union, Canada, Belgium, Switzerland and Israel, have made.

While education, health, the economy and governance are, each in their own right, pillars of sustainable development, they remain pieces of a much larger puzzle in Africa's struggle to break out of its current state of poverty and misery. If one of the greater resources of Africa is its people, the other is language. Sustainable development will not be achieved at the expense of the people of Africa, or at the expense of their languages. It will occur only when the majority of the people are educated enough, healthy enough, materially secure and aware of what is at stake to be able to take their destiny in their own hands. Fifty years of trying have shown that it is highly doubtful that these objectives can be achieved in a European language. How many more centuries can Africans afford to wait? Everyone is agreed that Africa needs to develop its own productive capacity, and that it can only do so efficiently through its own people. The actors of change remain the African people themselves; they are the ones who have to become more knowledgeable of new technologies and be able to take them up and adapt them to their needs and realities. They are the ones that will make Africa a developed continent, and it is most unwise to force upon them foreign linguistic and development models divorced from the local realities and that betray the very essence of their existence. As Devonish puts it:

> The language variety spoken as the language of everyday communication by the ordinary members of a community is the most effective language medium for releasing creativity, initiative and productivity among the members of such community. Such a language is also the most effective means of promoting popular participation in, and control of, the various decision-making bodies within the state. (Devonish, 1986: 35)

This reality is now widely recognised, even amongst those who felt that the White Man's Burden was to impose his language to the peoples of Africa. Pointing to the economic impact of using a non-native language, Jean-François Dehecq, Chief Executive of Sanofi-Aventis, goes so far as to assert:

> ... If you force people to speak in English, those who are native speakers function at 100% of their potential, those who speak it very well as a second language are at 50% of their potential, and the majority of people function at 10% of their potential. (Interview with *L'Expansion* magazine cited in Barbotin, 2004; my own translation)

It would be naive to believe that the use of African languages alone or their promotion to official status in the domains of education, health, the economy and governance will suddenly reverse the tragic situation that Africa faces, and the long-standing negative attitudes towards these languages. But to act in the next 50 years as if the linguistic situation of Africa was a foregone conclusion would be a mistake that could lead to even more tragic consequences than the current predicament. The denials of responsibility and the blame games have lasted for too long. The time has come to face up to the challenges of the present and plan for the future with courage, determination and intellectual probity. Historical wrongs, such as slavery, do not make present injustices by African governments on their own people right. As Léger (1987: 153) writes:

> The times we live in will be ruthless for the weak and the indecisive. Those who aren't able to master technological progress, assimilate, and enrich it with their own contribution, shall be dominated by it. And we all know that technology is not neutral and that it embodies the civilisation of the country it was created in. (Léger, 1987: 153; my own translation)[178]

There is much more to Africa than suffering and dim horizons, and there is no use bemoaning the past, as mutterings of one's discontent cannot be equated with actions. Beyond the figures, one has to look to the people of Africa for answers. If this book seems to have emphasised the failures, this was only to show the extent to which the current model of development is not working and how, in spite of this, the people of Africa are still managing to survive, maintaining and developing their own languages in the face of unimaginable odds. Africa tomorrow must refuse to be a prisoner of her past and must turn to the future resolutely; but the future will be fraught with difficulties, unless and until the language question is tackled with some degree of purpose and realism. Isn't it remarkable that the Church in Africa – especially the Catholic Church – well-known for its conservatism, was able to reconcile its reticence to change its Judeo-Christian traditions and embrace African languages and cultures, in order to make the Christian spiritual experience truly meaningful to the faithful? Why then is it that the same languages that can speak the language of the sacred texts and spread the word of God are not being used as media of dissemination of information to the masses?

Notes

1. In Sartre's view, only the oppressed can tell the truth about his plight.
2. The manuscripts are scattered in various locations in Timbuktu and its surroundings (only 18,000 of an estimated 700,000 manuscripts are in the Ahmed Baba Research Centre) and virtually exposed to the elements of the desert. In brittle condition, they have always been in urgent need of restoration, preservation, translation and publication. On the occasion of a state visit to Mali in 2001, the President of South Africa, Thabo Mbeki, offered to help the Malian government to preserve some 200,000 of these manuscripts. The two countries have set a five-year period to upgrade the Ahmed Baba Research Centre and finance the building of a new library at an estimated total cost R36 million (The South Africa-Mali Timbuktu Manuscripts Trust). The preservation of the manuscripts has become a South African Presidential Project, coordinated by the Presidency and the Department of Arts and Culture, through the National Archives in Pretoria. They have also been earmarked as the first official cultural project on the New Partnership for Africa's Development (NEPAD). The project is funded by the government of Luxembourg, the Norwegian Agency for Development Cooperation (NORAD), the Ford Foundation, the Norwegian Council for Higher Education's Programme for Development Research and Education (NUFU), and the United States Ambassador's Fund for Cultural Preservation. The Cooperative Africana Microfilm Project (CAMP) has digitised 200 of these manuscripts.
3. Fasold (1984: 7) adds that 'there is a definite relationship between linguistic uniformity and economic development'. Gellner (1983: 35) also locates the roots of linguistic homogenisation in 'the distinctive structural requirements of industrial society'. Coulmas writes:

    Language is an asset. But this must not be taken to mean that a multiplicity of languages is conducive to social wealth. Rather, the inverse connection seems to suggest itself and has, indeed been interpreted as a causal rather than merely an accidental correlation [...]. It is ruled out that a high level of socio-economic development is compatible with linguistic fragmentation. (Coulmas 1992: 25)

    He further asserts that:

    The underdevelopment of the languages of the Third World countries is an indication and part of their economic underdevelopment, since these languages cannot, on a level comparable to the Western common languages, enhance national unity, nor do they exhibit the differentiation necessary for a modern society. (Coulmas 1992: 50–51)

4. Spain and Portugal did not join the European Community (now European Union) until 1986. Spain did not become officially multilingual until the

182

Constitution of 1978, when Euskara (or Basque), Catalan and Galician were declared official alongside Castilian.

5. Except for Wɛ, I am using the labels of the traditional linguistic classification here. An in-depth discussion of this classification follows in Chapter 1.

6. My knowledge of Baoulé facilitated my understanding of Ewe. By passive knowledge, I mean that I can understand almost everything said in a conversation, but cannot speak the language fluently.

7. See Djité (2006b: 1–20) 'shifts in linguistic identities in a global world'. The phenomenon has spread well beyond the sort of hybrid identity that Mazrui (1975: 11) once referred to as 'Afro-Saxon', because growing up in English, French or Portuguese in Africa in the last 30 years does not necessarily mean identification with metropolitan English, French or Portuguese culture.

8. The *Office International de la Francophonie* (2007) claimed that 12.7 million Ivorians, or 71.93% of the total population of Côte d'Ivoire, were French-speaking in 2006, despite a 53.6% adult literacy rate (% ages 15 and above).

9. The Bretton Woods Agreement of 1944 helped structure the world economy and finance by creating three institutions: The International Monetary Fund (IMF), the World Bank and the General Agreement on Tariffs and Trade (GATT), which later became the World Trade Organisation (WTO).

10. The purpose of the World Trade Organisation (WTO) is to oversee the rules of international trade and promote free trade by persuading countries to abolish import tariffs and other barriers. Set up in 1995 and based in Geneva, the WTO replaces the General Agreement on Tariffs and Trade (GATT). Its current membership stands at 149 countries, including China, which formally joined the body in December 2001. Over the years, the WTO has become closely associated with 'globalisation', a concept discussed in detail in the Chapter 4, Language, the Economy and Development.

11. The report entitled *What Now? Another Development* was prepared on the occasion of the seventh extraordinary General Assembly of the United Nations and published in the journal of the Dag Hammarskjöld Foundation, *Development Dialogue* in 1975.

12. This was the case at least for Félix Houphouët Boigny of Côte d'Ivoire, Mobutu Sesse Séko of the former Zaire, Jean-Bedel Bokassa of the Central African Republic and Gnassingbé Eyadéma of Togo, and is currently the case for Omar Bongo of Gabon.

13. I was asked to translate a number of such letters from 1985 to 1988, when I was teaching at an American University.

14. This is an ideology transposed to the African continent from Europe. Whilst France is renowned for despising its 'dialects' and 'patois', the Italians considered the French language itself a 'barbarous' language, back in the 16th century. Similarly, German was conceived to be unsuitable for lofty thought (Blackall, 1978: 3–4). A long tradition in Britain also represented dialects as 'barbarous'.

15. Some countries, like Cameroon, adopted not one, but two languages from the former colonisers.

16. The linguistic information provided about most countries in Batibo's country-by-country case studies (Batibo, 2005: 68–84) are definitely the result of guesswork. For instance, contrary to his assertion, the dominant languages of Côte d'Ivoire (i.e. Anyi-Baule in the south and Dyula in the north) are not as

neatly geographically defined as is shown. It would be of great help to all, for the sake of scientific protocol, for Batibo and others to provide evidence of the so-called 'Daho-Doo' language in Côte d'Ivoire.

17. The Shona call themselves *vana vevhu* or 'children of the soil'.

18. This Centre, founded and directed by Kwesi Kwaa Prah, is based in Cape Town (South Africa). The CASAS book series has published a number of studies on African languages, mother-tongue education and development. The CASAS is currently involved in the harmonisation of orthographies and the development of common spelling systems of some of these languages, organising workshops to train writers and teachers to produce educational materials in the new orthographies.

19. National legislation is not translated into Romansh, and courts do not operate in Romansh.

20. The Malian astrophysicist, Cheikh Modibo Diarra, heads this programme and leads a team of linguistics and computer engineers at the University Cheikh-Anta-Diop of Dakar in Senegal.

21. The Vai script was standardised at the University of Liberia in 1962.

22. See Dalby (1967) and Battestini (1997) for a full discussion and description of African writing systems.

23. The two countries set a five-year period to upgrade the Ahmed Baba Research Centre and finance the building of a new library at an estimated total cost R36 million (The South Africa-Mali Timbuktu Manuscripts Trust). The preservation of the manuscripts has become a South African Presidential Project, coordinated by the Presidency and the Department of Arts and culture, through the National Archives in Pretoria. They have also been earmarked as the first official cultural project on the New Partnership for Africa's Development (NEPAD). This project is funded by the government of Luxembourg, the Norwegian Agency for Development Cooperation (NORAD), the Ford Foundation, the Norwegian Council for Higher Education's Programme for Development Research and Education (NUFU), and the United States Ambassador's Fund for Cultural Preservation. The Cooperative Africana Microfilm Project (CAMP) has digitised 200 of these manuscripts.

24. This reminds me of a discussion I had with an ICT expert on a train in Paris. He (the Expert) was excited being part of a team on its way to Timbuktu (Mali) to collect all the remaining old manuscripts in order to post them on the Internet. He looked baffled when I asked him whether the web page would also be in Arabic. Indeed, he assumed, as many do, that in Mali, 'they all speak French'. The research team he was working with received a large grant from an international organisation, and their sole objective was to save these precious manuscripts and make them available to researchers all around the globe. It did not matter whether the people of Mali would actually be afforded the same opportunity.

25. Lithuania re-established its independence in March 1990, Latvia in August 1991 and Estonia in 1991. Georgia was also absorbed into the Russian Empire in the 19th century, before briefly becoming independent from 1918 to 1921, then it was again forcibly incorporated into the USSR in 1921. Georgia regained its independence in 1991. Ukraine was absorbed into the Russian Empire in the 18th century, before briefly becoming independent from 1918 to 1919, then

forcibly being incorporated into the USSR again in 1921. Ukraine regained its independence in 1991.

26. See Djité, P. (1996) 'La loi Toubon et le pluralisme linguistique et culturel en francophonie'. The Loi Toubon (no. 94–665) on the use of the French language was passed on 4 August, 1994. This law was followed by a number of other instruments, including the Decree of 3 March, 1995, the Circular of 19 March 1996, the Decree of 1 July, 1998 modifying the Decree of 3 March, 1995 concerning international transportation, the Circular of 28 September, 1999 regarding the application of provisions of Articles 3 and 4 of the law, the Order of 25 June, 2001 concerning the renewal of the approval of Associations for the defence of the French language, and the Circular of 20 September 2001 regarding the application of Article 2 of the law.

27. According to Fabian (1986: 6), Swahili has been the dominant language among the African labour force in the Shaba (Congo) at least since the first quarter of the 20th century.

28. The French text reads: 'Remplacer le français comme langue officielle et langue d'enseignement n'est ni souhaitable ni possible si du moins nous ne voulons pas être en retard au rendez-vous de l'an 2000'.

29. Note the assumption inherent in the term 'overseas development aid', implying that all aid recipients are assumed to be 'overseas' in relation to the donors.

30. This quote is from Albaugh's PhD dissertation, which has subsequently been edited and published in the *Journal of Modern African Studies* (Albaugh, 2007).

31. This is in reference to Ghana's several decades of exemplary use of local languages as media of instruction, until 2001, when this policy was reversed and an English-only policy from the first year of primary school introduced.

32. The four official languages of the European Community were Dutch, German, French and Italian.

33. The seven additional languages were English, Danish, Greek, Spanish, Portuguese, Finnish and Swedish.

34. The ten additional languages were Estonian, Latvian, Lithuanian, Polish, Czech, Slovakian, Hungarian, Slovenian, Maltese and Irish.

35. Suddenly rediscovering Renan's rhetorical question: 'Can one not have the same feelings and the same thoughts, love the same things in different languages?' ('*Ne peut-on pas avoir les mêmes sentiments et les mêmes pensées, aimer les mêmes choses dans des langues différentes?*' Renan (1882), the French have even coined the term '*exception culturelle*'. After more than a century of imposition of the French language in France's colonial possessions and former colonies in Africa, some French intellectuals have now come to the realisation that 'the push for the use of a single language ... promotes the rise of a single mode of thought which has the potential, eventually, to become a single power, that is, a dictatorship' (Durand 2002), and that 'The languages of France contribute to the creativity and cultural influence of our country ... we hold them in common, they are part of the heritage of humanity' (2004 mission statement of the DGLFLF, cited in Adamson 2007: 34). In 2005, the *Rapport au parlement* of the *Délégation générale à la langue française et aux langues de France* (DGLFLF) stated that 'The multiplicity of languages is a reality which is seen increasingly positively in France, as an image of the past but also as a project for the future' (cited in Adamson, 2007: 34).

36. Also called the Sarkozy Law, 'Selective immigration' refers to a law tabled by the Minister of the Interior, Nicolas Sarkozy, and passed by the French National Assembly on 30 June, 2006 (Assemblée Nationale, 2006). In essence, this law states that France reserves the right to choose who can migrate onto its territory. The law has been denounced by most African leaders as a way of encouraging a brain drain from Africa.
37. The Mission for the African Academy of Languages (MACALAN) was originally created by Presidential Decree No. 00-630/PRM of 19 December, 2000 issued by Alpha Oumar Konaré when he was President of Mali. Mr Adama Samassekou was appointed Head of this mission by Presidential Decree 00-30/PRM of 26 January, 2001.
38. The process of empowerment coexists with knowledge' (Bacon, 1597, cited in Titelman, 1996).
39. With the exception of Ethiopia which, although it was briefly occupied by Italy (1936–1941), quickly regained its independence and so the colonial administration did not play a major part in the language-planning decisions.
40. These are Botswana, Gambia, Ghana, Kenya, Lesotho, Malawi, Nigeria, Sudan, Swaziland, Tanzania, Uganda, Zambia and Zimbabwe for the British colonies, and Burundi, the DRC and Rwanda for the Belgian colonies. African languages were also favoured in all the German colonies and/or protectorates (present day Tanzania, Rwanda, Burundi, Namibia, Cameroon and Togo), before the carving up of the continent at the Berlin conference (November 1884 to February 1885), and the re-allocation of these to other colonial administrations.
41. These are Benin, Burkina Faso, the Central African Republic, Chad, Côte d'Ivoire, Gabon, Guinea, Mali, Mauritania, Niger, the DRC, Senegal, Togo for the French colonies, Angola, Cape Verde, Guinea Bissau, Mozambique and Sao Tome e Principe for the Portuguese colonies, and Equatorial Guinea, the only country colonised by Spain in Africa.
42. Originally a German colony, after the Berlin Conference Cameroon was under French influence in the east and British influence in the west. The French influence in Cameroon was too strong for any of the local languages to be introduced into the education system. Originally a French colony, Seychelles came under the influence of British administration and hence the development and introduction of Kriol or Seychellois in the education system. Somalia was under Italian and British influence; and the predominance of the British influence led to the introduction of Somali in the education system. Namibia came under the influence of South Africa, which explains the use of African languages in education.
43. Batibo refers to Arabic as an 'indigenous language', thereby implying that the total neglect of millions of speakers of Berber languages spread across North Africa (including in Libya and Egypt) is justified or justifiable.
44. Following the establishment of an agreed orthography in the early 1980s, this project was developed among the Ngbaka people in 1984 by the Protestant and Catholic Churches and the Summer Institute of Linguistics. It now covers some 30,000 learners taught by 3000 voluntary teachers.
45. One of the five goals of the National Action Plan for Education is the 'Utilisation of local languages as co-vectors for instruction and acquisition of knowledge' (Cameroun, 2003: 23–24).

46. The number of speakers of French in Burundi, including French nationals living in the country, varies between 3 and 10% (Frey, 1993: 245).
47. The language policy of South Africa is also coupled with a Bill of Rights. Section 30 of this reads as follows: 'Everyone has the right to use the language and participate in the cultural life of their choice, but no one exercising these rights may do so in a manner inconsistent with any provision of the Bill of Rights' (available online at www.info.gov.za/documents/constitution/1996/96cons2.htm; accessed 12.2.06). The Constitution of the new South Africa was adopted in 1996 and Section 6 of Chapter 1 'Founding Provisions' laid down the principles of language policy.
48. This pilot programme, initially called *Primary Reading Programme* (PRP), was launched by the Ministry of Education to teach initial skills in reading and writing in the Kasama Province in the local language in Grade 1. The preliminary results were encouraging, and the programme had been extended to other schools in the country by 2003.
49. I find this paradoxical given UNESCO's well-known position that, wherever possible, children should be taught in their mother tongues in the first instance.
50. Summarises what is otherwise called 'Language Attitudes'. I owe the expression to Peter Plüdderman of PRAESA.
51. In the context of the current debate on globalisation, sociolinguistic research into the preference of the population of Francophone Africa (including the illiterates) for English or French as a language of international communication will no doubt settle this issue.
52. Bonjawo (2002 and 2005) and *Futurs Africains* (2003) suggest information and communication technologies (ICTs) as the one tool that will resolve Africa's education crisis. African governments are now going to be able to purchase ICTs in combination with localised software, affording the African child the opportunity to learn in her own language
53. In Chapter 1 I explain why I believe these to be fundamentally flawed.
54. Nadine Dutcher reviewed innovative language programs in 13 countries in 2001: Bolivia, Cameroon, Eritrea, Ethiopia, Guatemala, Indonesia, Côte d'Ivoire, Mali, Mexico, Namibia, Papua New Guinea, the Philippines and Vietnam (see Dutcher, 2004). I owe the expression 'pushed out' to Professor Casimir Rubagumya of Tanzania.
55. The first example is from an Ethiopian colleague, who, throughout high school, thought that this was the proper English expression for 'Please erase the blackboard for me'. The second is from a Togolese friend. The teacher was trying to say 'hippopotamus'. This is not to suggest that all teachers of European languages are incompetent. There are some very good teachers in the system, trying their very best to improve their own performance and that of their students. Too often, the good teachers are moved on to office jobs or recruited by political parties to run for public office.
56. This is despite claims about the number of speakers of European languages in Africa. According to the biennial report of the *Organisation Internationale de la Francophonie* (2007 there are six African countries among the ten leading the pack of French-speaking countries. They are the DRC, with 24.3 million speakers, Algeria (not a member of the Francophonie movement) with 16 million, Côte d'Ivoire with 12.7 million, Morocco with 10.1 million, Cameroon with 7.3 million and Tunisia with 6.3 million. There is no doubt that these are

'guestimates', because the proposition that 71.93% of the total population of Côte d'Ivoire (17,654 843 million inhabitants, according to the 2006 population census) is French-speaking is quite simply ludicrous. More importantly, with such statements, it is clear that the very concept of a French speaker will have to be revisited. The complacent assumption that European languages are the dominant languages is misleading.

57. I owe the expression to H. Ekkehard Wolff (2006). See Chapter 2 of ADEA (2006).
58. These measures are spelt out under sub-paragraphs i, ii and iii of the Charter (Council of Europe, 1992). The full text of the European Charter for Regional or Minority Languages and information about signatures and ratifications can be found on the Council of Europe website at: http://conventions.coe.int/Treaty/EN/CadreListeTraites.htm. Accessed 22.4.06.
59. This leads to a considerable brain drain at university level.
60. There are several aspects to the issue of African languages being used as languages of science and technology (for a detailed discussion see Alexander, 2005b). This section focuses on African languages in the information society.
61. _Computer Economics_ had already predicted that 57% of Internet surfers would speak a language other than English on the web by 2005.
62. Article 1 of the Universal Declaration on Cultural Diversity (UNESCO, 2002) reads as thus: 'Cultural diversity is as necessary for humankind as biodiversity is for nature. In this sense, it is the common heritage of humanity and should be recognised and affirmed for the benefit of present and future generations' (adopted at the 31st Session of the UNESCO General Conference held in Paris from 15 October to 3 November 2001).
63. This is the case for the Open Swahili Localisation Project (see http://www.kilinux.org/kiblog/index.html; accessed 25.6.07) and the Igbo open source translation project (http://igbo.sourceforge.net/; accessed 25.6.07).
64. I describe as 'altruistic' the efforts made by non-profit organisations that use open software in languages of cultural importance, where it is clear that there is no money to be made. Efforts such as those of the multinational company Microsoft and other private companies concentrate on languages of economic importance, where a lot of money can be made. In the case of African languages, these companies will go after 'prestige' in the first instance, taking the calculated risk that the money will follow.
65. Translate.org.za is a non-profit organisation in South Africa. It specialises in localising free and open source software into all 11 of South Africa's official languages. Translate.org.za also created a keyboard and font for the ciVenda language.
66. The Malian astrophysicist, Cheikh Modibo Diarra, heads this programme and leads a team of linguistics and computer engineers at the University Cheikh-Anta-Diop of Dakar, Senegal.
67. A Somali language word processor called 'Hikaadiye' already exists (Somitek, 1999).
68. Defined as 'a tactic of boundary maintenance, [that] involves institutionalising the linguistic patterns of the elite, either through official policy or informally established usage norms in order to limit access to socioeconomic mobility and political power to people who possess the requisite linguistic patterns' (Myers-Scotton 1990: 27)

69. The digital divide affects differently the written language (which implies a writing system, literacy, and then word processing software) and the oral language, since oral language can be digitalised directly.

70. These are the words of Sudeep Baneriee, the Indian Secretary of State for Education.

71. On 2 January 2007, the government of Rwanda committed to provide one laptop per child to all primary school children within five years.

72. This objective (a computer at $100) is yet to be achieved, as the cost of producing and distributing each XO computer is currently $175, and its running costs are estimated to be another $100. A rival project by the Industrial Development Corporation (IDC) instead plans to build a $400 computer, the Classmate PC, whilst the American company Dell is working on a $300 computer to be sold in China.

73. For example the Terminology project based at the Kiswahili Institute of Dar-Es-Salaam (Tanzania), the African Languages and Cyberspace project based in Addis Ababa (Ethiopia) and the Lexicography project based in Gabarone (Botswana).

74. The phrase means 'He who loses his language, loses his faith' [my own translation]

75. 'Un peuple s'instruit, se cultive, s'éduque plus vite s'il peut s'instruire, se cultiver et s'éduquer dans la langue qu'il parle' Ministère de l'éducation (sd: 6).

76. For instance, 30% of all health care services in Ghana are provided by hospitals run by missionaries – see Institute for Policy Alternatives, quoted in IRIN (WHO, 2006).

77. A situation made even worse, because Africa has only 4% of the world's health workers (WHO, 2006).

78. These countries are Chad, the Democratic Republic of Congo, the Central African Republic, Ethiopia, Mozambique, Guinea-Bissau, Burundi, Mali, Burkina Faso, Niger and Sierra Leone.

79. According to the 2006 World Health Report, 19of the 20 countries in the world with the highest rates of maternal mortality are located in sub-Saharan Africa.

80. 2006 International AIDS Conference held in Toronto, Canada. It was estimated that 25 million people were living with HIV infection in 2004, 90% of whom were adults and youths over the age of 15 years (UNAIDS). In some of the worst-hit countries, close to 20% of all children under the age of 17 had lost at least one parent to HIV/AIDS.

81. This figure dropped to 74% in 2006.

82. The controversy between South Africa and pharmaceutical companies concerning the protection of patents may have mobilised the world to look for more creative and flexible solutions, and a number of large pharmaceutical laboratories have begun investing in these neglected diseases (malaria, tuberculosis, meningitis, schistosomiasis, and the like). Some US$2.5 billion have already been spent on research and development in this area. In 2007, the Global Alliance for Vaccines and Immunization (Gavi), mainly funded by the Gates Foundation, launched a major vaccination drive in 12 West African countries (including Côte d'Ivoire, Guinea, Liberia, Mali, Senegal and Togo) against yellow fever, a deadly viral disease transmitted by mosquitos. On 16 May 2007, Gavi announced that it will fund a vaccination campaign to the tune of US$58 million. This funding will make it possible to gather some 11 million

doses to protect well over 48 million people. By December 2006, the Gates Foundation had donated US$7.8 million to health programmes under the theme 'Global Health'. In the same year, George Soros, through his foundation, the Open Society Institute, donated US$3 million to combat the XDR-TB, a super-resistant form of tuberculosis, in patients in Lesotho also infected by the AIDS virus. The charitable organisation, Partners in Health, and the Brigham and Women's Hospital of Boston, also participated in this initiative. Sanofis-Aventis and the Drugs for Neglected Diseases Initiative (DNDi) have formed a partnership to launch a new medicine, ASAQ – a mix of Artesunate (AS) and amodiaquine (AQ) – to combat malaria, a disease that kills 3000 children every day in Africa. ASAQ will cost less than a dollar for a three-day full treatment for adults and less than 50 cents for children. The Gates Foundation also donated US$4.1 million to the African Malaria Network Trust (Amanet). GlaxoSmithKline (GSK) now produces a new vaccine to combat the A, C and W135 strains of meningitis in Africa. The Gates Foundation, yet again, donated US$107.6 million to GSK for work on a vaccine against malaria. This new vaccine will replace Titanrix, which protects against hepatic B, diphtheria, pertussis and tetanus (DPT vaccine).

83. In September 2006, Britain threatened to withhold a payment of £50 million to the World Bank in protest at the conditions the bank attaches to aid for developing countries.

84. Statement by Alpha Omar Konaré, Chairperson of the African Union Commission, at the 55th Session of the WHO-AFRO Regional Committee for Africa, Maputo, Mozambique, August 22–26, 2005.

85. The 2002 per capita government expenditure on health at international dollar rate was US$240 for Bostwana, US$244 for Mauritius, US$232 for Namibia, US$280 for South Africa and US$207 for Tunisia.

86. 25% of African doctors and nurses now work in developed countries. Overall, some 25,000 skilled Africans settle in developed countries every year (African Union); according to the UNCTAD, each of these skilled immigrants represents a saving of US$184,000 to the receiving country.

87. According to Mr José Luis Rodriguez Zapatero, Prime Minister of Spain, this country forcibly returned 13,055 illegal immigrants from January to September 2006 (*AFP*, 2006, 20 September). In the Netherlands, would-be immigrants now have to pay 350 euros and sit a knowledge test on Dutch language and culture, although citizens of the European Union and the Swiss, as well as the Japanese, the Americans, New Zealanders and Canadians are exempted from such a test. In Australia, the Conservative Government has put in place what it calls the 'Pacific Solution', a policy forcing all refugee applicants to travel (at the Australian Government's expense) to the island state of Nauru or to Papua New Guinea where their applications are processed. In 2006, it increased the waiting period to four years and put in place a test of English proficiency for all new citizenship applicants, whilst the Leader of the Labour Opposition went so far as to suggest that all visitors should sign up to 'Australian Values' before they are issued with a visa to enter the country. In France, forced repatriation of illegal immigrants is a daily occurrence. The recently-adopted French official immigration policy (30 June, 2006) called 'Immigration choisie' seeks to determine who is entitled to settle in the country. In the United Kingdom, a similar law was adopted on 7 March 2006 and came into force in the summer of

2007. The French policy has been roundly criticised. Abdoulaye Wade, President of Senegal, calls it 'dishonest'. Abdou Diouf, Secretary General of the International Organisation of Francophonie finds it 'politically and morally unacceptable'. Alpha Oumar Konaré, Chairman of the Commission of the African Union, believes that it is a blatant 'attempt to deny Africa the right to development'. Ségolène Royal, a leading socialist, who ran for President in France in 2007, sees it as an 'unacceptable' ploy 'to plunder the skills of poor countries, after having plundered their raw materials'. In an opinion piece published in *Le Monde* (20 September 2006), Sandrine Mazetier believes that Sarkozy's new law will harm research in France, a country which, in her words, is now 'between countries that *innovate* in the area of technology and those that *imitate*' [my own translation]. Mazetier points out that the new visa called 'Ability and Talent' ignores the fact that 25% of doctoral students in France are foreigners, and that these students will now choose to go to the United States or Canada. Nevertheless, on 23 September 2006 Nicolas Sarkozy and his Senegalese counterpart, Ousmane Ngom, signed an agreement to control the flow of immigration between the two countries. Whilst hailed as 'historic' by Nicolas Sarkozy, the agreement has been roundly criticised by the local press as an agreement whose sole aim is to organise charters for the forced repatriation of illegal immigrants. Following Sarkozy's election as President of France in April 2007, a residence permit called 'Skills and Talents' (*'competences et talents'* in French) has been introduced. This permit will be issued only to students whose programme of study is sanctioned by a partnership agreement between France and the student's country of origin for a maximum period of six years. [The quotes in this paragraph are taken from news items in *Le Monde*, which does not allow general access to its archives.]

88. Figures released at the Colloquium organised by the *Agence Info-Sud*, Brussels, 8 December 2000. Future research in this area should also look into what could be called a 'leg and foot drain' in athletics and football.

89. Michel Sarkozy was the French Minister of the Interior in 2006. He was elected President of France in 2007.

90. Feely (2006) suggests that the shortage of medical staff in Southern Africa has more to do with high rates of death due to AIDS over the past 10 years than to the brain drain. He estimates that, at least for Zambia, and based on the figures from 2000, the number of deaths among nurses and midwives was nearly twice as high as the number of nurses who applied for registration in the United Kingdom in 2003–2004.

91. Australia, Belgium, Canada, France, Portugal, Spain, the United Kingdom and the United States are the favourite destinations for 94.2% of these doctors and nurses. Australia has just begun a pilot program to teach immigrant doctors how to be better understood by the Australian patient population and how to communicate with their Australian colleagues (Weaver, 2007). The programme is headed by the director of speech pathology at Toowoomba Base Hospital (Queensland) with doctors from Africa, India and South America.

92. And one nurse for 3648 inhabitants, one midwife for 1802 pregnant women (*Fraternité Matin*, 8 April, 2006).

93. According to the French Embassy in Zimbabwe, sub-Saharan African countries generally have a ratio of 1 medical doctor for 40,000 people (http://www.ambafrance-zw.org; accessed 9.5.06). In 2004, there were 1500 unemployed

medical doctors in Madagascar (WHO, 2006, cited in *Santé Sud*, 2006). In Côte d'Ivoire, in September 2006, following the scandal of the dumping of toxic waste in the port city of Abidjan by the Probo Koala, a Greek-owned vessel flying a Panama flag, operated by a Russian crew and chartered by Trafigura Beheer BV (a Dutch company with offices in three European cities), the Minister of Health offered to hire all the medical doctors, dentists and pharmacists who had been unemployed until that time (*Fraternité Matin*, 13 September, 2006). See Chapter 5 for further discussion on the toxic waste scandal.

94. See Annual Report of the Organe International de contrôle des stupéfiants (OICS, 2007). In 2007, the owner of the *Zambian Weekly Angels* claimed to have discovered an effective treatment for HIV/AIDS, which turned out to be Tetrasil, a pesticide used for disinfecting swimming pools (*AFP*, 2007e).

95. This NGO was created in 1994 by scientists, health professionals and associations for the fight against AIDS.

96. I am indebted to Dr Corentin GUI TEH for providing me with this list, which may not be as exhaustive now as it was when I received it.

97. All the names of Associations and NGOs have been translated by me.

98. Probably because they did not trust the researcher, or simply because of the prevailing general socio-political climate in Côte d'Ivoire at the time (2004–2005), as the country was still going through the difficult experience of a rebellion, and everyone was on high-security alert.

99. Part of the research protocol was to keep all details of personal communication confidential. Only AIBEF provided us with research material, the questionnaires of which had been translated into Dyula and Baoulé, two of the major regional languages of Côte d'Ivoire.

100. This is very much akin to 'shock' commercials on the effects of smoking or driving under the influence of alcohol in developed countries, where there is always a debate about the 'crude' or 'shocking' effect of some of the communicative strategies adopted.

101. Usually, this is a code for non-technical European languages; however, the crux of the problem remains the language of communication itself.

102. Also called *voertaal* in South Africa (see Herselman, 1996).

103. In Australia, where English is the *de facto* national language, and where professional health interpreters are used in hospitals only for the immigrant population, it is estimated that language/communication problems cause 20% of fatalities in hospitals.

104. In the absence of trained interpreters, any bilingual, or anyone purporting to be a bilingual, is used as an interpreter. After all, having an untrained interpreter is better than having no interpreter at all. Such shortcuts are not characteristic of Africa alone; they also occur in developed countries with supposedly sophisticated interpreter services, such as Australia, as witnessed by this author.

105. Entitled 'Improving Access to Services for Persons with Limited English Proficiency', the Executive Order was issued by President Clinton. It calls on the Federal Government and various Federal Agencies to ensure and improve access of government-funded services to individuals with limited English proficiency.

106. There are various minority ethnic groups within these countries. With a

population of 6 million people (July 2004), Laos for instance is believed to have up to 68 ethnic groups, 47 of which are officially recognised (see http:// en.wikipedia.org/). Although the constitution in Vietnam says that all ethnic groups have the right to use their own languages, and the government of Vietnam recognises and expresses strong commitment to the development of its 54 minority ethnic groups and languages (about 13% of the population), the use of ethnic minority languages in education is limited to a small number of schools. Guidelines restrict the language of instruction to Kinh (majority Vietnamese), and another eight minority languages are taught as school subjects. Some 28 languages have standardised writing systems, but few books exist outside the main minority languages (T^ y, Muong, Cham and Khmer), and there are not enough ethnic minority teachers because of difficulties in progressing through the education system (see Pinnock *et al.*, 2006)

107. Most Lao students rely on bilingual dictionaries written in the Thai language.
108. Except notably in the 2004 UNDP Human Development report, entitled 'Cultural liberty in today's diverse world' and the Report on the Millennium Development Goals, which make direct, positive reference to multilingualism (UNDP 2004, 2005).
109. A three-year UN Project entitled *Investing in Development: A Practical Plan to Achieve the Millennium Development Goals,* commissioned by the UN Secretary-General and sponsored by the United Nations Development Program on behalf of the UN Development Group. A team of 265 of the world's leading development experts produced and presented a report on this project in January 2005.
110. The adjective 'informal' itself is subject to controversy, as some argue that it has negative connotations – it conjures up all sorts of illegal activities, such as prostitution and the trafficking of firearms and precious stones. Some would rather substitute the word 'popular' as in 'popular economy', to stress the fact that the only difference here is that people in the 'formal economy' pay taxes, and people in the 'popular economy' do not.
111. According to the United Nations, the growth rate of the African population is set to remain above 1% in the long term, and its population will increase from 800 million to 2.1 billion people by 2075.
112. Note the inclusions of Ghana and Uganda, which were lauded as great successes in the implementation of structural adjustment measures. From 1980 to 1999, Ghana received 26 adjustment loans and Uganda received 20.
113. Again note the presence of Ghana and Uganda on this list.
114. See the 2006 Report of the United Nations Conference on Trade and Development (UNCTAD). 35 of the 50 least developed countries are located in Africa.
115. Sub-Saharan Africa is reliant on primary commodities for 89% of its total exports. From 6% of international trade in 1980, these have fallen to 2.4% in 2004.
116. The low sulphur content of West African crude makes it of further strategic importance.
117. Woodside, an Australian company, operates the Mauritanian oil fields.
118. In 2005, China became the first supplier of finished goods to the African continent, well ahead of France and Germany, establishing some 800 companies and signing investment agreements with 28 African countries.

China is also the second client for African exports. In 2005, Sino-African trade reached US$39.7 billion, an increase of 35% over the previous year. In the first half of 2006, this figure had already increased by 41% (*Pressafriq*, 19 October, 2006) and reached US$55 billion by the end of 2006.

119. See Chietigj Bajpaee's article in *Power and Interest News Report* of 7 October, 2005 and the paper 'Sino-US energy competition in Africa' written by a research associate at the Centre for Strategic and International Studies (CSIS) in Washington, DC. Also see Paul Mooney's 'China's African Safari' (Mooney, 2005).

120. It is argued that the last three Sino-African fora have brought Africa more benefits than the last 29 Franco-African Summits. In May 2007, China signed a technological and economic agreement with Côte d'Ivoire and cancelled the €18 million debt owed by the latter (40% of the total debt of the country); and provided another €10 million in aid (for the construction of two schools in the rural area and a hospital. This is in addition to €4.6 million Côte d'Ivoire received in January 2007 to fund several projects of bilateral cooperation (*AFP*, 2007b).

121. The author claimed that the title of his book was based on words spoken by Napoleon to this effect: 'China is a sleeping giant. Let the giant sleep, for when he awakes, he will amaze the world'. The French original reads: '*La Chine est un géant qui sommeille. Laissez-le dormir, car l'orsqu'il se réveillera, il étonnera le monde.*'

122. Verschave (1999) coined the words 'françafrique' (after 'France-Afrique') and '*mafiafrique*' (after 'mafia' and 'Africa'). Note the play on words with '*fric*' meaning 'money'.

123. In part because a number of donor countries now consider ODA as an extension to their foreign trade, and many African countries are made to accept 'tainted' aid (Beckman, 1992).

124. Only Denmark, Luxemburg, Norway, the Netherlands and Sweden are currently contributing 0.7% of their GDP. Ireland aims to reach this mark in 2007, Finland by 2010 and France by 2012.

125. At the request of the European Organisation for Economic Cooperation (EOEC, now OECD), the United States spent well over US$13 billion (the equivalent of US$100 billion in today's currency) on the reconstruction of 17 European countries between 1948 and 1951. This European Recovery Program is what was called the Marshall Plan, after General George Marshall who was then American Secretary of State.

126. There are those who take the view that the situation in Africa has nothing to do with poverty, but everything to do with maladministration and its consequences, and that, unless these issues are resolved, no amount of financial aid will solve the problem of poverty in Africa. Indeed, no amount of financial aid will solve the problem of poverty in Africa, unless bold steps are taken to empower the masses and thereby ensure that they are actively involved in an endogenous development process. One crucial way of achieving this is to open up the channels of communication in the formal domain by allowing the use of the language(s) the majority of the people understand.

127. Majid Rahnema (2003: 268) suggests that aid is only an expenditure, whose aim is to reinforce the structures that generate misery.

128. However, Gordon Brown failed to secure full backing, especially from the United States, for a new financing mechanism that would raise US$50 billion a year on the world capital markets to boost development aid.

129. Accusing an African leadership group, the New Partnership for Africa's Development (NEPAD) set up six years ago to manage development of wasting hundreds of millions of dollars and achieving nothing for the world's poorest continent, Senegal President Abdoulaye Wade declared in substance: 'I've decided no longer to waste my time going to meetings where nothing gets done. It's very agreeable to meet among ourselves but it doesn't drive things forward.' Wade said that NEPAD, which is meant to commit African leaders to promote democracy and good governance in return for increased Western investment, trade and debt relief, had proved no more than a talking shop, denouncing 'Expenses adding up to hundreds of millions of dollars have been spent on trips, on hotels. But not a single classroom has been built, not a single health centre completed. NEPAD has not done what it was set up for.'
130. Critics of this view often fail to acknowledge that there are different schools of thought when it comes to the concept of 'economic growth'.
131. Founded in 1959, the aim of the European Free Trade Association was to create a free trade area between the member countries, _under which individual tariffs of the member countries on imports from non-members are retained, but import duties on goods originating in any member country are eliminated_ [italics added].
132. A European institution created by the Treaty of Rome on 25 March 1957, based on the progressive rapprochement of the economic policies of member countries, the harmonious development of economic activities, continuous and balanced expansion, increasing stability, the accelerated improvement of the standard of living and closer cooperation between member states.
133. The 2003 UNDP report (page 155) reveals that a European cow receives 114 times more aid than an African person. Indeed, in 2000, the European Union granted its dairy farm producers US$913 per head of cattle, compared to US$8 per person in foreign aid to sub-Saharan Africa. Cattle and cotton farming in OECD countries received more assistance in 2000 than the entire population of sub-Saharan Africa. In 2000, the United States subsidised its cotton farms to the tune of US$10.7 million per day, as against US$3.1 million of foreign aid to sub-Saharan Africa. According to Austrian filmmaker Erwin Wagenhofer, every day in Vienna the amount of unsold bread sent back to be disposed of is enough to supply Austria's second-largest city, Graz – according to his 96-minute documentary film _We Feed the World_ about scarcity amid plenty (Wagenhofer, 2005). Jean Ziegler, the United Nations Special Rapporteur on the Right to Food, is quoted as saying that 'today's problem lies rather in unequal, dysfunctional production patterns and distribution systems, over-consumption, gross injustice, unfair international trade and subsidies' (see Abadie 2007, and the _Amplifier for Positive Change_ website).
134. Note that in 2003 the National Cotton Council was awarded the prize of the best lobby in the United States.
135. The Malaysian government invests 30% of its budget in research and 20% in education and training.
136. One could even argue that the final negotiations were limited to the 'top guns' or G2, the European Union and the United States.
137. Cotton is the main export product of Chad. It represents 75% of export income in Benin, 60% in Burkina Faso and 50% in Mali. The oil extracted from cotton is used as the major source of cooking oil in Mali, Chad, Burkina Faso and Togo,

as well as Côte d'Ivoire and Cameroon. Cotton by-product is also used for cattle feed.

138. Pool (1972) wrote: 'a country that is intrinsically heterogeneous is always underdeveloped and a country that is developed always has considerable uniformity'. What is true, though, is that the most indebted countries of the world are the richest; together, they share 93% of the world's debt or US$31.2 billion out of a total US$33.5 billion. The United States lead the pack with US$7.625 billion, followed by the United Kingdom, with US$6.145 billion. South Africa, with its US$3.95 billion comes only in 32nd position. Other most indebted countries are Germany, France, Italy, Japan, The Netherlands, Spain, Ireland, Belgium, Switzerland, Canada, Sweden, Austria and Australia, in that order. Of course, what matters is debt as a ratio of total output or relative to GDP, and hence how manageable the debt burden is.

139. This is a system of saving invented by the Italian Banker, Lorenzo Tonti, in the 17th century. In Africa, this system takes the form of a periodic payment – usually monthly – into a communal pot. Each participant waits for his turn to take all the money collected.

140. Commissioned under the auspices of the ILO Inter-Sectoral Task Force on the Informal Economy, and prepared by Pat Horn, Shirin Motala and Jantjie Xaba, in preparation for the general discussion on the informal economy at the 90th International Labour Conference (ILC) in Geneva, in June 2002 (Xaba *et al.*, 2002). Data was obtained from Angola, Botswana, the Democratic Republic of Congo, Cameroon, Gabon, Gambia, Ghana, Kenya, Mozambique, Nigeria, South Africa, Swaziland, Tanzania, Uganda, Zambia and Zimbabwe.

141. By 1990, 40 countries in sub-Saharan Africa had agreed to follow rigorous IMF restructuring plans. IMF recommendations saw the continent's currencies drop by an average of 50%, the selling off of government-owned industries, and the slashing of government spending.

142. The devaluation of the CFA Franc (currency used in former French African colonies) in 1994 worsened the structural imbalances of the 14 countries concerned, 11 of which are among the HIPCs.

143. In the 1990s the informal economy was reported to contribute between 25 and 40% of Mexico's GDP and 60% of Peru's GDP.

144. Also see Fifth African Development Forum on Youth and Leadership in the 21st century, held in Addis Ababa from 16–18 November 2006, organised by the Economic Commission for Africa and the African Union. According to the ILO report, only 1 in 10 young people in sub-Saharan Africa earns enough to lift themselves and their families above the poverty level. The number of these young working poor, living on less than a US$1 a day, has increased from 36 million in 1995 to 45 million in 2005 (ILO, 2006). One should be aware that two thirds of the African population is less than 25 years old.

145. The African Growth and Opportunity Act (AGOA), enacted in 2000, is a trade agreement with the United States, which allows qualifying sub-Saharan African countries to export most products to the United States duty-free. Qualifying countries are those that are deemed to be making progress toward an improved rule of law, human rights, core labour standards and child labour. The US Congress broadened the benefits provided under this legislation in 2002 (known as AGOA II). In June 2004, this was further extended until 2015 (AGOA III). Thirty-seven countries currently qualify for AGOA benefits.

146. Especially Article 22, which stipulates: 'The Union shall respect cultural, religious and linguistic diversity' and paragraph 4 of Article 41, which reads: 'Every person may write to the institutions of the Union in one of the languages of the Treaties and must have an answer in the same language' (Treaty of Rome, 1957). See also Articles 126 and 128 of the Treaty of Rome, and Article 21 of the Treaty of Nice (2001).

147. French films are reported to have secured a 38.4% share of the market in 2004, as against 35% in 2003. The share of the market for American films fell to 47.2% in 2004 in France, as against 52.8% in 2003.

148. NEPAD deals with the concepts of 'democracy' and 'good governance' from an economic perspective, and gives the impression that economic mismanagement is the only reason for Africa's poverty. It is interesting to note that a major framework such as NEPAD, based on the key concept of 'partnership', was conceived and put forward without consulting the people. Everything is done as though only the political representatives knew what is best for their people, but do they?

149. In the area of political governance, the study notes that, although law enforcement agencies continue to violate the rights of the people in many countries and the protection of the rights of women and children remains a challenge, there is:
    • stronger adherence to constitutionalism;
    • greater understanding that democratic and multiparty elections are the only acceptable means of alternation of power, and voter participation is getting stronger;
    • greater transparency and credibility in the electoral process and political institutions and the political space is becoming more liberalised, more inclusive and diverse;
    • stronger participation of civil societies in the decision-making process;
    • significant improvement in human rights.
    In the area of economic governance, the study concludes that, although corruption continues to undermine socio-economic growth and development, and in spite of poor infrastructural development and service delivery, there is:
    • greater commitment to macro-economic stability;
    • better public financial management, with a more equitable tax system, smaller budget deficits, and resource mobilisation;
    • more focus on poverty reduction;
    • greater incentives for private sector development;
    • greater independence for monetary and financial institutions, such as central banks, and better integrity and accountability.
    The study also indicates that in 62% of the 28 countries it covered, institutional effectiveness and accountability is improving, that the powers of the Executive are being checked and that the legislature and judiciary are increasingly becoming independent, although there are significant challenges in strengthening the human and resource capacities of both the legislature and the judiciary and providing better access to justice for the poor. The Study identifies 10 priority areas for action in building capable and accountable states:
    (1) strengthening the capacity of electoral institutions to efficiently perform their core functions, i.e. the electoral process;
    (2) deepening legal and judicial reforms;

(3) improving public sector management;
(4) improving the delivery of public services;
(5) removing bottlenecks to private enterprise;
(6) tapping the potential of information and communication technologies;
(7) fostering credible and responsible media;
(8) maximising the contribution of traditional modes of governance;
(9) confronting the governance dimension of HIV/AIDS;
(10) getting partners to live up to their commitments.
For full details see *Striving for Good Governance in Africa* (UNECA, 2005a).

150. See also World Bank (2005b: 27), which reads: Africans believe democracy is good for the economy and prefer democratic political systems to authoritarian alternatives. The African public expects democracy to deliver access to the basic necessities of life, like food, water, shelter and education. The value surveys also show that Africans care about equity and public action to reduce poverty. They are less comfortable with wide wealth differentials, and have a strong commitment to political equality. About 75% of the respondents agree that African governments are doing too little for people trapped in poverty.

151. It is a misnomer to call them '(political) leaders'.

152. Estimates of speakers of English, French, Portuguese and Spanish in Africa over the last 50 years still vary between 20% to a low 5% (Bamgbose, 1971: 38–39; Heine, 1992: 27; Heugh, 1999: 75–76). According to Simire (2003), about 33% of the total population of Nigeria are literate in English, but only 15% can really use Standard English effectively in professional and administrative activities.

153. The recent events in Togo (where Faure Gnassingbé was handed power after the death of his father), the events in Côte d'Ivoire (where a rebellion has partitioned the country into north and south), the continued hold on power or return to power by the same individual either by altering the constitution or by force, in countries like Burkina Faso, Cameroon, Gabon and Congo (Brazzaville), and the probable resolutions of these state of affairs are not particularly promising, especially when the promoters of a Peer Review Mechanism (NEPAD) are at loggerheads with regard to how best to ensure political transition (e.g. the disagreement between Thabo Mbeki of South Africa and Abdoulaye Wade of Senegal about how best to resolve the conflict in Côte d'Ivoire).

154. Félix Houphouët-Boigny is most remembered for the 'basilica in the bush', the largest basilica in the world, in his hometown of Yamoussoukro during an economic downturn in Côte d'Ivoire, and then donating it to the Vatican (who accepted it!). This benevolent despot was widely admired for his 'softly-softly' approach, always trying to bring everyone – including political dissidents – under the same tent, and his advocacy for dialogue and peace. One of his former (disgraced) ministers once said: 'They do not know the "Old Man"; he would rather take away your dignity and pride, the dignity and pride of your family, and make you all suffer right here on Earth. Now, that is worse than killing you' (personal communication).

155. Most seriously corrupt African countries in 2006 were Algeria, Burkina Faso, Cameroon, Kenya, Morocco, South Africa and Uganda. Most vulnerable in 2006 were Sudan, Democratic Republic of Congo, Côte d'Ivoire, Chad, Somalia, Guinea, Liberia, Central African Republic, Burundi and Sierra Leone.

Countries are deemed to be vulnerable on the basis of the status of their economy, health, life expectancy, education and violent conflicts.

156. For example, there have been unjustified increases in the cost of road work in Tanzania, ranging from 101% to 353%. Ten of thousands of fictional civil servants and soldiers were used to inflate the civil service and military payrolls in Uganda and the DRC, respectively. In Nigeria, the construction of a steel mill was overcharged by US$1.6 billion (Oti, 2000).

157. A prominent example provided in the report is that of Houphouët-Boigny of Côte d'Ivoire, with US$7 to US$11 billion. In Transparency International's Corruption Perceptions Index 2005 (pp. 5–6), Côte d'Ivoire ties for 152nd out of 159 rated countries, along with Equatorial Guinea and Nigeria.

158. It is an irony, if an interesting one, that Wolfowitz, who took control of the World Bank on promises of curbing corruption and combat poverty, had to resign, following accusations of nepotism and violation of the Bank's ethics, for giving his girlfriend, Shaha Riza, a generous secondment package. Robert Zoellick was soon after nominated by President Bush to replace Paul Wolfowitz (30 June 2007). Zoellick was the former American Trade Representative (2001 to 2005), number two of the State Department, and then international adviser for Goldman Sachs since 2006.

159. Some of these ruthless dictators are Sani Abacha (Nigeria, 1993–1998), Issayas Afewerki (Eritrea, since 1991), Omar Al Bachir (Sudan, since 1989), Idi Amin (Uganda, 1971–1979), Said Mohammed Barre (Somalia, 1969–1991), Paul Biya (Cameroon, since 1975), Jean-Bedel Bokassa (Central African Republic, 1966–1979), Samuel Doe (Liberia, 1980–1990), Gnassingbé Eyadéma (Togo, 1963 and 1967–2005), Muammar Gaddafi (Libya, since 1969), Hissène Habré (Chad, 1982–1990), Laurent Kabila (the DRC, 1997–2001), Haile Mariam Mengitsu (Ethiopia, 1974–1991), Joseph Désiré (Sessé Séko) Mobutu (Zaire, now the DRC, 1965–1997), Robert Mugabe (Zimbabwe, since 1980), Daniel Arap Moi (Kenya, 1978–2002), Teodoro Nguema (Equatorial Guinea, since 1979), Charles Taylor (Liberia, 1997–2003), Sékou Touré (Guinea, 1958–1984), Lansana Conté (Guinea, since 1984), Moussa Traoré (Mali, 1968–1991), Omar Bongo (Gabon, since 1967), Denis Sassou-Nguesso (Congo, 1979–1992 and since 1997) and Blaise Compaoré (Burkina Faso, since 1987).

160. According to press reports (*AFP, Reuters, Le Monde, Soir Info, Jeune Afrique*), the ship belonged to the Greek company, Prime Marine Management INC. It was chartered by Trafigura Beheer BV, a Dutch company having its headquarters in Lucerne (Switzerland), flew a Panama flag and was operated by a Russian crew. Trafigura Beheer BV was implicated in the United Nations' 'Oil for Food' scandal in Iraq. Côte d'Ivoire, on the other hand, is no stranger to corruption scandals. Another well-publicised case dates back to the late 1990s, when funds from the European Union for the rehabilitation of the health system were embezzled under the watch of the government of former President Henri Konan Bédié.

161. Trafigura settled the case with the Ivorian government on 13 February 2007 and paid US$203.6 million in damages. Nevertheless, on 18 April 2007, lawyers for 94 Ivorian victims lodged a complaint against X in a Paris Court, for corruption of public servant and involuntary homicide and injuries. Legal proceedings were also under way in Estonia, the Netherlands and the United Kingdom.

162. It is estimated that 10% of maritime freight consists of such dangerous

substances, which are dumped all around the continent in exchange for smaller payment than what the operators responsible for this traffic would have to pay in their countries of origin.

163. From the title of the Ayi Kwei Armah's novel: _The beautyful ones are not yet born_ (Collier Books, New York, 1969).

164. I owe the expression 'white men in black skins behaving badly' to my mother. By this, she means all those who hide under the cloak of the European language and take advantage of the ignorance of the people. In my mother tongue, we say of anyone who speaks French and holds a job 'ó kpa kwi wɛ' [he is now a white man].

165 The Millennium Challenge Account of the Millennium Challenge Corporation has made good governance a priority and will now direct aid only to countries where governments take the lead in the fight against corruption and where the level of corruption is low. Similarly, in October 2006, Mo Ibrahim, founder of Celtel International, established a prize (US$5 million) for good governance in Africa, to be awarded to any Head of State leaving office and having made a significant contribution in the areas of education, economic development, health and human rights.

166. According to Transparency International, Mobutu managed to embezzle US$5 billion in 32 years of reign, some 40% of total foreign aid, whilst the GNP of Zaire was US$100 per capita.

167. Guillaume Soro (whose partner, Sylvie Tagro, is from the south) and Louis André Dakoury-Tabley, the leaders of the rebellion are both Christians, whilst Mamadou Coulibaly (President of the National Assembly) and Laurent Dona-Fologo (President of the Commission for Economic and Social Affairs), considered to be the hawks of the regime are both from the north (the former is Muslim and the latter Christian).

168. My own translation. The original words in French were: '_Cette guerre ivoirienne sent à plein nez le pétrole_' (_Le Patriote_, 2006).

169. It has been argued that, in issuing these edicts, both Kings Edward III and François I were not interested in promoting lateral communication between themselves and their subjects, but in extracting taxes and maintaining the peace (Gellner, 1983: 10).

170. Based on the research of the Indian economist and Nobel Prize winner, Amartya Sen, the concept of human development takes into account indicators such as life expectancy at birth, level of education, average length of schooling and the literacy rate, in addition to quantitative and economic criteria.

171. In Kenya, Uganda, Tanzania and many other countries trying to introduce the mother tongue in education, a number of schools, especially private schools, are able to circumvent the stated language policy and implement a European language as the sole language of education.

172. I am fully aware of the difference between the two situations, and especially of the elitist nature of the French policy. My emphasis here is on the opportunities offered to the majority to have a voice in the public affairs of their respective countries.

173. As far as cost is concerned, one needs to realise that it is not just the cost of using additional languages that is involved, but the alternative cost of not using them, which can be calculated in terms of exclusion, inefficiency, and wasted or

unutilised human potential. Furthermore, priorities have to be matched by budget decisions and spending.

174. These were Bété (4 minutes and 9 seconds), Dyula (3 minutes and 15 seconds), Ebrié (9 minutes and 44 seconds), Sénoufo (11 minutes and 36 seconds), Mooré (10 minutes and 48 seconds) and Baoulé (20 minutes). The variable length of the translations have led to speculations of propaganda targeting some of these ethnic groups (Silué, 2006).

175. The full quote is as follows: Unless things improve it will take sub-Saharan Africa until 2129 to achieve universal primary education, until 2147 to halve extreme poverty and until 2165 to cut child mortality by two thirds. For hunger no date can be set because the region's situation continues to worsen.

176. Asked about the future of African literature in African languages, in April 1980, Robert Cornevin declared: '*La littérature dans les langues africaines, c'est la rigolade. Elle ne peut être qu'une littérature subalterne ... Si vous scolarisez votre enfant en baoulé, il restera au village*' ['Literature in African languages *is a joke. It can only amount to second rate literature* ... If you educate your child in Baoulé, that child will stay in the village'] (interview with *Fraternité Matin*, 1980; emphasis added).

177. This subtitle is borrowed from the title of a book chapter published in 2006 (see Djité, 2006a).

178. The original French passage reads: '*L'époque sera impitoyable pour les faibles et les velléitaires: qui ne saura pas maîtriser le progrès technologique, l'assimiler et l'enrichir de son propre apport, sera dominé par lui et chacun sait que la technologie n'est pas neutre, qu'elle porte avec elle la marque, la civilisation du pays qui l'a sécrétée*' (Léger, 1987: 153).

References

Abadie, R. (2007) Les dérives de l'agroalimentaire mondial. In *L'humanité*, 25 April. Available online at www.humanite.fr/2007-04-25_International_-La-famine-sur-la-planete-est-un-massacre-absurde. Accessed 20.5.07.

Acemoglu, D. (2005) The form of property rights: Oligarchic vs. democratic societies. MIT mimeo, April.

Adamson, R. (2007) *The Defence of French: A Language in Crisis?* Clevedon: Multilingual Matters Ltd.

ADB (African Development Bank) (2005) *African Development 2005: Public Sector Management in Africa*. Oxford: Oxford University Press.

ADB (2007) *African Economic Outlook 2007*. African Development Bank and Development Centre of the OECD. Available online at www.oecd. org/dev/publications/africanoutlook. Accessed 20.3.07.

ADEA (Association for the Development of Education in Africa) (2006) Optimising learning and education in Africa: The language factor: A stocktaking research on mother tongue and bilingual education in sub-Saharan Africa. UNESCO Institute for Education and Deutsche Gesellschaft für Technische Zusammenarbeit. Working document B-3.1.

Adegbite, W. (2003) Enlightenment and attitudes of the Nigerian elite on the roles of languages in Nigeria. *Language, Culture and Curriculum* 5 (2), 185–196.

African Union (2001) *Abuja Declaration on HIV/AIDS and Framework for Action for the Fight Against HIV/ AIDS, Tuberculosis and other Related Infectious Diseases in Africa: Global Crisis – Global Action*. 21 April. Abuja: AU. Available online at www.un.org/ga/aids/coverage/FinalDeclarationHIVAIDS.html. Accessed 25.6.07.

African Union (2002) Draft African Union Convention on Preventing and Combating Corruption, Ministerial conference, 18–19 September, 2002, Addis Ababa, Min/Draft/AU/Conv/Comb/Corruption (II) Rev. 5. Available online at www.africanreview.org/docs/corruption/convention.pdf. Accessed 27.12.05.

African Union (2007) Statement by the African Union, delivered to the 60th World Health Assembly in Geneva by H.E. Advocate Bience Gawanas, Commissioner for Social Affairs of the African Union Commission. 16 May. Available online at www.doh.gov.za/docs/sp/2007/sp0516.html. Accessed 30.5.07.

Afristat and DIAL (2003) *Le secteur informel dans les principales agglomérations de sept Etats membres de l'UEMOA: Performances, insertion, perspectives*. Dakar: Afristat and DIAL.

AFP (2006) L'Espagne a rapatrié 13055 émigrants clandestins africains depuis janvier 2006. *Agence France Press*. Available online at http://www.interet-general.info. Accessed 22.12.05.

AFP (2007a) Microsoft propose des logiciels à 3 dollars. *Agence France Press*, 20 April.

AFP (2007b) Chine/Côte d'Ivoire: Pékin annule 18 m EUR de dette et prévoit 10 M d'aide. *Agence France Press*, 14 May.

AFP (2007c) Le G8 s'inquiète d'une nouvelle spirale de surendettement. *Agence France Press*, 19 May.

AFP (2007d) Au pays du pétrole, la pauvreté tue. *Agence France Press*, 23 May.

AFP (2007f) Le Nigeria réclame 7 milliards de dollars de dommages au laboratoire Pfizer. *Agence France Presse*, 5 June 2007.

AFP (2007e) Zambie: Un prétendu traitement contra side se révèle être un pesticide. *Agence France Press*. Available online at www.aegis.com/NEWS/AFP/2007/AF070601_FR.html. Accessed 3.6.07.

Ainsworth-Vaughn, N. (2001) The discourse of medical encounters. In D. Schiffrin, D. Tannen and H. Hamilton (eds) *The Handbook of Discourse Analysis* (pp. 453–469). Oxford: Blackwell Publishers.

Ainsworth, M. and Over, M. (1998) AIDS and development: The role of government. *AIDS/IAS Newsletter* 9, 12 (5), 12–13.

Albaugh, E. (2006) The colonial image reversed: Changing ideas about multilingual education in Africa. Unpublished paper derived from Chapter 5 of *The Colonial Image Reversed: Advocates of Multilingual Education in Africa*. PhD dissertation, Duke University, May 2005.

Alexander, N. (2000) *English Unassailable but Unattainable: The Dilemma of Language Policy in South African Education*. Occasional Papers 3. Cape Town: PRAESA/University of Cape Town.

Alexander, N. (2003) The African renaissance, African languages and African education. In E. Wolff (ed.) *Tied Tongues, the African Renaissance as a Challenge for Language Planning* (pp. 21–37). Münster: Lit.

Alexander, N. (ed.) (2005) *The Intellectualisation of African Languages: The African Academy of Languages and the Implementation of the Language Plan of Action for Africa*. Cape Town: PRAESA/ University of Cape Town.

Alexandre, P. (1972) *An Introduction to Languages and Language in Africa*. London: Heinemann.

Alidou, H. (1997) Education language policy and bilingual education: The impact of French language policy in primary education in Niger. PhD thesis, University of Illinois Urbana-Champaign. Ann Arbor, MI (UMI number 9737030).

Alidou, H. and Brock-Utne, B. (2006) Teaching practices: Teaching in a familiar language. In *Optimising Learning and Education in Africa: The Language Factor* (pp. 75–86). Commissioned by ADEA, GTZ, Commonwealth Secretariat.

Alidou, H. and Mallam, M. (2003) Assessment and observations of experiences of utilization of African languages in basic education. Working paper for the ADEA Biennial 2003, Grand Baie, Mauritius, 3–6 December.

Altenroxel, L. (2000) Aids taking a toll on student nurses. *Star*, September 4.

Amnesty International News for Health Professionals (2004) Physicians for human rights: Action plan to prevent brain drain: Building equitable health systems in Africa. *AI Bulletin* 7 (14). Available online at http://allafrica.com/sustainable/resources/view/00010242.pdf. Accessed 12.4.06.

Amplifier for Positive Change + New Learning. Website at http://www.pnyv.org/index.php. Accessed 4.6.07.

Anyaegbunam, C., Mefalopulos, P. and Moetsabi, T. (2001) Participatory rural communication appraisal. SADC Centre of Communication for Development and FAO Regional Project. Working document GCP/RAF/297/ITA.

Armstrong, D. and Armstrong, R. (2003) *Life for Rent*. Warner Chappell Music Ltd.

Arndt. C. and Lewis, J. (2000) The macro implications of HIV/AIDS on South Africa: A preliminary assessment. *South African Journal of Economics* 68 (5), 856–887.

Arndt. C. and Lewis, J. (2001) The HIV/AIDS pandemic in South Africa: Sectoral impacts and unemployment. *Journal of International Development* 13 (4), 427–449.

Assemblée Nationale (2006) Projet de Loi relatif à l'immigration et à l'intégration, présenté au nom de M. Dominique de Villepin, Premier ministre, par M. Nicolas Sarkozy, ministre d'État, ministre de l'intérieur et de l'aménagement du territoire enregistré à la Présidence de l'Assemblée nationale le 29 mars. Paris, Assemblée Nationale. (Final version of the Law available online at http://www.senat.fr/leg/tas05-132.html. Accessed 15.4.06.)

AUCMC (2005) *Déclaration de Nairobi sur la culture, l'intégration et la renaissance africaine*. AUCMC/Decl. 1. Rev. 3, p. 3. Issued on 14 December, Nairobi, Kenya.

Ayittey, G. (2005) *Africa Unchained: The Blueprint for Africa's Future*. New York: Palgrave/Macmillan.

Bajpaee, C. (2005) Sino–US energy competition in Africa. In *Global Policy Forum. Monitoring Policy Making at the United Nations. Power and Interest News Report*. October 7.

Baker, C. and Jones, S. (1998) *Encyclopedia of Bilingualism and Bilingual Education*. Clevedon: Multilingual Matters.

Baldauf, R. and Luke, A. (eds) (1990) *Language Planning and Education in Australasia and the South Pacific*. Clevedon: Multilingual Matters.

Baldwin, J. (1966) Unnameable objects, unspeakable crimes. *Ebony: The White Problem in America* (pp. 173–181). Chicago: Johnson.

Balit, S. (1988) *Rethinking Development Support Communication. Development Communication Report* 62. Arlington, VA: CDC.

Bamgbose, A. (1971) The English language in Nigeria. In J. Spencer (ed.) *The English Language in West Africa* (pp. 35–48). London: Longman.

Bamgbose, A. (1985) Barriers to effective education in West African languages. In K. Williamson (ed.) *West African Languages in Education* (pp. 22–38). Vienna: University of Vienna.

Bamgbose, A. (1991) *Language and the Nation: The Language Question in Sub-Saharan Africa*. Edinburgh: Edinburgh University Press.

Bamgbose, A. (2000) *Language and Exclusion*. Muenster: LIT Verlag.

Bamgbose, A. (2001) Review of Robert Phillipson (ed.) *Rights to Language Equity Power and Education* and M. Kontra, R. Phillipson, T. Skutnabb-Kangas and T. Varady (eds) *Language, a Right and a Resource: Approaching Linguistic Human Rights. South African Journal of African Languages* 21 (2), 197–202.

Bamgbose, A. (2003) The future of multilingualism in South Africa: From policy to practice. Paper read at the Language Conference of the Department of Arts and Culture, Kopanong, Johannesburg, 12–13 June 2002.

Bamgbose, A. (2004) Language of instruction policy and practice in Africa. Available online at http://www.unesco.org/education/languages_2004/languageinstruction_africa.pdf. Accessed 22.2.06.

Bamgbose, A. (2005a) Mission and vision of the African Academy of Languages. In N. Alexander (ed.) *The Intellectualisation of African Languages: The African Academy of Languages and the Implementation of the Language Plan of Action for Africa* (pp. 15–20). Cape Town: PRAESA.

Bamgbose, A. (2005b) Mother-tongue education: Lessons from the Yoruba experience. In B. Brock-Utne and R. Hopson (eds) *Languages of Instruction for African Emancipation: Focus on Postcolonial Contexts and Considerations* (pp. 210–234). Cape Town: CASAS.

Barbotin, L. (2004) Jean-François Dehecq: L'industrie pharmaceutique doit être citoyenne. *L'Expansion*, 28 October.

Barro, R. and Lee, J. (2002) IMF lending: Who is chosen and what are the effects? Mimeo, Harvard University, April.

Batibo, H. (2005) *Language Decline and Death in Africa: Causes, Consequences and Challenges*. Clevedon: Multilingual Matters Ltd.

Batibo, H. (2006) Marginalisation and empowerment through educational medium: The case of the linguistically disadvantaged groups of Botswana and Tanzania. In M. Pütz, J. Fishman and J. Neff-van Aertselaer (eds) *Along the Routes to Power: Explorations of Empowerment through Language* (pp. 261–283). Berlin: Mouton de Gruyter.

Battestini, S. (1997) *Ecriture et Texte: Contribution africaine*. Québec et Ottawa: Les Presses de l'Université Laval, in collaboration with Présence Africaine.

Baugh, A. (1959) *A History of the English Language* (2nd edn). London: Routledge and Kegan Paul Ltd.

BBC News (2004) Swahili baffles African leaders. Available online at http://bbc.co.uk/go/pr/fr/-/2/hi/africa/3871315.stm. Accessed 3.10.07.

Beckman, B. (1992) Empowerment or repression? The World Bank and the politics of African adjustment. In P. Gibbon, B. Yusuf and O. Arve (eds) *Authoritarianism, Democracy and Adjustment: The Politics of Economic Reform in Africa* (pp. 83–105). Uppsala: Nordiska Afrikainstitutet.

Benabou, R. (1996) Inequality and growth. In B. Bernanke and J. Rotemberg (eds) *NBER Macroeconomics Annual 1996* (pp. 11–74). Cambridge: MIT Press.

Berdichevsky, N. (2004) *Nations, Language and Citizenship*. Jefferson, NC: McFarland & Company, Inc.

Bergman, H. *et al.* (2002*) Les langues nationales à l'école primaire: Evaluation de l'école expérimentale*. Edition Albasa s/c MEB-GTZ/2PEB. Niamey: Ministère de l'éducation de base.

Birdsall, N. (1999) Education: The people's asset. *CSED Working Paper 5*. Washington, DC: Brookings Institution.

Birdsall, N. and Hamoudi, A. (2002) Commodity dependence, trade and growth: When 'openness' is not enough. *CSED Working Paper 7*. Washington, DC: Center for Global Development.

Birdsall, N., Ross, D. and Sabot, R. (1995) Inequality and growth reconsidered: Lessons from East Asia. *World Bank Economic Review 9* (3), 477–508.

Bischoff, A., Bovier, P., Isah, R., Françoise, G., Ariel E. and Louis, L. (2003) Language barriers between nurses and asylum seekers: Their impact on symptom reporting and referral. *Social Science and Medicine* (57), 503–512.

Blackall, E. (1959/1978) *The Emergence of German as a Literary Language 1700–1775*. Ithaca: Cornell University Press.

Blommaert, J. (1999a) *State Ideology and Language in Tanzania: East African Languages and Dialects* (Vol. 10). Köln: Rüdiger Köppe Verlag.

Blommaert, J. (ed.) (1999b) *Language Ideological Debates*. Berlin: Mouton de Gruyter.

Blommaert, J. (1999c) The debate is closed. In J. Blommaert (ed.) *Language Ideological Debates* (pp. 425–438). Berlin: Mouton de Gruyter.

Bloom, D. and Canning, D. (2000) The health and wealth of nations. *Science* 287 (5456), 1207–1209.

Bobda, A. (2006) Life in a Tower of Babel without a language policy. In M. Pütz, J. Fishman and J. Neff-van Aertselaer (eds) *Along the Routes to Power: Explorations of Empowerment through Language* (pp. 357–372). Berlin: Mouton de Gruyter.

Bokamba, E. (1984) Language and literacy in West Africa. In R. Kaplan (ed.) *Annual Review of Applied Linguistics* (Vol. 4; pp. 4–77). Rowley: Newbury House.

Bokamba, E. (1991) French colonial language policies in Africa and their legacies. In D. Marshall (ed.) *Language Planning: Festschrift in Honour of Joshua A. Fishman on the Occasion of his 65th Birthday* (Vol. 3; pp. 175–215). Amsterdam: John Benjamins.

Bonjawo, J. (2002) *Internet, une Chance pour l'Afrique.* Paris: Editions Karthala.

Bonjawo, J. (2005) *L'Afrique du XXIe siècle: L'Afrique de nos volontés.* Paris: Editions Karthala.

Bonnel, R. (2000) HIV/AIDS: Does it increase or decrease growth in Africa? Mimeo. Washington: World Bank.

Bot, M. and Schindler, J. (1997) *Baseline Study: Macro Indicators 1991–1996.* Braamfontein: Centre for Policy Development, Evaluation and Management.

Bourdieu, P. (1980/1990) *Le sens pratique.* Paris: Editions de Minuit (Available in English: *The Logic of Practice* (R. Nice, trans.). Stanford: Stanford University Press, 1990.)

Bourdieu, P. (1982/1991) *Ce que parler veut dire: L'économie des échanges linguistiques.* Paris: Fayard. 1991. (Available in English: *Language and Symbolic Power.* (J. Thompson ed.; G. Raymond and M. Adamson, trans.). Cambridge: Harvard University Press, 1991.)

Bourguignon, F. and Verdier, T. (2000) Oligarchy, democracy, inequality and growth. *Journal of Development Economics* (62) 2, 285–313.

Brach, C., Fraser, I. and Paez, K. (2005) Crossing the language chasm. An in-depth analysis of what language-assistance programs look like in practice. *Health Affairs* 24 (2), 424–434.

Bratton, M. and Logan, C. (2006) Voters but not yet citizens: The weak demand for political accountability in africa's unclaimed democracies. A comparative series of national public attitude surveys on democracy, markets and civil society in Africa. Working paper no. 63. Cape Town: IDASA, CDD Ghana and MSU. Available online at www.globalbarometer.net/afro.htm. Accessed 15.12.06..

Brecht, B. (1988) An die Studenten der Arbeiter – und Bauernfakultät (To the Students of the Workers' and Peasants' Faculty). In B. Brecht, *Die Gedichte von Bertolt Brecht in einem Band* (5th edn, pp. 1026–1027).Frankfurt am Main: Suhrkamp.

Breton, R. (2005) Unis dans la diversité: devise des Européens comme des Indiens. Paper presented at the International Esperanto Congress at Boulogne sur Mer, 25 March.

Brock-Utne, B. (2000) *Whose Education for All? Recolonization of the African Mind.* London: Falmer Press.

Brock-Utne, B. (2002) Stories of the hunt: Who is writing them? In C. Odora Hoppers (ed.) *Indigenous Knowledge and the Integration of Knowledge Systems: Towards a Philosophy of Articulation* (pp. 237–257). New Africa Education: Claremont.

Brock-Utne, B. (2005) Language-in-education policies and practices in Africa with a special focus on Tanzania and South Africa: Insights from research in progress. In L. Angel and P. Martin (eds) *Decolonisation, Globalisation: Language-in-Education Policy and Practice* (pp. 173–193). Clevedon: Multilingual Matters.

Brock-Utne, B., Desai, Z. and Qorro, M. (eds) (2004*)* *Researching the Language of Instruction in Tanzania and South Africa*. Vlaeberg: African Minds.

Brunot, F. (1967) *Histoire de la langue française des origines à nos jours* (Vol. ix): *La Révolution et l'Empire*. Paris: Armand Colin.

Bruthiaux, P. (2003) 21st century trends in language and economics. In A. Liddicoat and P. Bryant (eds) *Language Planning and Economics. Current Issues in Language Planning* Volume 4 (1), 84–90.

Calvet, L-J. (1985) *Les langues du marché*. Paris: Université René Descartes.

Calvet, L-J. (1987) *La guerre des langues et les politiques linguistiques*. Paris: Payot.

Cameron, R. and Williams, J. (1997) Sentence to ten cents: A case of relevance and communicative success in non-native speaker interactions in medical settings. *Applied Linguistics* 18 (4), 416–445.

Cameroun (2003) *Plan d'action national de l'éducation pour tous*. Yaoundé: Ministère de l'éducation.

CBS Broadcasting Inc. (2006) The State of the Union Address. Available online at http://www.cbsnews.com/stories/2006/01/31/politics/main1264706.shtml. Accessed 2.2.06.

CCFD (Comité Catholique contre la Faim et pour le Développement) (2007) Biens mal acquis, profitent trop souvent. La fortune des dictateurs et les complaisances occidentales. Working document. Direction des études et du plaidoyer. March 2007.

Césaire, A. (1956/89) *Discours sur le colonialisme*. Paris: Présence Africaine. (Available in English as *Discourse on Colonialism*. New York: Monthly Review Press,1989.)

CESCR (Committee on Economic, Social and Cultural Rights of the United Nations' Economic and Social Council) (2000) The right to the highest attainable standard of health (article 12 of the International Covenant on Economic, Social and Cultural Rights). General Comment No. 14 (2000) *E/C.12/2000/4*. 22nd session, Geneva, 25 April to 12 May. Available online at www.unhchr.ch/tbs/doc.nsf/ (symbol)/E.C.12.2000.4.En. Accessed on 30.9.06.

Charbi, S. (2007) Le poids de l'économie informelle. *Jeune Afrique*, 18 March. Available online at http://www.jeuneafrique.com/jeune_afrique/article_jeune _ afrique.asp?art_cle=LIN18037lepoiellemr0. Accessed 23.3.07.

Charmes, J. (2000) Size, trends and productivity of women's work in the informal sector and in old and new forms of informal employment. An outlook of recent empirical evidence. Paper presented at the International Association for Feminist Economics, Istanbul, August.

Chaudenson, R. (1987) Industries de la langue, éducation et développement. In R. Chaudenson et D. de Robillard (eds) *Langues et développement: Langues, économie et développement (tome 1)* (pp. 147–188). Aix-en-Provence: Institut d'études créoles et francophones et Didier Erudition.

Chaudenson, R. (1989) *1989: Vers une Révolution Francophone?* Paris: Editions l'Harmattan.

Chekaraou, I. (2004) Teachers' appropriation of bilingual educational reform policy in sub-Saharan Africa: A socio-cultural study of two Hausa-French schools in Niger. PhD thesis. Bloomington: Indiana University.

Chen, M. (2001) Women in the informal sector: A global picture, the global movement. *SAIS Review* 21 (1), 71–82.

Chimhundu, H. (1992) Early missionaries and the ethnolinguistic factor during the invention of tribalism in Zimbabwe. *Journal of African History* 33, 87–109.

Chimhundu, H. (ed.) (1997) *Language Policies in Africa: Intergovernmental Conference on Language Policies in Africa, Harare, Zimbabwe, 17–21 March 1997. Final Report (revd.)* (web version edited by Karsten Legère). Harare: UNESCO.

Chiswick, B. and Miller, P. (2002) Immigrant earnings: Language skills, linguistic concentrations and the business cycle. *Journal of Population Economics* 15, 31–57.

Chiswick, B. and Repetto, G. (2001) Immigrant adjustment in Israel: The determinants of literacy and fluency in Hebrew and their effects on earnings. In S. Djajic (ed.) *International Migration: Trends, Policies and Economic Impact* (pp. 204–288). London: Routledge.

Chiswick, B., Partinos, H. and Hurst, M. (2000) Indigenous language skills and the labour market in a developing economy: Bolivia. *Economic Development and Cultural Change* 48 (2), 349–367.

Choi, E. (2002) Trade and the adoption of a universal language. *International Review of Economics and Finance* 11, 265–275.

Chomsky, N. (1966) *Cartesian Linguistics: A Chapter in the History of Rational Thought.* New York: Harper and Row.

Chomsky, N. (1975) *The Logical Structure of Scientific Theory.* New York: Plenum Press.

Cohen, A., Rivara, F., Marcuse, E., McPhillips, H. and Davis, R. (2005) Are language barriers associated with serious medical events in hospitalized pediatric patients? *Pediatrics* 116 (3), 575–579.

Colgan, A-L. (2002) Hazardous to health: The World Bank and IMF in Africa. *Africa Action Position Paper* (April 2002). Available online at http://www.africa action.org/action/sap0204.htm. Accessed 22.4.06

Commission on Macroeconomics and Health (2001) *Macroeconomics and Health: Investing in Health for Economic Development.* Report. Geneva, WHO, 200p.

Cordellier, S., Didiot, B. *et al.* (2004) *L'Etat du monde: Annuaire économique et géopolitique mondial.* Paris: Editions La Découverte.

Coulmas, F. (1992*) Language and Economy.* Oxford: Blackwell.

Coulmas, F. (2001) Literacy in Japan: Kanji, Kana, Romaji, and Bits. In D. Olson and N. Torrance (eds) *The Making of Literate Societies* (pp. 101–120). Oxford: Blackwell Publishing.

Council of Europe (1992) *European Charter for Regional or Minority Languages.* European Treaty Series 148. Strasbourg: Council of Europe. Available online at http://ec.europa.eu/education/policies/lang/languages/langmin/files/charter_en.pdf. Accessed 30.5.07.

Crystal, D. (1997) *English as a Global Language.* Cambridge: Cambridge University Press.

Dalby, D. (1967) A survey of the indigenous scripts of Liberia and Sierra Leone. *African Language Studies* VIII, 1–51.

Dávila, A. and Mora, M. (2000) English fluency of recent Hispanic immigrants to the United States in 1980 and 1990. In *Economic Development and Cultural Change*, 48: 369–389.

DeGraff, M. (2003) Against Creole exceptionalism. *Language* 79 (2), 391–410.

De Klerk, V. (2002) Part 2: The teachers speak. *Perspectives in Education* 20 (1), 15–27.

Department of Education (1997) *Language-in-education Policy.* Pretoria: DoE. Available online at http://www.uni-wuerzberg.de/law/sf00000_html. Accessed 3.2.06.

Department of Education (2005) *Curriculum 2005.* Pretoria: DoE. Available online at http://education.pwv.gov.za/DoE_Sites/Curriculum/New_2005/draft_revised_national_curriculu.htm#overview. Accessed 18.06.06.

Descartes, R. (1637) *Le discours de la méthode: Pour bien conduire sa raison et chercher la vérité dans les sciences.* Leyde: Imprimerie de Ian Maire.

Devarajan, S., Dollar, D. and Holmgren, T. (eds) (2001) *Aid and Reform in Africa.* Washington, DC: World Bank.

Devonish, H. (1986) *Language and Liberation: Creole Language Politics in the Caribbean.* London: Karia Press.

Diki-Kidiri, M. and Baboya, E. (2003) Les langues africaines sur la toile. *Cahiers du Rifal* 23, 5–32. Available online at www.rifal.org/3_information.html. Accessed 10.2.06.

Djité, P. (1987) Francophonie in Africa: Some obstacles. *Journal of the Washington Academy of Sciences* 77 (1), 40–46.

Djité, P. (1988) Correcting errors in language classification in Africa: Monolingual nuclei and multilingual satellites. *Language Problems and Language Planning* 12 (1), 1–13.

Djité, P. (1989) The spread of Dyula and popular French in Côte d'Ivoire. *Language Problems and Language Planning* 2 (3), 213–225.

Djité, P. (1992) The Arabization of Algeria: Linguistic and socio-political motivations. *International Journal of the Sociology of Language* 98 (2), 16–32.

Djité, P. (1993) Language and development in Africa. *International Journal of the Sociology of Language* 100 (101), 149–166.

Djité, P. (1994) De quel côté se lèvera le soleil ? *Afrique 2000, Revue africaine de politique internationale* 17, 99–102.

Djité, P. (1996) La loi Toubon et le pluralisme linguistique et culturel en francophonie. *Afrique 2000, Revue africaine de politique internationale* 24, 83–102.

Djité, P. (2006a) Living on borrowed tongues? A view from within. In M. Pütz, J. Fishman and J. Neff-van Aertselaer (eds) *Along the Routes to Power: Explorations of Empowerment through Language* (pp. 405–420). Berlin: Mouton de Gruyter.

Djité, P. (2006b) Shifts in linguistic identities in a global world. *Language Problems and Language Planning* 30 (1), 1–20.

Djité, P. and Kpli, J.-F.Y.K. (2007) The language situation in Côte d'Ivoire since 2000: An update. In R.B. Kaplan and R.B. Baldauf, Jr (eds) *Language Planning and Policy in Africa, Vol. 2: Algeria, Côte d'Ivoire, Nigeria and Tunisia* (pp. 185–189). Clevedon: Multilingual Matters.

Douglass, F. (1852) The meaning of July Fourth for the Negro. Speech delivered to the leading citizens of Rochester, New York. Available online at http://www.pbs.org/wgbh/aia/part4/4h2927t.html. Accessed 21.5.07.

Drennan, M. (1998) Reproductive health: New perspectives on men's participation. *Population Reports* Series J, no. 46. Baltimore: Johns Hopkins University, Population Information Program.

Dumont, P. (1990) *Le français langue africaine*. Paris: L'Harmattan.
Dumont, R. (1980) *L'Afrique étranglée: Zambie, Tanzanie, Sénégal, Côte d'Ivoire, Guinée-Bissau, Cap-Vert*. Paris: Editions du Seuil.
Dumont, R. (1986) *Pour l'Afrique, j'accuse*. Paris: Plon.
Dumont, R. (1991) *Démocratie pour l'Afrique*. Paris: Seuil.
Durand, C-X. (2002) La manipulation mentale par la destruction des langues. Article 19, *Dossier: Mondialisation et démocratie linguistique* (14 Septembre). Available online at http://www.voxlatina.com/vox_dsp2.php3?art=1573. Accessed 15.3.06.
Dustmann, C. (1994) Speaking fluency, writing fluency and earnings of migrants. In *Journal of Population Economics* 7: 133–156.
Dustmann, C. and van Soest, A. (2001) Language fluency and earnings: Estimation with misclassified language indicators. *Review of Economics and Statistics*, 83: 663–674.
Dutcher, N. (2004) *Expanding Educational Opportunity in Linguistically Diverse Societies*. Washington, DC: Center for Applied Linguistics.
Easterlin, R. (1981) Why isn't the whole world developed? *Journal of Economic History* 41 (1), 1–19.
Easterly, W. (2002) What did structural adjustment adjust? The association of policies and growth with repeated IMF and World Bank adjustment loans. Working paper. Washington, DC: Center for Global Development, Institute for International Economics.
Easterly, W. (2005) Inequality does cause underdevelopment. Working paper. Washington, DC: Center for Global Development, Institute for International Economics.
The Economist (2001) Finance and economics: Tongue-tied. 7 April, p. 83.
The Economist's View (2005) Will the dollar lose its position as the dominant reserve currency? 29 September. Available online at http://economistsview.typepad.com/economistsview/2005/09/will_the_dollar.html. Accessed 6.2.06.
Edwards, J. (1985) *Language, Society and Identity*. Oxford: Basil Blackwell.
Edwards, J. (1989) *Language and Disadvantage* (2nd edn). London: Cole & Whurr.
Eisemon, T., Cleghorn, A. and Nyamate, A. (1989) A note on language of instruction, teaching and cognitive outcomes of science of instruction in primary schools in the Kisii and Kwale districts of Kenya. *Kenya Journal of Education* 4, 153–65.
Errington, J. (2001) Colonial linguistics. *Annual Review of Anthropology* 30, 19–39.
Fabian, J. (1983) Missions and the colonization of African languages: developments in the Former Belgian Congo. *Canadian Journal of African Studies/Revue Canadienne des Etudes Africaines* 17 (2), 165–187.
Fabian, J. (1986) *Language and Colonial Power: The Appropriation of Swahili in the Former Congo 1880–1938*. Cambridge: Cambridge University Press.
Fadegnon, D. (2006) Le point de la situation, hier matin : 8 décès, 68 hospitalisations, 77. 776 consultations. *Soir Info*, 26 September.
Fairclough, N. (2001) *Language and Power* (2nd edn). London: Longman and Pearson Education Ltd.
Fantognan, X. (2005) A note on African languages on the worldwide web. In J. Paolillo, D. Pimienta, D. Prado *et al.*, *Measuring Linguistic Diversity on the Internet* (pp. 105–108). Montreal: UNESCO.
FAO (Food and Agriculture Organisation) (2001) *World Food Report 2000*. Rome: Food and Agriculture Organisation.

Fardon, R. and Furniss, G. (1994) Introduction. Frontiers and boundaries: African languages as political environment. In R. Fardon and G. Furniss (eds) *African Languages, Development and the State* (pp.1–32). London: Routledge.

Fasold, R. (1984) *The Sociolinguistics of Society.* Oxford: Blackwell.

Feeley, F. (2006) Fight AIDS as well as the brain drain. *The Lancet* 368 (9534), 435–436.

Fenton, S. (ed.) (2004) *For Better or Worse: Translation as a Tool for Change in the South Pacific.* Manchester: St Jerome Publisher.

Ferguson, G. (2000) The medium of instruction in African education: The role of the linguist. In S. Makoni and N. Kamwangamalu (eds) *Language and Institutions in Africa* (pp. 95–111). Cape Town: Centre for Advanced Studies of African Society.

Ferreira, M. and Makoni, S. (2002) Towards a cultural and linguistic construction of late-life dementia in an urban African population. In S. Makoni and K. Stroeken (eds) *Ageing in Africa: Sociolinguistic and Anthropological Approaches* (pp. 21–42). Burlington: Ashgate.

Filmer, D. and Pritchett, L. (1998) Educational attainment profiles of the poor (and rich): DHS evidence from around the globe. Unpublished mimeo.

Finlayson, R. and Slabbert, S. (2004) Is instruction in the mother tongue always the optimal choice? South African case studies with reference to the inclusion/ exclusion debate. *LAUD Series A: General and Theoretical Paper* 60. Essen: University of Duisburg-Essen.

Fishman, J. (1991) Theoretical recapitulation: What is reversing language shift (RLS) and how can it succeed? In J. Fishman *Reversing Language Shift: Theoretical and Empirical Foundations of Assistance to Threatened Languages* (pp. 381–419). Clevedon: Multilingual Matters.

Fishman, J. (1995) On the limits of ethnolinguistic democracy. In T. Skutnabb-Kangas and R. Phillipson (eds) *Linguistic Human Rights: Overcoming Linguistic Discrimination* (pp. 49–61). Berlin: Mouton de Gruyter.

Fogel, W. (1966) The effects of low educational attainment on incomes: A comparative study of selected ethnic groups. *Journal of Human Resources* 1, 22–40.

Foster, P. (1972) Problems of literacy in sub-Saharan Africa. In T. Sebeok (ed.) *Current Trends in Linguistics* (Vol. 8; pp. 587–617). The Hague: Mouton.

Fraternité Matin (1980) La littérature africaine en langues africaines. Interview with Robert Cornevin, 1 April.

Fraternité Matin (2006) 1200 médecins chômeurs: Non au concours d'entrée. Fratmat – La Côte d'Ivoire au quotidien (article by Nimatoulaye Ba). No. 12450, 8 May.

Frey, C. (1993) Trois langues et plusieurs normes pour une minorité grandissante de francophones au Burundi. In D. de Robillard and M. Beniamino (eds) *Le français dans l'espace francophone* (Vol. 1; pp. 243–259). Paris: Champion.

Friends of the Earth (2004) Blair must push Bush to act on climate change. Press release, Friends of the Earth, Nov. 11. Available online at www.foe.co.uk/resource/ press_releases/blair_must_push_bush_to_ac_10112004.html. Accessed 3.12.06.

Futurs Africains (2003) *Afrique 2025: Quels futurs possibles pour l'Afrique au Sud du Sahara?* Paris: Editions Karthala.

Gallup, J. and Sachs, J. (2001) The economic burden of malaria. *American Journal of Tropical Medicine and Hygiene* 64 (1–2), 85–96.

Gelb, I. (1952) *A Study of Writing.* Chicago: The University of Chicago Press.

Gellner, E. (1983) *Nations and Nationalism.* Oxford: Basil Blackwell.

Gill, H. (1999) Language choice, language policy and the tradition-modernity debate in culturally mixed postcolonial communities: France and the 'Franco-phone' Maghreb as a case study. In Y. Suleiman (ed.) *Language and Society in the Middle East and North Africa* (pp. 122–136). London: RoutledgeCurzon.

Gobineau J-A. (Comte de) (1853–1855/1967) *Essai sur l'inégalité des races humaines.* Paris: Éditions Pierre Belfond.

Gordon, J. (1981) *Verbal Deficit: A Critique.* London: Croom Helm.

Government of Senegal (1971) Décret n° 71-566 du 21 mai 1971 relatif à la transcription des langues nationales, modifié par décret n° 72-702 du 16 juin 1972.

Graham, S. (2000) Social network analysis: More toward an application to sociolinguistic research and language development assessment. In G. Kindell and M. Lewis (eds) *Assessing Ethnolinguistic Vitality: Theory and Practice; Selected Papers from the Third International Language Assessment Conference* (pp. 131–166). *Publications in Sociolinguistics* 3. Dallas: SIL International.

Graddol, D. (2006) *English Next: Why Global English may mean the end of English as a Foreign Language.* London: British Council. Available online at www.british council.org/files/documents/learning-research-english-next.pdf. Accessed 3.1.07.

Grainger, K., Atkinson, K. and Coupland, N. (1990) Responding to the elderly: Troubles talk in caring contexts. In H. Giles, N. Coupland and J. Wiemann (eds) *Communication, Health and the Elderly* (pp. 192–212). Manchester: Manchester University Press.

Greenfield, W. (1830) *A Defence of the Surinam Negro-English Version of the New Testament.* London: Samuel Bagster.

Grenier, G. (1984) The effect of language characteristics on the wages of Hispanic-American males. *Journal of Human Resources* 19, 25–52.

Grillo, R. (1989) *Dominant Languages: Language and Hierarchy in Britain and France.* Cambridge: Cambridge University Press.

Grimes, B. (1992) *Ethnologue: Languages of the World.* Dallas, TX: Summer Institute of Linguistics.

Grimes, B. (ed.) (2000) *Ethnologue: Languages of the World.* Dallas, TX: Summer Institute of Linguistics.

Grin, F. (1996) Economic approaches to language and language planning: An introduction. *International Journal of the Sociology of Language* 121, 1–16.

Grin, F. (1997) Diversité linguistique et théorie économique de la valeur. In J. Hatem (ed.) *Lieux de l'Intersubjectivité* (pp. 155–174). Paris: L'Harmattan.

Grin, F. (1999) Market forces, language spread and linguistic diversity. In M. Kontra, R. Phillipson, T. Skutnabb-Kangas and T. Varády (eds) *Language: A Right and a Resource* (pp. 169–186). Budapest: Central European University Press.

Grin, F. (2003) Language planning and economics. In A. Liddicoat and P. Bryant (eds) *Language Planning and Economics, Current Issues in Language Planning* 4 (1), 1–66.

Grin, F. (2005) The economics of language policy implementation: Identifying and measuring costs. In N. Alexander (ed.) *Mother Tongue-Based Bilingual Education in Southern Africa: The Dynamics of Implementation* (pp. 11–25). Proceedings of a symposium held at the University of Cape Town, 16–19 October 2003. Cape Town: Volkswagen Foundation & PRAESA.

Grin, F. and Sfreddo, C. (1998) Language-based earnings differentials on the Swiss labour market: Is Italian a liability? *International Journal of Manpower* 19 (7), 520–532.

Grin, F. with Jensdóttir, R. and Ó Riagáin, D. (2003) *Language Policy Evaluation and the European Charter for Regional and Minority Languages*. London: Palgrave, Macmillan.

Halaoui, N. (2003) Relevance of education: Adapting curricula and use of African languages. Background paper for the ADEA Biennial 2003, Grand Baie, Mauritius, 3–6 December.

Hamoudi, A. and Birdsall, N. (2002) HIV/AIDS and the accumulation and utilization of human capital in Africa. Working paper 2. Washington: Center for Global Development.

Hampton, J. (1990) Living positively with AIDS. *Strategies for Hope* 2, 5.

Harel, X. (2006) *Afrique, pillage à huis clos: Quand le pétrole africain finance le monde occidental*. Paris: Fayard.

Harries, P. (1987) The roots of ethnicity: Discourse and the politics of language construction in South Africa. *African Affairs*, 25–52.

Harris, R. (1980) *The Language-makers*. Ithaca, NY: Cornell University Press.

Harris, R. (1981) *The Language Myth*. London: Duckworth.

Hart, K. (1973) Informal income opportunities and urban employment in Ghana. *Journal of Modern African Studies* 11, 61–89.

Hastings, A. (2001) Christianity and nationhood: Congruity or antipathy? *Journal of Religious History* 25 (3), 247–260 (14).

Haugen, E. (1966) Linguistics and language planning. In W. Bright (ed.) *Sociolinguistics* (pp. 50–71). The Hague: Mouton.

Hechter, M. (1975) *Internal Colonisation*. London: Routledge & Kegan Paul.

Heine, B. (1992) Language policies in Africa. In R. Herbert (ed.) *Language and Society in Africa: The Theory and Practice of Sociolinguistics* (pp. 23–35). Johannesberg: Witwatersrand University Press.

Heine, B. and Nurse, D. (eds) (2000) *African Languages: An Introduction*. Cambridge: Cambridge University Press.

Herrntein, R. and Murray, C. (1994). *The Bell Curve: Intelligence and Class Structure in American Life*. New York: Free Press.

Herselman, S. (1996) Some problems in health communication in a multicultural clinical setting: A South African experience. *Health Communication* 8 (2), 153–170.

Heugh, K. (1995a) From unequal education to the real thing. In K. Heugh, A. Siegruhn and P. Plüddermann (eds) *Multilingual Education for South Africa* (pp. 42–52). Johannesburgh: Heinemann.

Heugh, K. (1995b) Disabling and enabling: Implications of language policy trends in South Africa. In R. Mesthrie (ed.) *Language and Social History: Studies in South African Sociolinguistics* (pp. 329–350). Cape Town: David Philip.

Heugh, K. (1999) Languages, development and reconstructing education in South Africa. *International Journal of Educational Development* 19, 301–313.

Heugh, K. (2000) Giving good weight to multilingualism in South Africa. In R. Phillipson (ed.) *Equity, Power and Education* (pp. 234–238). Mahwah, NJ: Lawrence Erlbaum Associates.

Heugh, K. (2002) The case against bilingual and multilingual education in South Africa: Laying bare the myths. *Perspectives in Education* 20 (1), 171–96.

Heugh, K. (2003) Language policy and democracy in South Africa: The prospects of equality within rights-based policy and planning. Doctoral dissertation. Stockholm University Centre for Research on Bilingualism.

Heugh, K. (2006) Language education models in Africa: Research, design, decision-making, outcomes and costs. In H. Alidou, A. Boly, B. Brock-Utne, Y. Diallo, K. Heugh and E. Wolff (eds.) *Optimising Learning and Education in Africa: The Language Factor* (pp. 47–73). Commissioned by ADEA, GTZ and the Commonwealth Secretariat for the ADEA 2006 Biennial Meeting in Libreville, Gabon, 27-31 March.

Hutchinson, J. (1983) Educational reform for Niger's société de développement. Boston: The Walter Rodney African Studies Seminar (unpublished).

Hyltenstam, K. and Stroud, C. (2004) SIDA policy document proposal. Multilingualism in development (unpublished draft).

Hymes, D. (1984) Linguistic problems in defining the concept of 'Tribe'. In J. Baugh and J. Sherzen (eds) *Language in Use: Readings in Sociolinguistics* (pp. 7–27). Englewood Cliffs: Prentice Hall.

IAI (Institute for African Initiatives) (2003) Debating NEPAD: New agenda. *South African Journal of Social and Economic Policy* 9 (first quarter).

ICCAF (Inter-Church Coalition on Africa) (1993) *Beyond Adjustment: Responding to the Health Crisis in Africa*. Toronto: ICCAF.

Ilboudo, P. (2003) Etude de cas national, Burkina Faso. Pertinence de l'éducation. Adaptation des curricula et utilisation des langues africaines: Le cas de l'éducation bilingue au Burkina Faso. Working document for the ADEA, Biennial, Grand Baie, Mauritius, 3–6 December.

ILO (International Labour Organisation) (1972) *Employment, Incomes and Equity: A Strategy for Increasing Productive Employment in Kenya*. Geneva: ILO.

ILO (International Labour Organisation) (2004) *Global Employment Trends for Youth 2004*. Geneva: ILO.

ILO (International Labour Organisation) (2006) *Global Employment Trends for Youth*. Geneva: ILO.

Irvine, J. and Gal, S. (2000) Language ideology and linguistic differentiation. In P.V. Kroskrity (ed.) *Regimes of Language: Ideologies, Polities, and Identities* (pp. 35–83). Oxford: James Currey.

Isham, J., Woolcock, M., Pritchett, L. and Busby, G. (2005) The varieties of resource experience: Natural resource export structures and the political economy of economic growth. *The World Bank Economic Review* 19,141–174.

Jeater, D. (2001) Speaking like a native: Vernacular languages and the State in Southern Rhodesia, 1890–1935. *The Journal of African History*, 42: 449–468.

Jeune Afrique (2006a) Le Soudan, pays le plus vulnérable du monde. Jeune afrique.com. Accessed 2.5.06.

Jeune Afrique (2006b) Immigration, Françafrique, Côte d'Ivoire ... Sarkozy n'élude aucun sujet. Propos recueillis par François Soudan et Marwane Ben Yahmed. Jeuneafrique.com. Accessed 8.11.06.

Jeune Afrique (2007) Côte d'Ivoire: Les promesses de l'or noir. 14 April .

Jozana, X. (1999) Democratic consolidation in South Africa: Weaknesses and pitfalls. In K. Adenauer (ed.) *Consolidating Democracy in South Africa* (pp. 7–8). Stiftung seminar papers (unpublished).

Kabou, A. (1991) *Et si l'Afrique refusait le développement?* Paris: L'Harmattan.

Kamwangamalu, N. (2000) A new policy, old language practices: Status planning for African languages in a multilingual South Africa. *South African Journal of African Languages* 20 (1), 50–60.

Kamwendo, G. (2004) Language policy in health services: A sociolinguistic study of a Malawian referral hospital. PhD thesis. Institute for Asian and African Studies No. 6, Helsinki: Helsinki University Printing House.

Kapur, D., Lewis, J. and Webb, R. (1997) *The World Bank: Its First Half Century, Vol. 1: The History.* Washington, DC: The Brookings Institution.

Kaufmann, D. (2005) Back to basics: 10 myths about governance and corruption. *Finance and Development* 42 (3).

Kelly, M. (1991) *Education in Declining Economy: The Case of Zambia 1975–1985.* Washington, DC. The International Bank for Reconstruction and Development and The World Bank.

Kerber, L. (1997) The meanings of citizenship. *Journal of Dissent* 33–37.

Keulder, C. and Wiese, T. (2005) Democracy without democrats? Results from the 2003 Afrobarometer survey in Namibia. A comparative series of national public attitude surveys on democracy, markets and civil society in Africa. *Afrobarometer Working Paper* 47. Cape Town: IDASA, CDD Ghana and MSU. Available online at pdf.usaid.gov/pdf_docs/PNADF396.pdf. Accessed 2.6.05.

Killick, T., Gunatilaka, R. and Marr, A. (1998) *Aid and the Political Economy of Policy Change.* London: Routledge.

Ki-Zerbo, J. (1990) *Eduquer ou périr.* Paris: Unesco et Unicef.

Ki Zerbo, J. (2003) *A quand l'Afrique?* Interview with René Holenstein. Paris: Editions de l'Aube.

Kodjo, E. (1986) *..et demain l'Afrique.* Paris: Stock.

Koelle, S. (1854) *Outlines of a Grammar of the Vei Language.* London: Church Missionary House.

Konaré, A. (2005) Statement at the 55th Session of the WHO-AFRO Regional Committee for Africa, Maputo, Mozambique (unpublished). August 22–26.

Ku, L. and Flores, G. (2005) Pay now or pay later: Providing interpreter services in health care. *Health Affairs* 24 (2), 435–444.

Kuhn, T. (1962) *The Structure of Scientific Revolutions.* Chicago: University of Chicago Press.

Laitin, D. (1992) *Language Repertoires and State Construction in Africa.* Cambridge: Cambridge University Press.

Lamb, D. (1987) *The African.* New York: Random House.

La Porta, R. Lopez-de-Silanes, F., Shleifer, A. and Vishny, R. (1998) Law and finance. *Journal of Political Economy* 106 (6), 1113–1155.

La Porta, R. Lopez-de-Silanes, F., Shleifer, A. and Vishny, R. (1999) The quality of government. *Journal of Law, Economics and Organization* 15, 222–279.

Léger, J-M. (1987) *La Francophonie: Grand dessein, grande ambiguité.* Ville de LaSalle: Hurtubise HMH.

Lieberson, S. (1980) Procedures for improving sociolinguistic surveys of language maintenance and language shift. *International Journal of the Sociology of Language* 25, 11–27.

Lo Bianco, J. (1987) *National Policy on Languages.* Canberra: Australian Government Publishing Service.

Lo Bianco, J. (1991) Language policy: Australia's experience. In R. Baldauf and A. Luke (eds) *Language Planning and Education in Australia and the South Pacific* (pp. 47–79). Clevedon: Multilingual Matters.

Lo Bianco, J. (2002) Destitution, wealth, and cultural context: Language and development connections. In J. Lo Bianco (ed.) *Voices From Phnom Penh. Development and Language: Global Influences and Local Effects. Reflections from a Conference in Phnom Penh on the Complex Interaction between Economically Conceived Progress and Indicators of Communication-language* (pp. 3–22). Melbourne: Language Australia Ltd.

Macdonald, C. (1990) *English Language Skills Evaluation: A Final Report of the Threshold Project*. Pretoria: Human Sciences Research Council.

Macdonald, C. and Burroughs, E. (1991) *Eager to Talk and Learn and Think: Bilingual Primary Education in South Africa*. Cape Town: Maskew Miller Longman.

McCullagh, D. (2005) MIT's Nicholas Negroponte and UN's Kofi Annan announce details of hand-cranked laptop for children in developing world. *CNET News.com*. Accessed 15.5.06

McLaughlin, F. (2001) Dakar Wolof and the configuration of an urban identity. *Journal of African Cultural Studies* 14 (2), 153–172.

McLean, D. and McCormick, K. (1996) English in South Africa 1940–1996. In J. Fishman, A. Conrad and A. Rubal-Lopez (eds) *Post-Imperial English: Status Change in Former British and American Colonies, 1940–1990* (pp. 303–308). New York: Mouton de Gruyter.

Maho, J. (2004) How many languages are there in Africa, really? In K. Bromber and B. Smieja (eds) *African Languages and Globalisation: Risks and Benefits* (pp. 179–96). Berlin and New York: Mouton de Gruyter.

Makoni, S. (1998) Conflict and control in intercultural communication: A case study of compliance-gaining strategies in interactions between Black nurses and White residents in a nursing home in Cape Town, South Africa. *Multilingua* 17 (2–3), 227–248.

Makoni, S. (2000) In the beginning was the missionary's word: The European invention of an African language: The case of Shona in Zimbabwe. In K. Prah (ed.) *Between Distinction and Extinction: The Harmonisation and Standardisation of African Languages* (pp. 157–65). *Casas Book Series* 1. Cape Town: The Centre for Advanced Studies of African Society.

Makoni, S., Brutt-Griffler, J. and Mashiri, P. (2007) The use of 'indigenous' and urban vernaculars in Zimbabwe. *Language in Society* 36: 25–49.

Makoni, S., Dube, B. and Mashiri P. (2006) Zimbabwe colonial and post-colonial language policy and planning practices. *Current Issues in Language Planning* 7 (4), 377–414.

Makoni, S. and Meinhof, U. (2004) Western perspectives in applied linguistics in Africa. *AILA Review* 17 (1), 77–104.

Makoni, S. and Pennycook, A. (2005) Disinventing and (re)constituting languages. *Critical Inquiry in Language Studies* 2 (2) 137–156.

Makoni, S. and A. Pennycook (eds) (2007) *Disinventing and Reconstructing Languages*. Clevedon: Multilingual Matters.

Malik, K. (2000) Let them die. *Prospect* 57 (November), 16–17.

Manguelle, D. (1989) *L'Afrique a-t-elle besoin d'un programme d'ajustement culturel?* Paris: Editions Nouvelles du Sud.

Mankell, H. (2003) Waiting room of death. *SPIEGEL* in-depth interview with Henning Mankell about his love for Africa, the necessity of Western aid and the pride of the poorest people on earth. Spiegel Online International 14 July. Available online at http://www.spiegel.de/international/spiegel/0,1518,256 728,00. html. Accessed 21.5.07.

Mazrui, A. (1975) *The Political Sociology of the English Language: An African Perspective*. The Hague: Mouton.

Mazrui, A. (1997) The world bank, the language question and the future of African education. *Race and Class* 38 (3), 35–48.

Mazrui, A. (2001) The African Renaissance: A triple legacy of skills, values and gender. In S. Saxena (ed.) *Africa Beyond 2000: Essays on Africa's Political and Economic Development in the Twenty-First Century* (pp. 29–60). Delhi: Kalinga Publishers.

Mazrui, A. (2002) The English language in African education: Dependency and decolonization. In J.W. Tollefson (ed.) *Language Policies in Education: Critical Issues* (pp. 267–281). Mahwah, NJ: Lawrence Erlbaum Associates.

Mazrui, A. (2003) Maintaining linguodiversity: Africa in the twenty-first century. In H. Tonkin and T. Reagan (eds) *Language in the 21st century* (pp. 99–113). Amsterdam: Benjamins.

Mazrui, A. and Mazrui, A. (1998) *The Power of Babel: Language and Governance in African Experience*. Oxford: James Currey.

Memmi, A. (1989) *Portrait du colonisé*. Paris: ACCT.

Microsoft Corporation (2004) Microsoft enables millions more to experience personal computing through local language program. PressPass, Information for Journalists. Available online at http://www.microsoft.com/presspass/press/2004/mar04/03-16LLPPR.asp. Accessed 16.3.04.

Ministère de l'éducation (s.d.) *L'école du peuple, structures et fonctionnement*. Brazzaville: Ronéo.

Ministry of Education (1994) *The Structure of the New School Curriculum*. Lusaka: Government Printers.

Ministry of Education (1996) *Educating Our Future: National Policy on Education*. Lusaka: Government Printers.

Ministry of Education (2000) *The Basic School Curriculum Framework: Curriculum*. Lusaka: Government Printers.

Le Monde (Economie) (2007) Le G8 s'inquiète du surendettement de l'Afrique et épingle la Chine. *Le Monde et AFP*. Available online at http://www.lemonde.fr/web/article/0,1-0@2-3234,36-912507@51-912509,0.html. Accessed 20.5.07.

Mooney, P. (2005) China's African safari. *YaleGlobal Online*, 3 January. Yale: Yale Centre for the Study of Globalisation.

Mothibeli, A. (2005) Cross-country achievement results from the SACMEQ II project,2000 to 2002. A quantitative analysis of education systems in Southern and Eastern Africa. *Edusource Data News* 49 (October).

MSF (Médecins sans frontières) (2006) MSF appelle le gouvernement angolais à prendre des mesures beaucoup plus importantes contre le choléra. Les Missions de MSF dans le monde. Country Profile: Angola, 13 April. Available online at www.msf.be. Accessed 20.5.06.

Multilingual Action Group (2003) Media statement (10 February). Available online at www.litnet.co.za/taaldebat/magE.asp. Accessed 23.12.05

Mutembei, A., Emmelin, M., Lugalla, J. and Dahlgren, L. (2002) Communicating about AIDS: Changes in understanding and coping with help of language in urban Kagera, Tanzania. *Journal of Asian and African Studies* 37 (1), 1–16.
Muthwii, M. (2002) *Language Policy and Practices in Education in Kenya and Uganda.* Nairobi: Phoenix.
Mwinsheikhe, H. (2002) *Science and the Language Barrier: Using Kiswahili as a Medium of Instruction in Tanzania Secondary Schools as a Strategy of Improving Student Participation and Performance in Science.* Report 10/1, *Education in Africa.* Oslo: Institute for Educational Research.
Myers-Scotton, C. (1993) Elite closure as a powerful language strategy: The African case. *International Journal of the Sociology of Language* 103, 149–163
NCCRD (National Centre for Curriculum Research and Development) (2000) *Language in the Classroom: Towards a Framework for Intervention.* Research Report. Pretoria: Department of Education.
NEPAD (2001) *The New Partnership for Africa's Development.* Abuja, October. Available online at www.nepad.org. Accessed 20.6.06.
Nettle, D. (2000) Linguistic fragmentation and the wealth of nations: The Fishman-Pool Hypothesis re-examined. *Economic Development and Cultural Change* 48 (2), 335–348.
Nettle, D. and Romaine, S. (2000) *Vanishing Voices: The Extinction of the World's Languages.* Oxford University Press.
Ngalasso, M. (1989) Le dilemne des langues africaines. *Notre Librairie* 98, 15–21.
OAU (Organisation of African Unity) (2002a) *Report of the 4th General Assembly of the African Population Commission.* Decisions of the 76th Ordinary Session of the OAU Council of Ministers / Eleventh Ordinary Session of the AECCM/Dec. 661–670. Durban, South Africa. Available online at www.au2002.gov.za/docs/summit_council/cmdec2.htm. Accessed 5.5.06.
OAU (Organisation of African Unity) (2002b) *The New Partnership for Africa's Development (NEPAD): Declaration on Democracy, Political, Economic and Corporate Governance.* Adopted at the 38th Ordinary Session, Assembly of Heads of State and Government, July 8. Durban, South Africa.
Obanya, P. (1980) Research on alternative teaching in Africa. In E. Yoloye and K-H. Flechsig (eds) *Educational Research for Development* (pp. 67–112). Bonn: Deutsche Stiftung für Internationale Entwicklung.
OECD (Organisation for Economic Co-operation and Development) (2006) *African Economic Outlook 2005/2006.* Development Centre, Paris. Available online at www.oecd.org/bookshopsales@oecd.org. Accessed 10.1.07.
OECD (Organisation for Economic Co-operation and Development) (2007) Development aid from OECD countries fell 5.1% in 2006. Development Co-operation Directorate (DCD-DAC). Available online at http://www.oecd.org/document/17/0,3343,en_2649_33721_38341265_1_1_1_1,00.html. Accessed 15.4.07.
OECD and ADB (2005) Organisation for Economic Co-operation and Development (OECD) and African Development Bank (ADB) (2005) *African Economic Outlook 2004/2005.* Development Centre, Paris. Available online at www.oecd.org/bookshopsales@oecd.org. Accessed 10.1.07.
Ohly, R. (1992) Diagnostic and therapeutic aspects of sociolinguistics in pre-independence Namibia: The effects of first and second order observation. In R. Herbert (ed.) *Language and Society in Africa* (pp. 49–69). Johannesburgh: Witwatersrand University Press.

OICS (Organe International de contrôle des stupéfiants) (2007) *Rapport annuel 2006*. E/INCB/2006/1. New York: OICS. Available online at http://www.incb.org/ pdf/f/press/2007/annual-report-press-kit-2006-fr-4.pdf. Accessed 10.6.07.

Omoniyi, T. (2004) *The Sociolinguistics of Borderlands*. Trenton, NJ: Africa World Press.

Ong, L., de Haes, C., Hoos, A. and Lammes, F. (1995) Doctor–patient communication: A review of the literature. *Social Science and Medicine* 40 (7), 903–918.

Onwuejeogwu, M. (1987) Indigenous socio-economic and political organisations and their relevance to development in contemporary Nigeria. Paper presented at the Nigerian Anthropological and Sociological Association on Strategies of Authentic Development in Nigeria. University of Ilorin, November 30 to December 2.

Organisation Internationale de la Francophonie (2007) *La francophonie dans le monde en 2006–2007*. Paris: Editions Nathan. Available online at www.francophonie. org/actualites/nouvelle.cfm?der_id=1325. Accessed 15.6.07.

Orsenna, E. (2006) *Voyage au pays du coton: Petit précis de mondialisation*. Paris: Fayard.

Oti, D. (2000) Corruption en Afrique. La légitimité des États est mise en péril. *Afrique Expansion* 7 (2nd quarter), 36.

Ouédraogo, M. (2002) L'utilisation des langues nationales dans les systèmes éducatifs en Afrique. *IIRCA-UNESCO Bulletin*. December 4 (4).

Over, M. (1992) The macro-economic impact of AIDS in sub-Saharan Africa. Technical working paper 3. Washington, DC: The World Bank, Africa Technical Department, Population, Health, and Nutrition Division.

Oxfam (2006) Four million more health professionals need worldwide. Oxfam Press Release. Available online at http://www.oxfam.org.uk/press/releases/world_health_day070406.htm. Accessed 2.6.07.

Palmer, S. (1997) Language of work: The critical link between economic change and language shift. In J. Reyhner (ed.) *Teaching Indigenous Languages* (pp. 263–287). Flagstaff, AZ: Northern Arizona University.

Le Patriote (2006): La guerre ivoirienne sent le pétrole, Célébration de la messe de la paix. Cardinal Bernard Agré (Archevêque d'Abidjan), 1 January.

Pennycook, A. (1994) *The Cultural Politics of English as an International Language*. London: Longman.

Pennycook, A. (2002) Mother tongues, governmentality, and protectionism. *International Journal of the Sociology of Language* 154: 11–28.

Pennycook, A. and Makoni, S. (2005) The modern mission: The language effects of Christianity. *Journal of Language, Identity & Education* 4 (2), 137–155.

People's Daily Online (2005) US targets oil in Africa. Available online at http://english.peopledaily.com.cn/200508/05/eng20050805_200508.html. Accessed 2.06.

Perotti, R. (1996) Growth, income distribution and democracy: What the data say. *Journal of Economic Growth* 1, 149–187.

Person, Y. (1982) Colonisation et décolonisation en Côte d'Ivoire. *Le mois en Afrique* 188–89, 15–30.

Persson, T. and Tabellini, G. (1994) Is inequality harmful for growth? *The American Economic Review* 84, 600–621.

Peyrefitte, A. (1973) *Quand la Chine s'éveillera ... le monde tremblera*. Paris: Fayard.

Peyrefitte, A. (1996) *La Chine s'est éveillée*. Paris: Fayard.

220

The Sociolinguistics of Development in Africa

Pinnock, H., Thao, D. and Bich, N. (2006) Les politiques et les pratiques du Vietnam *Id21 Insights Education 5, Communicating Development Research*. Available online at www.id21.org/insights/insights-ed05f/art05.html. Accessed 10.6.07.

Pool, J. (1972) National development and language diversity. In J. Fishman (ed.) *Advances in the Sociology of Language* (Vol. 2; pp. 213–230). The Hague: Mouton.

Prah, K. (2003) Going native: Language of instruction for education, development and African emancipation. In B. Brock-Utne, Z. Desai and M. Qorro (eds) *The Language of Instruction in Tanzania and South Africa (LOITASA)* (pp. 14–35). Dar es Salaam: E & D Publishers.

Prah, K. (ed.) (2000) *Between Distinction and Extinction: The Harmonisation and Standardisation of African Languages. Casas Book Series* 1. Cape Town: The Centre for Advanced Studies of African Society (CASAS).

Prah, K. (ed.) (2002) *Rehabilitating African Languages. Casas Book Series* 18. Cape Town: The Centre for Advanced Studies of African Society (CASAS).

Pretorius, L. and Patel, S. (2004) *The New Partnership for Africa's Development (NEPAD): A Critical Review.* Cape Town: Labour Research Service, AIDC.

Probyn, M. (2001) Teachers' voices: Teachers' reflections on learning and teaching through the medium of English as a second language. *International Journal of Bilingual Education and Bilingualism* 4 (4), 249–266.

Probyn, M (2005) Language and the struggle to learn: The intersection of classroom realities, language policy, and neocolonial and globalisation discourses in South African schools. In L. Angel and P. Martin (eds) *Decolonisation, Globalisation: Language-in-Education Policy and Practice* (pp. 153–172). Clevedon: Multilingual Matters.

Probyn, M., Murray, S., Botha, L., Botya, P., Brooks, M. and Westphal, V. (2002) Minding the gaps: An investigation into language policy and practice in four Eastern Cape districts. *Perspectives in Education* 20 (1), 29–46.

Prophet, R. and Dow, J. (1994) Mother-tongue language and concept development in science: A Botswana case study. *Language, Culture and Curriculum* 7 (3), 205–17.

Przeworski, A. and Vreeland, J. (2000) The effect of IMF programs on economic growth. *Journal of Development Economics* 62, 385–421.

Pugh, R. (1996) *Effective Language in Health and Social Work.* London: Chapman and Hall.

Pugh, R. and Jones, E. (1999) Language and practice: Minority language provision within the Guardian and Litem service. *The British Journal of Social Work* 29 (4), 529–545.

Rahnema, M. (2003) *Quand la misère chasse la pauvreté.* Paris: Fayard/Actes Sud.

Rassool, N. (2004) Countering globalization: Linguistic diversity and the assertion of local voices in development. In K. Fraurud and K. Hyltenstam (eds) *Multilingualism in Global and Local Perspectives* (pp. 31–46). Stockholm: Rinkeby Institute of Multilingual Research.

Ray, P. (1968) Language standardisation. In J. Fishman (ed.) *Readings in the Sociology of Language* (pp. 754–765). The Hague: Mouton.

Raynaud, A., Marion, P. and Béland, R. (1969) La répartition des revenus selon les groupes ethniques au Canada. Unpublished manuscript. Ottawa: Commission royale d'enquête sur le bilinguisme et le biculturalisme.

Renan, E. (1882) Qu'est-ce qu'une nation? Lecture given at the Sorbonne on 11 March 1882. Available online at http://ourworld.compuserve.com/home pages/bib_lisieux/nation01.htm. Accessed 27.4.06.

Reuters (2007) China's shadow hangs over German G8 meeting. 19 May. Available online at http://today.reuters.com/news/articlenews.aspx? Accessed on 20.5.07.

Ricardo, D. (1817) *On the Principles of Political Economy and Taxation*. London: John Murray.

Robbins, L. (1935) *Essay on the Nature and Significance of Economic Science*, 2. London: Macmillan.

Robert, A-C. (2004) *L'Afrique au secours de l'Occident*. Paris: Editions de l'Atelier.

Robinson, C. (1996) *Language Use in Rural Development: An African Perspective*. Berlin: Mouton de Gruyter.

Romaine, S. (1994) *Language in Society: An Introduction to Sociolinguistics*. Oxford: Oxford University Press.

Rosen, Y. (2002) Judge strikes down Alaska's official English law. *Reuters News Service*, March 26, 2002.

Roy-Campbell, Z. (1998) Attitudes towards the use of African languages as media of instruction in secondary schools. In K. Prah (ed.) *Between Distinction and Extinction: The Harmonization & Standardization of African Languages* (pp. 255-264). Johannesburg: Witwatersrand University Press.

Roy-Campbell, Z. (2000) The language of schooling: Deconstructing myths about African languages. In S. Makoni and N. Kamwangamalu (eds) *Language and Institutions in Africa* (pp. 111–31). *Casas Book Series* 5. Cape Town: The Centre for Advanced Studies of African Society (CASAS).

Roy-Campbell, Z. (2003) Promoting African languages as conveyors of knowledge in educational institutions. In S. Makoni, G. Smitherman, A. Ball and A. Spears (eds) *Black Linguistics: Language, Society and Politics in Africa and the Americas* (pp. 83–102). London: Routledge.

Rubagumya, C. (1994) Introduction. In C. Rubagumya (ed.) *Teaching and Researching Language in African Classrooms* (pp. 1–5). Clevedon: Multilingual Matters.

Rubagumya, C. (2003) English-medium primary schools in Tanzania: A new 'linguistic market' in education? In B. Brock-Utne, Z. Desai and M. Qorro (eds) *The Language of Instruction in Tanzania and South Africa (LOITASA)* (pp. 149–70). Dar es Salaam: E & D Publishers.

Sachs, J. (2007) L'aide peut être efficace. In *Jeune Afrique/l'Intelligent*, 21 Janvier 2007. Available at www.jeuneafrique.com/jeune_afrique/article_jeune_afrique.asp? Accessed 25.1.07.

Said, E. (1985) An ideology of difference. *Critical Inquiry* 12 (1), 38–58.

Santé Sud (2006) Madagascar, 'l'effet tâche d'huile'. Trimestriel, Numéro 72, décembre: pp. 1, 6. Available online at www.santesud.org. Accessed 30.5.07.

Saohatse, M. (1997) African language varieties at Baragwanath Hospital: A sociolinguistic analysis. Unpublished PhD Thesis, University of South Africa.

Saohatse, M. (1998) Communication problems in multilingual speech communities. *South African Journal of African Languages* 18 (4), 111–117.

Saohatse, M. (2000) Solving communication problems in medical institutions. *South African Journal of African Languages* 20 (1), 95–102.

Sartre, J.-P. (1948) *Orphée noir*, Situations III. Paris: Gallimard.

de Saussure, F. (1916/1986). *Course in General Linguistics* (C. Bally, A. Sechehasye and A. Riedlinger, ed. and R. Harris, trans.). La Salle, IL: Open Court.

Schaefer, B. (2003) Economic freedom: The path to African prosperity. Paper delivered in January at the conference on AGOA: The NGO Perspective on Implementation, Progress and Future Objectives in Phoenix, Mauritius.

Schultz, T. (1961) Investment in human capital. *American Economic Review* 51 (1), 1–17.

Schultz, T. (1989) Education investments and returns. In H. Chenery and T. Srinivasan (eds) *Handbook of Development Economics* (Vol. 1; pp. 543–630). Amsterdam: North Holland Publishing.

Sen, A. (1999) *Development as Freedom*. Oxford: Oxford University Press.

Sidaction, UNAIDS and WHO (2005) *Expanding Access to HIV Treatment through Community-based Organizations*. A joint publication of Sidaction, the Joint United Nations Programme on HIV/AIDS (UNAIDS) and the World Health Organisation (WHO). Geneva: UNAIDS Best Practice Collection.

Silué, B. (2006) Propagande: L'étrange rediffusion du discours de Banny en langues nationales. *Le Courrier d'Abidjan* 22 November. Available online at http://news.abidjan.net/h/224218.html. Accessed 23.11.06.

Simire, G. (2003) Developing and promoting multilingualism in public life and society in Nigeria. *Language, Culture and Curriculum* 16 (2), 231–244.

Skutnabb-Kangas, T. (2000) *Linguistic Genocide in Education, or Worldwide Diversity and Human Rights?* London: Lawrence Erlbaum Associates.

Smith, A. (1776/1976) *An Inquiry into the Nature and Causes of the Wealth of Nations*. Oxford: The Clarendon Press.

Smith, S. (2003) *Négrologie: Pourquoi l'Afrique se meurt*. Paris: Calmann-Lévy.

Smith, T. and Fortein, T-L (2005) Pandor's African languages plan faces big hurdles. *The Cape Argus* May 18, 2005.

Sokoloff, K. and Engerman, S. (2000) Institutions, factor endowments, and paths of development in the new world. *Journal of Economic Perspectives* 14 (3), 217–232.

Somitek (Somali Information Technology) (1999) Hikaadiye, a complete word-processor with Somali and English spell checking capability. Available online at www. somitek.com. Accessed 25.5.06.

Spilpunt (2007) *Weekly World Bank Briefings on dub-Saharan Africa* 14 June. Available online at http://spilpunt.blogspot.com/2007/03/weekly-world-bank-briefings-on-sub.html. Accessed 18.6.07.

Spolsky, B. (2003). *Language Policy*. Cambridge, UK: Cambridge University Press.

Spurr, N. (2001) Durban Unicity gets to work in the informal economy. *Khanyisa*, 1 September 2001. Available online at: http://www.idasa.org.za/. Accessed 15.6.07.

Standing, G. (1999) *Global Labour Flexibility: Seeking Distributive Justice*. New York: St Martin's Press.

Starkey, H. (2002) *Democratic Citizenship, Language Diversity and Human Rights. Language Policy Division Monographs*. Strasbourg: Council of Europe.

Stelhi, J-S. (2006) Patriotisme linguistique: En ces temps de défense de l'entreprise France, il n'est pas bien vu, pour nos patrons, de parler anglais. *L'Express* 30 March. Available online at www.lexpress.fr/info/societe/dossier/langue/dossier.asp?ida=437557. Accessed 5.5.06.

Stiglitz, J. (2002) *Globalization and its Discontents*. New York: Norton.

Suleiman, Y. (2004) *War of Words: Language and Conflict in the Middle East*. Cambridge: Cambridge University Press.

Tadadjeu, M. (ed.) (1990) *Le Défi de Babel au Cameroun*. Collection PROPELCA 53. Yaoundé: SIL Publication.

Thompson, C. and Pledger, L. (1993) Doctor–patient communication: Is patient knowledge of medical terminology improving? *Health Communication* 5, 88–89.

Titelman, G. (1996) *Random House Dictionary of Popular Proverbs and Sayings.* Random House: New York.

Tollefson, J. (1991) *Planning Language, Planning Inequality.* New York: Longman.

Tollefson, J. (ed.) (1995) *Power and Inequality in Language Education.* Cambridge: Cambridge University Press.

Tokman, V. (ed.) (1992) *Beyond Regulation: The Informal Economy in Latin America.* Geneva: World Employment Program, ILO.

Tonkin, H. (2006) Language inclusion and individual exclusion: Patterns of communication in bilingual and multilingual polities. Unpublished mimeo.

Tonkin, H. and Reagan, T. (eds) (2003) *Language in the 21st century.* Amsterdam: Benjamins.

Transparency International (2006) *The Global Corruption Report 2006.* London: Pluto Press.

Treaty of Nice (2001) Full text available online at www.eurotreaties.com/nicetext. html. Accessed 15.2.06.

Treaty of Rome (1957) Consolidated text available online at http://europa.eu.int/ eur-lex/en/search/search_treaties.html. Accessed 20.3.06.

Truman, H. (1949) Inaugural address, delivered in person at the Capitol. Provided courtesy of The American Presidency Project. John Woolley and Gerhard Peters. University of California, Santa Barbara. On WWW at www.trumanlibrary.org/ calendar/viewpapers.php? Accessed 19.04.06.

TWN *Africa* (2005) EC trade director 'stunned' in Dar as African Ministers oppose Singapore issues in EPAs. Political Economy Unit (ATA, January) 23 March. Available online at www.twnafrica.org/news_detail.asp?twnID=785. Accessed 16.2.06.

UK Commission on Africa (2005) *Our common interest.* Available at: http:// commissionforafrica.org (visited 12 March 2005).

UNAIDS (Joint United Nations Programme on HIV/AIDS) (2004) *2004 Report on the Global AIDS Epidemic.* Geneva: United Nations.

UNAIDS (Joint United Nations Programme on HIV/AIDS) (2006) *Report on the Global AIDS Epidemic.* In cooperation with the World Health Organisation. A UNAIDS 10th anniversary special edition. Geneva: United Nations.

UNCTAD (United Nations Conference on Trade and Development) (2001) Energy services in international trade: development implications. Geneva, 2001. Available at http://www.unctad.org. Accessed 30.4.07.

UNCTAD (United Nations Conference on Trade and Development) (2006) Least Developed Countries Report 2006: Developing Productive Capacities. Geneva: United Nations.

UNDP (United Nations Development Programme) (1992) *Human Development Report 1992.* Oxford: Oxford University Press.

UNDP (United Nations Development Programme) (1996) *Human Development Report 1996.* Oxford: Oxford University Press.

UNDP (United Nations Development Programme) (1999) *Human Development Report 1999.* Oxford: Oxford University Press.

UNDP (United Nations Development Programme) (2000a) *Overcoming Human Poverty.* Oxford: Oxford University Press.

UNDP (United Nations Development Programme) (2000b) *Human Development Report 2000:* Oxford: Oxford University Press.

UNDP (United Nations Development Programme) (2002) *Botswana Human Development Report 2002*. Oxford: Oxford University Press

UNDP (United Nations Development Programme) (2003) *Human Development Report 2003: Millennium Development Goals: A Compact Among Nations to End Human Poverty* New York: UNDP.

UNDP (United Nations Development Programme) (2004) *Human Development Report 2004: Cultural Liberty in Today's Diverse World*. New York: UNDP.

UNDP (United Nations Development Programme) (2005) *Millennium Project 2005. Investing In Development: A Practical Plan to Achieve the Millennium Development Goals*. New York: UNDP.

UNDP (United Nations Development Programme) (2006) *Millennium Development Goals Report*. New York: UNDP.

UNDP and UNPF (The United Nations Development Programme and the United Nations Population Fund) (2002) Recommendation by the Executive Director: Assistance to the Government of South Africa. First regular session 2002, 28 January to 8 February, New York: United Nations population fund proposed projects and programmes. Available online at www.unfpa.org/exbrd/2002/firstsession/dpfpazaf2.doc. Accessed 4.10.07.

UNECA (United Nations Economic Commission for Africa) (1989) *Economic Report on Africa 1989*. Addis Ababa: UNECA.

UNECA (United Nations Economic Commission for Africa) (2003) *The Bamako 2002 Declaration*. Addis Ababa: UNECA. Available online at www.uneca.org/codi/documents/pdf/bamako2002declarationen.pdf. Accessed on 5.2.07.

UNECA (United Nations Economic Commission for Africa) (2005a) *Striving for Good Governance in Africa: Synopsis of the 2005 African Governance Report*, Prepared for the African Development Forum IV. Addis Ababa: UNECA.

UNECA (United Nations Economic Commission for Africa) (2005b) *Economic Report on Africa 2005: Meeting the Challenges of Unemployment and Poverty in Africa*. Addis Ababa: UNECA.

UNESCO (United Nations Educational, Scientific and Cultural Organization) (1953) *The Use of Vernacular Languages in Education*. Paris: UNESCO.

UNESCO (United Nations Educational, Scientific and Cultural Organization) (1996) *The Universal Declaration of Linguistic Rights*. Paris: UNESCO. Available online at http://www.unesco.org/cpp/uk/declarations/linguistic.pdf. Accessed 30.5.07.

UNESCO (United Nations Educational, Scientific and Cultural Organization) (2000a) *The World Education Forum. Education for All: Meeting our Collective Commitments*. United Nations Educational, Scientific and Cultural Organisation Held in Dakar, 26–28 April. Available online at unesdoc.unesco.org/images/0012/001211/121147e.pdf. Accessed 3.3.06.

UNESCO (United Nations Educational, Scientific and Cultural Organization) (2000b) *World Education Report 2000: The Right to Education: Towards Education for All throughout Life*. Paris: UNESCO.

UNESCO (United Nations Educational, Scientific and Cultural Organization) (2002) *The Universal Declaration of Cultural Diversity: Common Heritage, Plural Identities*. Paris: UNESCO. Available online at unesdoc.unesco.org/images/0012/001271/127160m.pdf. Accessed on 15.4.07.

UNESCO (United Nations Educational, Scientific and Cultural Organization) (2003a) *Education in a Multilingual World*. Paris: UNESCO.

UNESCO (United Nations Educational, Scientific and Cultural Organization) (2003b) *Cultural and Linguistic Diversity in the Information Society.* UNESCO Publications for the World Summit on the Information Society. Paris: UNESCO.

UNESCO (United Nations Educational, Scientific and Cultural Organization) (2005) *Measuring Linguistic Diversity on the Internet.* A collection of papers by John Paolillo, Daniel Pimienta, Daniel Prado *et al.* UNESCO Publications for the World Summit on the Information Society. Edited with an introduction by UNESCO Institute for Statistics. Montreal, Canada.

UNESCO (United Nations Educational, Scientific and Cultural Organization) (2006) *Intergovernmental Conference on Language Policies in Africa; Final Report.* Harare, Zimbabwe 17–21 March 1997. Intangible Heritage Section, document CLT.2006/WS/5 REV. Catalogue Number: 145746.

UNICEF (United Nations' Children's Fund) (2005) *L'enfance en peril: La situation des enfants des enfants dans le monde.* New York: UNICEF. Available online at www.unicef.org/french/sowc05/fullreport.html. Accessed 25.6.07.

Vaillancourt, F. (1980) *Difference in Earnings by Language Groups in Quebec, 1970: An Economic Analysis.* Québec: Centre international de recherche sur le bilinguisme (publication B-90).

Vaillancourt, F. (1996) Language and socioeconomic status in Quebec: Measurement, findings, determinants, and policy costs. *International Journal of the Sociology of Language* 121, 69–92.

Vaillancourt, F. and Grin, F. (2000) *The Choice of a Language of Instruction: The Economic Aspects.* Distance Learning Course on Language Instruction in Basic Education. Washington, DC: The World Bank Institute.

Van der Veken, A. and de Schryver, G-M. (2003) Les langues africaines sur la Toile: étude des cas haoussa, somali, lingala, et isixhosa. *Cahiers du Rifal* 23, 33–45. Available online at tshwanedje.com/publications/Toile.pdf. Accessed 8.6.06

Van Parijs, P. (1999) Lingua franca. *La Revue nouvelle* 9, 114–119.

Van Parijs, P. (2000) The ground floor of the world: On the socio-economic consequences of linguistic globalisation. *International Political Science Review* 21 (2), 217–233.

Van Parijs, P. (2002) Linguistic justice. In W. Kymlicka and A. Patten (eds) *Language Rights and Political Theory* (pp. 153–168). Oxford University Press.

Van Parijs, P. (forthcoming) Must Europe be Belgian? On democratic citizenship in multilingual polities. To be published in I. Hampsher-Monk (ed.) *The Demands of Citizenships.* London: Cassell.

Vawda, Y. and Patrinos, A. (1999) Producing educational materials in local languages: Costs from Guatemala and Senegal. *International Journal of Educational Development* 19, 287–299.

Verschave, F-X. (1994) *Complicité de génocide? La politique de la France au Rwanda.* Paris: La Découverte.

Verschave, F-X. (1999) *La Françafrique: Le plus long scandale de la République.* Paris: Stock.

Verschave, F-X. (2000) *Noir silence.* Paris: Les Arènes.

Verschave, F-X. (2001a) *Noir procès: Offense à chefs d'Etats.* Paris: Les Arènes.

Verschave, F-X. (2001b) L'envers de la dette: Criminalité politique et économique au Congo-Brazza et en Angola. *Dossier noir de la politique africaine de la France 16.* Agone, 225 p.

Verschave, F-X. (2002) *Noir Chirac.* Paris: Les Arènes.

Verschave, F-X. (2004a) *De la Françafrique à la Mafiafrique.* Paris: Tribord.

Verschave, F-X. (ed.) (2004b) *La santé mondiale entre racket et bien public.* Paris: Editions Charles Léopold Meyer.
Verschave, F-X., Tobner, O. and Diop, B. (2005a) *Négrophobie, réponse aux 'Négrologues', journalistes françafricains et autres falsificateurs de l'information.* Paris: Les Arènes.
Verschave, F-X. and Coret, L. (2005b) *L'horreur qui nous prend au visage: L'Etat français et le génocide, Rapport de la Commission d'enquête citoyenne sur le rôle de la France dans le génocide des Tutsi au Rwanda.* Paris: Karthala.
Wa Thiong'o, Ngùgí (1986) *Decolonising the Mind: The Politics of Language in African Literature.* London and Nairobi: James Currey/Heinemann.
Wagenhofer, E. (2005) *We Feed the World Documentary* Allegro Film and Austrian Film Commission. Available online at www.we-feed-the-world.at/en/team. htm. Accessed 20.5.07.
Walter, C. (1998) The universal declaration of linguistic rights. *Global Issues in Language Education* 30, 16–17.
WCED (World Commission on Development and the Environment) (1987) *Our Common Future. The Brundtland Report.* London: Oxford University Press.
Weaver, C. (2007) Scheme to help overseas doctors talk like Orstrayans. *The Sunday Telegraph* (Australia), 10 June, p. 26.
Weber, M (1924) *Wirtschaftsgeschichte: Abriss der universalen Sozial- und Wirtschafts-geschichte* (S. Hellmann and M. Palyi, eds). Munich: Duncker & Humbolt.
Westley, D. (1992) Language and education in Africa: A selected bibliography, 1980–1990. *Comparative Education Review* 36 (3), 355–367.
Whittaker, R. (1974) New world in the morning. BMG Music.
WHO (World Health Organisation) (1999) *World Health Report 1999: Making a Difference.* Geneva: WHO.
WHO (World Health Organisation) (2002) *The World Health Report 2002: Reducing Risks, Promoting Healthy Life.* Geneva: WHO. Available online at www.who.int/whr/2002/en/. Accessed on 12.2.06.
WHO (World Health Organisation) (2005a) *The World Health Report 2005: Make Every Mother and Child Count.* Geneva: WHO.
WHO (World Health Organisation) (2005b) *Strategic Orientations for WHO Action in the African Region: 2005–2009.* Addis Ababa: WHO Regional Office for Africa.
WHO (World Health Organisation) (2006) *The World Health Report 2006 – Working together for health.* Geneva: WHO.
WHO (World Health Organisation) (2007) *World Health Statistics 2007.* New York: WHO. Online at www.who.int/healthinfo/statistics/en/. Accessed 25.6.07
Whorf, B. (1956) *Language, Thought and Reality.* (J. Carroll, ed.). Cambridge, MA: MIT Press.
Williams, G. (1986) Language planning or language expropriation? *Journal of Multilingual and Multicultural Development* 7 (6), 509–518.
Wolff, E. (1981) Die Berbersprachen. In B. Heine, T. Schadeberg and E. Wolff (eds) *Die Sprachen Afrikas* (pp. 171–185). Hamburg: Helmut Buske Verlag.
Woolcock, M., Pritchett, L. and Isham, J. (2001) The social foundations of poor economic growth in resource-rich economies. In R. Auty (ed.) *Resource Abundance and Economic Development* (pp. 76–92). *UNU/WIDER Studies in Development Economics.* Oxford: Oxford University Press.
World Bank (1980) *Annual Report 1980.* Washington, DC: World Bank.

World Bank (2001a) *World Development Report (WDR) 2000/2001: Attacking Poverty.* Washington, DC: World Bank. Available online at http://go.worldbank.org/L8RGH3WLI0. Accessed 18.6.06.

World Bank (2001b) *World Development Indicators.* Washington, DC: World Bank.

World Bank (2002) *The Case for Aid: Building a Consensus for Development Assistance.* Washington, DC: World Bank.

World Bank (2005a) In their own language: education for all. *Education Notes.* June. Available online at http://siteresources.worldbank.org/EDUCATION/Resources/Education-Notes/EdNotes_Lang_of_Instruct.pdf. Accessed 12.12.06.

World Bank (2005b) *Meeting the Challenge of Africa's Development: A World Bank Group Action Plan, Africa Region* (pp.32–33). Washington, DC: World Bank. Available online at siteresources.worldbank.org/INTAFRICA/Resources/aap_final.pdf. Accessed 3.06.05.

World Bank (2006a) *World Development Report 2006: Equity and Development.* World Bank and Oxford University Press. Washington DC.

The World Bank (2006b) Discussion avec Meera Shekar sur la malnutrition. Nouvelles/Médias, 7 mars 2006. Available online at www.banquemondiale.org/EXT/French.nsf/DocbyUnid/40B815DD540198D18525713300675F2D. Accessed 15.4.07.

World Bank (2007) *Global Development Finance 2007.* Washington, DC: World Bank Publications.

World Bank Group (1988) *World Bank Development Report 1988.* World Bank Publication Series. New York: Oxford University Press.

WSIS (World Summit on the Information Society) (2003) Building the Information Society: A global challenge in the new Millennium. Declaration of Principles: Our Common Vision of the Information Society. Geneva: WSIS. Document WSIS-03/GENEVA/DOC/4-E. 12 December. Available online at www. wsis-si.org/DOCS/science-en.pdf. Accessed 25.6.07.

Xaba, J., Horn, P. and Motala, S. (2002) The informal sector in sub-Saharan Africa. *Working Paper on the Informal Economy.* Employment Sector, Geneva: ILO.

Yao, E. (2006a) Paludisme en Côte d'Ivoire: 74 enfants de moins d'un an meurent chaque jour. *Soir Info, Quotidien Ivoirien d'Informations Générales.* 2 May.

Yao, E. (2006b) Tous clament leur innocenc. *Soir Info, Quotidien Ivoirien d'Informations Générales.* 26 Septembre.

Yngve, V. (1996) *From Grammar to Science: New Foundations for General Linguistics.* Amsterdam: John Benjamins.

Youdelman, M. and Perkins, J. (2002) Providing language interpretation services in health care settings: Examples from the field. US National Health Law Programme unpublished report.

Zeleza, P. (2006) The inventions of African identities and languages: The discursive and developmental implications. In O. Arasanyin and M. Pemberton (eds) *Selected Proceedings of the 36th Annual Conference on African Linguistics* (pp. 14–26). Sommerville, MA: Cascadilla Proceedings Project.

Ziegler, J. (2002) *Les nouveaux maîtres du monde, et ceux qui leur résistent.* Paris: Editions Fayard et Points.

Ziegler, J. (2005) *L'Empire de la honte.* Paris: Fayard.

CPSIA information can be obtained at www.ICGtesting.com
Printed in the USA
BVOW04s1848130914

366359BV00004B/12/P